OUR

FUNDAMENTAL

PROBLEM

OUR FUNDAMENTAL PROBLEM

A Revolutionary Approach to Philosophy

NICHOLAS MAXWELL

McGill-Queen's University Press
Montreal & Kingston • London • Chicago

ISBN 978-0-2280-0151-5 (cloth)
ISBN 978-0-2280-0152-2 (paper)
ISBN 978-0-2280-0286-4 (ePDF)
ISBN 978-0-2280-0287-1 (ePUB)

Legal deposit second quarter 2020
Bibliothèque nationale du Québec

Printed in Canada on acid-free paper that is 100% ancient forest free
(100% post-consumer recycled), processed chlorine free

Funded by the   Financé par le
Government   gouvernement   Canada   Canada Council   Conseil des arts
of Canada   du Canada   for the Arts   du Canada

We acknowledge the support of the Canada Council for the Arts.
Nous remercions le Conseil des arts du Canada de son soutien.

Library and Archives Canada Cataloguing in Publication

Title: Our fundamental problem : a revolutionary approach to philosophy / Nicholas
Maxwell.
Names: Maxwell, Nicholas, 1937– author.
Description: Includes bibliographical references and index.
Identifiers: Canadiana (print) 20200186736 | Canadiana (ebook) 20200186744
    | ISBN 9780228001522 (paper) | ISBN 9780228001515 (cloth) | ISBN
    9780228002864 (ePDF) | ISBN 9780228002871 (ePUB)
Subjects: LCSH: Philosophy.
Classification: LCC B72.M39 2020 | DDC 100—dc23

This book was typeset in 10.5/13 Sabon.

For Extinction Rebellion

Contents

Figures

Preface

How can our human world – the world we experience and live in – exist and best flourish embedded as it is in the physical universe? That is our fundamental problem. It encompasses all others of science, thought, and life. This is the problem I explore in this book. I put forward some suggestions as to how aspects of this problem are to be solved. And I argue that this is the proper task of philosophy: to try to improve our conjectures about how aspects of the problem are to be solved, and to encourage everyone to think, imaginatively and critically, now and again, about the problem. We need to put the fundamental problem centre stage so that our best ideas about it interact fruitfully, in both directions, with our attempts to solve even more important more specialized and particular problems of thought and life.

This book is intended to be a fresh, unorthodox introduction to philosophy – an introduction that will, I hope, interest and even excite an intelligent sixteen-year-old, as well as any adult halfway interested in intellectual, social, political, or environmental issues. Scientists and professional philosophers should find it of interest as well. The idea of the book is to bring philosophy down to earth and demonstrate its vital importance, when done properly, for science, for scholarship, for education, for life, for the fate of the world.

If everything is made up of fundamental physical entities, electrons and quarks, interacting in accordance with precise physical law, what becomes of the world we experience – the colours, sounds, smells, and tactile qualities of things? What becomes of our inner experiences? How can we have free will, and be responsible for what we do, if everything occurs in accordance with physical law, including our bodies and brains? How can anything be of value if everything in the universe is, ultimately, just physics? These are some of the questions we will be tackling in this book.

These questions arise because of this great fissure in our thinking about the world. Our scientific thinking about the physical universe clashes in all sorts of ways with our thinking about our human world. The task is to discover how we can adjust our ideas about both the physical universe and our human world so that we can resolve clashes between the two in such a way that justice is done both to what science tells us about the universe and to all that is of value in our human world – the miracle of our life here on earth – and the heartache and tragedy.

It is all but inevitable that even the smallest adjustments either to what we take science to tell us about the universe or to what we hold to be the nature and value of our human world will have all sorts of repercussions, potentially, for fields outside philosophy – for science, for thought, for life. And indeed this book does develop revolutionary ideas from its exploration of our fundamental problem.

There is, first, a revolution for philosophy. A new kind of philosophy emerges which I call *critical fundamentalism*. This tackles our fundamental problem, and in doing so seeks to resolve the fundamental fissure in the way we think about the universe and ourselves in such a way that there are multiple, fruitful implications for thought and life. Second, there is a revolution in what we take science to tell us about the world: science is concerned not with everything about everything, but only with a highly specialized aspect of everything. This is the subject of chapter 3. Third, there is a revolution in our whole conception of science, and the kind of science we should seek to develop – the subject of chapter 4. Fourth, there is a revolution in biology, in Darwin's theory of evolution, so that the theory does better justice to helping us understand how life of value has evolved. This is the subject of chapter 5. Fifth, there is a revolution in the social sciences. These are not sciences; rather, their basic task is to promote the cooperatively rational solving of conflicts and problems of living in the social world. An additional task is to discover how progress-achieving methods, generalized from those of natural science (as these ought to be conceived) can be got into social life, into all our other social endeavours, government, industry, the economy, and so on, so that social progress toward a more enlightened world may be made in a way that is somewhat comparable to the intellectual progress in knowledge made by science. Social inquiry emerges as social *methodology* or *philosophy* and not, fundamentally, social science. Sixth, there is a much broader revolution in academic inquiry as a whole. We need a new kind of academic enterprise rationally designed and devoted to helping us resolve the grave global conflicts and problems that confront us: habitat destruction; loss of wildlife; extinction of species; the menace of nuclear weapons; the lethal character of modern war; gross inequality; pollution of earth, sea and air; and above all the impending disasters of climate change. These problems have arisen in part because of the gross structural irrationality of our institutions of learning devoted as they are to the pursuit of knowledge instead of taking, as their basic task, to help humanity resolve conflicts and problems of living in increasingly cooperatively rational ways, thus making progress toward as good, as wise, a world as possible. Seventh, there is the all-important social revolution that might gradually emerge if humanity has the wit to develop what it so urgently needs: academic inquiry rationally devoted to helping us make progress toward a better, more civilized world. These fifth, sixth, and seventh revolutions are the subject of chapter 7.

Academic philosophy, whether so-called analytic or Continental philosophy, is not noted for its fruitful implications for other areas of thought and life. How come, then, that philosophy as done here, critical fundamentalism, has these dramatic revolutionary implications for science, for academic inquiry, for our capacity to solve the global problems that menace our future? I do what I can to answer this question in chapters 2 and 9.

Why has academic philosophy lost its way so drastically that it has failed to put the richly fruitful conception of philosophy, as done here, into practice? What caused academic philosophy to lose its way? I give my answer to this question in the appendix.

My chief hope in writing this book, however, is that the reader will be beguiled or provoked into thinking imaginatively and critically – that is, rationally – about our fundamental problem, not obsessively, but from time to time.

OUR

FUNDAMENTAL

PROBLEM

Our Human World in the Physical Universe

Introductory discussion of the problem

How can our human world, the world as it appears to us, the world we live in and see, touch, hear, and smell, the world of living things, people, consciousness, free will, meaning, and value – how can all of this exist and best flourish embedded as it is in the physical universe?

This is the problem we are going to explore in this book. It is our fundamental problem, of both thought and life. All other problems, I will argue, are parts or aspects of this most fundamental of all problems. Because it is so important, so basic, so all embracing, it deserves a name. Let us call it "the human world/physical universe" problem, or just "our fundamental problem."

Not everyone will agree that this is our fundamental problem. For example, those who believe in God may not agree. I will say more about that below.

Here is the problem, expressed a bit more vividly and dramatically, as it arises for me one summer afternoon:

I sit in my garden in north London with my wife, Christine. Behind me, honeysuckle tumbles over the garden wall and fills the air with its sweet scent. Bumble bees buzz and blunder among the honeysuckle flowers. A gentle breeze sifts through the tree above, and sunlight filters through the leaves. It is summer. The sky is dark blue. I stretch and say, "This is heaven," and Chris replies, "How right it is to take the garden as an image of Paradise." Put all this into the physical universe and what do we have? Both Chris and I seem to disappear altogether. I am made up of billions of cells, which are in turn made up of billions of highly complex molecules, in turn made up of atoms, in turn made up of tiny, mysterious particles called electrons, protons, and neutrons, the protons and neutrons in turn made up of even tinier particles called quarks.[1] Everything I am, everything I do, think, experience, see, feel, imagine, decide, understand are just billions of electrons and quarks interacting with each other in accordance with the laws of physics. And likewise for Chris. I see the blue sky, the green leaves, flowers and ferns; I smell the honeysuckle, and hear bees buzzing, and say "This is heaven." But what is happening? Light of various wavelengths, reflected from various surfaces, enters my eyes where it causes molecular processes to occur in my optic nerves; these in turn cause more such molecular processes to occur in the back of my brain, which lead to more such processes occurring in my brain which, in turn, lead to muscles being contracted, air being expelled, vocal chords vibrating, vibrations of molecules in the air that cause Chris's eardrums to vibrate, in turn causing tiny bones in her middle ear to vibrate, leading to complex molecular processes to occur in her brain. Ultimately, all that has occurred is that billions upon billions of electrons and quarks interacting with one another have produced light of such and such frequency, which, after travelling short distances, has affected the way further billions of electrons and quarks interacted. Colours disappear; sounds and smells disappear; perceptions, experiences, sensations, feelings, consciousness, intentions, decisions, and actions disappear; *we* disappear, and there remain merely electrons and quarks interacting, these interactions being mediated by forces such as electromagnetism, the nuclear, weak and strong forces, and gravitation, vibrations in the electromagnetic force travelling from one vast conglomeration of electrons and quarks to another. All meaning and value, everything required to have anything meaningful or of value, have vanished, leaving only cold physics behind.

How is our precious human world to be rescued from this insidious and terrifying assault from physics?

That is our problem.[2]

It is your problem too. Here you are, reading this book, wondering, perhaps, what it is going to be about. But again, both the book and you are made up of molecules, in turn made up of atoms, each in turn made up of electrons spinning around a central nucleus made up of protons and neutrons, which are in turn made up of quarks. Light – or rather, waves in the electromagnetic field – spreads out from the book. Some waves, right now, enter your eyes and cause neurological processes to occur in your brain that lead you to cough, or turn the page, or scroll down the screen if you are reading this on Kindle. You, your thoughts and feelings, seem to disappear, leaving behind this vast, complex system of electrons and quarks interacting with one another in extraordinarily complex ways.

How can we exist and live lives that are meaningful and of value if the world really is as modern physics seems to tell us it is?

This is our fundamental problem because all other problems we encounter, in thought and life, are, as I have already indicated, more or less specialized versions of this most basic problem. First of all, problems of physics are included. It is physics that poses the fundamental problem in the first place. But problems from other branches of natural science are included as well: cosmology, astronomy, geology, biology, chemistry, paleontology, ecology, neuroscience, the study of animal behaviour.[3] All these sciences play a crucial role in filling in details of our fundamental problem, in helping us clarify the nature of the problem, and in helping us to grope toward the solution to the problem. Evolutionary biology in particular, as we shall see, has a crucial role to play in helping us to understand how we can exist embedded as we are in the physical universe, in part at least, tiny fragments of the universe. All of natural science is included in our fundamental problem. Furthermore, the problems of mathematics and logic are included: natural science is inconceivable without these disciplines. And the problems of the social sciences and the humanities are included as well: anthropology, archeology, sociology, psychology, history, cultural studies, philosophy. The nature of our human world, our human life on earth, is as crucial a part of the fundamental problem as the nature of the physical universe, and we need the social sciences and humanities to improve our understanding of the nature of our human world. And we need more: we need literature, biography, drama, poetry, and other art forms as well.

The problems of all these branches of science, thought, and art are components of our fundamental problem. They are inherent in our fundamental problem. But all that is only a part of what is involved. For this human world/physical universe problem also concerns how human life can best *flourish* – how we can best realize what is genuinely of value to us in life. All the problems, the struggles, the suffering, the heartache, and aspirations of humanity are inherent in our problem as well. Our fundamental problem concerns not just how we can exist but also how we need to act, to live, to flourish, to achieve what is of value in life. And that brings in as well ideas, techniques, and problems that arise in connection with efforts to help solve problems of living: problems of medicine, psychiatry, technology, politics and political philosophy, law, industry and agriculture, education. All our problems of living are included, personal, social, national, and global; problems of politicians, office workers, parents, children, lovers, creative artists, bus drivers: every section and aspect of life is included.

If our fundamental problem does indeed incorporate all other problems – this multitude of more and less specialized and particular problems of human knowledge and human life – how can anyone hope to think intelligently, or at all, about the fundamental problem? Would this not require a vast knowledge of human thought and human life, beyond the capacity of any one person to acquire in a lifetime? No! In order to think intelligently about our fundamental problem, in a way which can be fruitful, it is essential to pare away detail – just as I have done in formulating the problem at the beginning of this chapter. Everyone should be introduced to the problem at school, when young, to be given the opportunity to think about the problem whatever background knowledge or ignorance one may have. We are all, essentially, in the same boat, the erudite scientist or scholar burdened with a great weight of expertise, and the five-year-old blithely unaware of almost everything: we all share immense ignorance. In fact in order to learn as we should learn, it is vital that we do have before us our fundamental problem, so that we may organize what we learn, sift out what is significant from what does not matter so much, and direct our learning to help us improve our tentative attempts at solving our fundamental problem as best we can. Without our fundamental problem before us, we may well lose our way, become lost in detail, or lose interest altogether. It is a scandal that education, in schools and universities, is not conducted in this way. I shall have more to say about this scandal in chapters 7 and 9.

Anyone can think in a worthwhile way about this most fundamental physical universe/human world problem. And we should all think about it – from time to time at least. Rich rewards are to be gained from exploring the problem intellectually, in our imagination.

There is, to begin with, all that modern science has to tell us about this strange universe we inhabit. Long ago, in 1610, Galileo discovered that the Milky Way, that faint wisp of misty light that stretches across the sky, is made up of stars, each a sun more or less like our sun.[4] The Milky Way is our local galaxy, a great spiral disk of 300 billion[5] stars, approximately 120,000 light years[6] across, slowly rotating so that it takes our sun some 220 million years to go round once. The universe is very, very big. Light, travelling at a velocity of 186,000 miles per second, takes 1.3 *seconds* to travel from the moon to the earth, 8.3 *minutes* to travel from the sun to the earth, 4.32 *years* to travel from the nearest star to earth, and 120,000 years to travel across our galaxy. Not far away in cosmic terms, there is another galaxy called Andromeda, much like ours: light takes 2.5 *million years* to travel from Andromeda to earth. And it would take light approximately 46.5 *billion years* to travel from the edge of the observable universe to us.

Scattered about in this vast cosmos, there are some 170 billion other galaxies, each composed of hundreds of billions of suns. Very recently, we have discovered that some nearby stars in our galaxy, a mere 40, 50, or 60 light years away, have planets rotating around them, as the planets of our solar system rotate around our sun. The universe, it seems, contains billions upon billions of planets rotating around stars. Do some of these planets support life, even conscious beings, societies, and civilizations? We do not know. And everywhere we look, there are mysteries.

One baffling mystery is the rotation of our galaxy. It may rotate so slowly that it takes 220 million years to complete one revolution, but actually it rotates much too quickly. Our sun travels round the galaxy at a velocity of 483,000 miles an hour: this rate of rotation of the galaxy is so fast that gravitation is not strong enough to hold it together. Our galaxy should fly apart. And the same goes for other galaxies. Scientists speculate that each galaxy, including ours, is immersed in a great ball of invisible matter, mistakenly called "dark" matter, that provides the extra mass and gravitational pull to hold the galaxy together. Dark matter makes up roughly 85 percent of the total mass of matter in the universe; all the matter we ordinarily know, which makes up the earth and everything on it, the moon, the planets, the sun, all the other stars, gas, and interstellar dust consists of a mere 15 percent of the total. What is this mysterious dark matter, 85 percent of all that there is? No one knows.

And there are other mysteries. We have discovered that the universe is expanding. Light from distant galaxies is "stretched" toward the red end of the spectrum; the further away the galaxies are, the more the wavelengths of light are increased. This means other galaxies are receding from us, the further away they are, the faster they recede. All galaxies recede from each other everywhere: the entire universe is expanding. This means that in the past, galaxies were much closer together, so much so that once upon a time, some 13.8 billion years ago, the entire universe, now over 90 billion light years across, was compressed into a space no bigger than an atom. Our universe began with the "big bang," as it is called, and we have detected radiation, not from the big bang itself, but from a time not long after the big bang, a mere 377,000 years after the big bang. But what caused the big bang? And what existed before the big bang? No one knows.

Another profound mystery concerns the rate of expansion of the universe. It has been discovered, by means of observations of very distant galaxies, that the rate of expansion is *increasing*. This is baffling, because the gravitational pull of galaxies on each other should be slowing down the rate of expansion. All of space, it seems, must be imbued with energy – called "dark" energy – which has the effect of exerting an increasingly repulsive force on galaxies, to counteract gravitation and cause them to fly apart ever more rapidly. But what is this dark energy? No one knows. What we do know is that if we invoke Einstein's famous equation, $E = mc^2$, which tells us what the mass equivalence is of a body of energy, then dark energy amounts to 68 percent of the total mass, dark matter 27 percent, and the matter we know, the whole world we know of planets, suns, stars and galaxies, a mere 5 percent. Almost everything that exists, 95 percent in fact, is unknown to us, a mystery.

And there are even stranger mysteries when we come to consider what science tells us about, not the very big, the cosmos, but the very small – the atoms, the electrons, protons and neutrons, the quarks and gluons, out of which everything we do know is made.

Since the middle of the eighteenth century we have discovered that all the myriads of different sorts of substances there are on earth and in the heavens are made up of no more than ninety-eight elements.[7] We have discovered that elements are composed of atoms, each atom a tiny solar system composed of protons and neutrons in a minute nucleus in the centre surrounded by a cloud of electrons. And each proton and neutron is composed of three quarks, held together by the so-called "strong" force, which operates by exchanging between quarks particles called "gluons" – particles that "glue" the quarks together. (So strong is this glue that it does not permit individual quarks to escape its strong grip.) The atom of each element has its own specific number of positively charged protons in the nucleus (and the same number of surrounding, negatively charged electrons, if the atom is electrically neutral overall). We understand why atoms combine together in specific ways to form molecules, the constituents of chemical compounds. We know why substances, in appropriate conditions, form gases, liquids, and solids. We have a good understanding of why different compounds have the diverse properties that they do have. We have discovered that electricity and magnetism are two aspects of one force, the electromagnetic force. We have discovered that light is just waves in the electromagnetic field of force, these waves being light of different colours from red to violet, or a vast range of invisible rays, from radio waves, infrared rays, ultraviolet rays, X-rays to gamma rays, as we go from very long to very short wavelengths.

But what are all these particles – electrons, protons, neutrons, quarks, gluons, and photons (particles of light)? No one knows. Their behaviour is utterly mysterious. Send one electron at a photographic plate, and it will be recorded as a tiny dot. Direct the electron at a screen with two slits in it and, if the electron travels past the screen and hits the photographic plate beyond, it will again be recorded as a tiny dot. So far, the electron behaves as a respectable particle. But now send many electrons at the two-slitted screen, one after the other, all with the same velocity, and beyond, on the photographic plate, the dots accumulate into a pattern of bands, regions where there are lots of dots interleaved with places where there are very few, if any. This can only be explained, it seems, if the electron is really a wave-like entity before it hits the photographic plate. This wave-like entity goes through both slits; at the photographic plate, there are regions where the waves reinforce each other (because a crest from one slit arrives simultaneously with a crest from the other slit); there are inter-leaved regions where the waves cancel each other out (because a crest from one slit arrives simultaneously with a trough from the other slit): where the waves reinforce each other it is most likely that the electron will be detected as a dot. The overall effect is one of alternative bands of lots of dots, interleaved with bands of few dots.

Just this "interference" effect (as it is called) can be obtained with *any* wave-like motion, with waves of light, for example, or waves of water. This two-slit experiment can be done in the bath, or in a harbour with two entrances. Ocean waves come into the harbour via both entrances. At some places on the beach, waves are high because whenever a crest from one entrance arrives, so too a crest from the other entrance arrives as well. At other places on the shore, whenever a crest arrives from one entrance, a trough arrives from the other entrance, the two cancel each other out, and the water is permanently still.

The electron is a particle. But it is also a wave. But we only ever detect the wave aspect of the electron via a great number of particle-like detections. Miraculously, it is both. And this is true of all these fundamental particles: not just electrons, but protons, neutrons, quarks, gluons, nuclei, atoms, even molecules (groups of atoms stuck together). In the case of the photon, the "particle" of light, it may become one of the biggest objects in the universe – indeed, so big that it is almost as big as the universe itself. Consider a photon emitted by an early star not long after the big bang. It travels off in different directions, at the speed of light, for some 13 billion years, reaching the gigantic size of over 26 billion light years across until some thoughtless person, looking up at the night sky, absorbs it into her eye and, across the universe, it vanishes. Can we really believe that there can be such physical entities, minute particles that also stretch right across the universe, but which, at any moment, might be detected as a tiny particle, or might just vanish?

What are these fundamental particles of physics: electrons, protons, photons, gluons, atoms, molecules? No one knows. The more fundamental our scientific knowledge becomes, the more bafflingly mysterious things seem to be. What is everything made up of? We know, but we don't know, because we don't know what these fundamental "particles" really are.[8] Even worse, as I have said, 95 percent of what exists is entirely unknown. And we don't know what caused the big bang, and what existed beforehand.

In view of all this scientific mystery, do we really know enough to know that what physics tells us about the world poses a threat to the meaning and value – even the existence – of our human world? We do, as will become clear in later chapters. Scientific mysteries mainly arise in connection with the most fundamental aspects of science, at the edges of scientific knowledge, as it were. There is an enormous amount that we do know about the universe, and ourselves as a part of the universe.

We have discovered that all of life on earth has evolved by means of the Darwinian mechanisms of inherited variations and natural selection during some 3.8 billion years from some original, primitive cell. Variations that are well adapted to survive do survive and reproduce; variations less well adapted fall by the wayside and fail to reproduce. But how life began is still a mystery, although there are tantalizingly plausible speculations about the matter.[9] We have vastly enhanced our knowledge of the millions of diverse species now living on earth, and our knowledge of extinct species alive in the past, and how evolution has taken place. We have an amazingly detailed knowledge of processes taking place in living things. We have a good understanding of the workings of muscles, nerves, the eye, the ear, the immune system, and so on. Recently, we have come to understand electronic and molecular processes associated with photosynthesis, that astonishing process that goes on all around us in every green leaf and grass blade, transforming sunlight and carbon dioxide into sugar and oxygen, upon which almost all life depends.[10] We know that all living things, apart from viruses, consist of cells, the nucleus of each cell consisting of DNA, that miraculous, molecular spiral that determines the characteristics of the individual in question. We know what the composition and structure of the DNA molecule is, and what the mechanisms are that translate information from the DNA molecule to specific proteins that go to make up multicell plants and animals – why, in plants, some cells form leaves, others roots, others stems, and why, in animals, some cells form muscles, others skin, others bone, and so on. We know what occurs when a new individual mammal or person is conceived, and what goes on in the womb to transform the fertilized egg into an infant. We have vastly increased our knowledge of disease, whether infectious like polio, or noninfectious like cancer, and we have transformed our capacity to cure and prevent disease. We have discovered a great deal about the structure and history of the earth. We know that the continents float on semimolten rock and slowly move with respect to each other, creating oceans when they move apart, and pushing up mountains when they collide. We know why there are earthquakes and volcanoes. We know that conditions on earth have changed dramatically in the past over billions of years: there have been ice ages and times of tropical heat. We know that the oxygen in the atmosphere was created in the distant past by algae as a result of photosynthesis. It took these blue-green algae a billion years to transform the atmosphere in this way, and thus make it possible for us and other animals, billions of years later, to breathe and live.

Our fundamental problem, then, is to understand how our miraculous and tragic human world can exist and best flourish immersed as it is in this fascinating but coldly impersonal universe of science. And in order to enhance our understanding of this problem, its scope and import, we need to ransack, not just the scientific picture of the universe, but also our human reality, in all its rich diversity, its heartache, its splendour. We need to explore the glorious achievements of humanity, the cathedrals, the gardens, the magnificent cities, the music, the art, the drama, the joy, the laughter, good times and bad times, families, institutions of liberty, democracy and justice, the habits of friendliness and civilization – this whole caboodle of the miraculous, the mundane, and the unspeakable. In our quest for the human heart we need above all to plunge into literature: Shakespeare, Tolstoy, Jane Austen, Dostoevsky, Stendhal, D.H. Lawrence, Chekhov, Flaubert, Proust, Kafka, Scott Fitzgerald, George Orwell, Turgenev, Thomas Hardy, James Joyce, George Eliot – and so many others. We need to enter imaginatively into the lives of others so that we feel at least a whisper of their joy, their pain, their hopes and fears, what they think and experience as they struggle to make something of their lives. We need to try to acquire some empathic understanding, not just of those who live lives like ours, but also of those whose lives are very different: much poorer, perhaps, or wealthier, or enmeshed in traditions, cultures, or circumstances very different from ours. We need to ransack the past: ancient civilizations, the Babylonians, the ancient Egyptians, the ancient Greeks, the latter so civilized and so barbaric, the inventors of mathematics, philosophy, theatre, and democracy. We need to be prepared to confront the dark places of the past: the wars, the massacres, the torture, the Nazi death camps. But we also need to consider those who struggled to care for others; those who provoked happiness and joy in others; those who fought for justice, for an end to slavery, exploitation, unnecessary suffering, deprivation, and death. Somehow, we need to embrace in our imagination the good, the bad, and the indifferent, the noble souls and the monsters, what is miraculous in existence and what provokes dismay or horror.

We need to consider, too, what we might one day be able to achieve. Is it realistic to hope that one day we might have a world free of war, starvation, dictatorships, gross inequality, unnecessary suffering and death, a world in which people care for the environment and each other, and everywhere have the opportunity to realize the wonderful things life has to offer? Could the physical universe permit such a human world one day to come into existence? Or is this a utopian fantasy, something our human nature, inherited from our evolutionary past, will not permit us to create? This possibility of a better world needs to be pondered, especially in view of doubts we may well have about the reality of free will in view of the fact that we are, whatever else we may be, integral bits of the physical universe.

We need, too, to put our human world into the broader context of all sentient life. We are not the only beings who see and act, experience joy, pain, and terror. So do foxes, otters, rabbits, elephants, sheep, and mammals of thousands of other species. We humans are mammals too, and we share this planet with our fellow mammals, our fellow sentient beings – except that there is this long history of our horrific casual brutality to our fellow sentient beings. Those of us who eat meat are mammalian cannibals. And then there are birds, and reptiles, and even fish to consider. They may be sentient too. We ought not to dissociate ourselves from the rest of life on this planet.

This precious life, this sparkling wonder of conscious and sentient living in a universe almost everywhere bereft of life: it is this miracle immersed in lifeless physics that we have to understand: how it can exist and best flourish.

There is a tendency these days for scientists to present science to the public as something that is full of excitement, astonishment, and mystery. Having discovered, perhaps, that the public listens only to pop stars and comedians, scientists now assume the garb of the pop star or the comedian and present science as space opera. Perhaps I have given in to this tendency a little myself, in this chapter. Actually, doing science mostly involves lots of painstaking, hard work and repeated failure, with only very occasional glimpses of something exciting and new. It is true, however, as I have tried to show, that modern science does present us with an astonishing vision of the universe around us, its history, the history of our earth, the history of life and our life. There is much that we know and much that remains a mystery.

But what tends not to be emphasized is the very grim message that science seems to bring to us about the reality of our human world. It seems to drain away all the colour, the sound and fury, the meaning and value, our whole world of inner experience, feeling, sensation, and thought, our very capacity to act, to decide ourselves what we will do and then do it, and leaves only a pale simulacrum of these things behind – ultimately, the lawful, lifeless dance of electrons,

photons, protons, and the rest. Everything that gives colour, meaning, and value to life seems to become a mere will-o-the-wisp, a thin
illusion, a dream that fades as science awakens us. It is simply dishonest not to acknowledge this nightmare threat from science. It is
dishonest to pretend the threat does not really arise.

This threat that comes from science is, it has to be admitted,
weirdly philosophical and esoteric in character. We follow the
argument, and are appalled. We blink, and it is the argument that
becomes a will-o-the-wisp, and life returns as a reality, in all its richness and frustrating complexity. But there is another threat to our
existence that stems from science that is of a kind that is much more
substantial and down to earth, much more difficult to deny.

We are confronted by grave global problems: population growth;
the destruction of natural habitats and the extinction of species; the
lethal character of modern war and terrorism; extreme inequality of
wealth and power around the globe; the threat of modern armaments,
conventional, chemical, biological and nuclear; threats to democracy
posed by social media; pollution of earth, sea, and air; and, above
all, the impending menace of climate change. These global problems,
taken together, are so severe they threaten what shards of civilization
we have managed to put together so far. Millions, possibly billions,
may die if we do not discover how to resolve our conflicts and problems a bit more intelligently, effectively, and humanely than we have
managed so far.

A decisive point to notice is that all these problems have been
made possible by the astonishing intellectual successes of modern
science and technology. Much that is of great benefit has come from
science. It has made the modern world possible. But science and
technology have made possible modern industry and agriculture,
modern hygiene and medicine, modern armaments and the Internet,
and these in turn have led to population growth, destruction of
habitats, lethal modern war, global warming, and the other global
problems we face. None of these global problems would have come
to be without modern science.

We should not be surprised by this outcome. Modern science and
technology give, to some of us, unprecedented powers to act. This
can have great benefit, in medicine or agriculture, for example. But,
without the capacity to act *wisely*, science and technology will, as
often as not, lead, not to human welfare, but to human suffering and

death – whether intended, as in modern war, or unintended, initially at least, as in the impending disasters of climate change.

In concerning ourselves with how our human world can best flourish immersed as it is in the world as depicted by science, we cannot ignore these global problems, and the role that science has played in the genesis of these problems. Science enhances our power to act, but not our power to act *wisely*, and therein lies the key disaster of our times, the disaster behind all the others. Before the advent of modern science, lack of wisdom did not matter too much. We lacked the power to do too much damage to the planet and ourselves. Now that we have science, and the powers to act it has bequeathed to us, wisdom has become, not a private luxury, but a public necessity.

Essentially, we need to *learn* how to solve these problems. And for that, we need *new institutions of learning*. We need to bring about a revolution in our schools and universities so that they become rationally devoted to helping us learn how to make progress toward as good a world as possible. Science, the pursuit of knowledge, needs to be transformed into something I shall call "wisdom-inquiry." That is the subject of chapter 7.

Some Ideas as to How Our Fundamental Problem Is to Be Solved

∞ Five approaches to its solution: physicalism, dualism, idealism, naive realism, and the two-aspect view ∞

Philosophy can hope to solve only a very meagre *aspect* of all that is involved in our fundamental problem.

For consider: the human world/physical universe problem is made up of all our problems of living – the problems we encounter as we live – and all our problems of thought. The second lot is, in a sense, a subsection of the first. We *think* as a part of *life*. Problems of living are solved by what we do, or what we refrain from doing: they will remain open and unresolved for as long as there are people around to continue to live. Problems of thought can arise out of a concern to solve problems of living; they may arise as we explore imaginatively possible actions in an attempt to discover what to do in order to achieve some desirable, or at least desired, objective. Problems of thought may also arise, however, out of curiosity, the desire to know, to understand, for its own sake, without this impulse being tied too specifically to any problem of *action* or *living*. Problems of thought, like problems of living, will remain open and unresolved as well to a considerable extent as long as there are still people to live, think, imagine and wonder.

In other words, almost *everything* associated with our fundamental problem must inevitably remain untouched and unresolved by what follows in this book – and what is contained in all philosophical books ever to be published in the future! Our concern here is only with a very, very thin slice of our fundamental problem – the *abstract, philosophical* aspect, that aspect of the problem that remains when all life, detail, and substance have been drained away, and only a whisper of the problem remains. We are concerned here, above all, with *possibility*: How is it *possible* that our human world can exist and best flourish embedded as it is in the physical universe? Everything singular, specific, detailed must be pared away until just enough remains for us to highlight and concentrate on this important issue of *possibility*.

The really important problems we face are the particular problems that confront us as we grapple with difficulties in life. But our fundamental philosophical problem is significant, too, in part because how good or bad our answer is to it, given implicitly in what we do in life, may well have a bearing on our capacity to solve our particular, urgent problems of living – a point I will seek to emphasize in what follows. As a result of improving our tentative solution to our fundamental philosophical problem, we may be able to improve our capacity to solve much more specific and urgent problems of living, and thus improve our lives.

Our concern is with the collision of two continents. On the one hand, there is the continent of science – the universe as depicted by science, including ourselves and everything around us conceived of as a part of the physical universe. On the other hand, there is the continent of human life and human experience, the world of consciousness, free will, meaning, and value. These two continents collide. They clash. It is all but impossible to see how these two worlds can coexist in one coherent world. That this basic clash of continents exists indicates that there are some very serious and pervasive things wrong with the way we think about the world – either the universe of physics, or our human world, but much more likely, both worlds together, both aspects of the universe. Exploring this clash of continents can be fruitful because it can lead us to uncover systematic mistakes we are making in the way we think about vast domains of existence: the physical universe, and our human world. We may be able to improve our ideas about the universe, our human existence, what is of most value in life, and how it is to be achieved.

We need to represent this clash of continents in as accurate and rich a way as possible, to do justice to the nature of the clash; at the same time we need to represent the clash in as simple and spare a way as possible, uncluttered by irrelevant detail, so that we can go straight to the heart of the clash, and so that we can play around with our simplified representations of these two continents, bend them and mould them this way and that until we find shapes that fit beautifully together to stand potentially for our one coherent actual world.

Two final remarks about the nature of our problem before we plunge into the investigation into how to solve it.

First, I have emphasized that the correct solution to the *philosophical* aspect of the problem – the solution that specifies correctly how it is *possible* for our human world and the physical universe to coexist in a coherent whole – would leave almost everything else untouched and unresolved. But this emphasis on the sterility of philosophy, its uselessness as far as everything else is concerned, can be taken too far (as I have also indicated). Any modification in one or other continent, however slight, that takes us a bit nearer to a reconciliation of the two continents is almost bound to have far-reaching fruitful implications for the continent that is modified. The problem we are tackling takes us to the very heart of our understanding of our world. It concerns a quite fundamental fissure in our thinking. Even a minor modification to one or other continent is almost bound to have far-reaching implications, for thought or for life – or for both. What are I hope fruitful implications will emerge from the discussion of this book – fruitful implications for our understanding of the universe, our understanding of science, our understanding of how we can learn to make progress toward a better, wiser world. These implications, mentioned in the preface and indicated during the course of the book, are gathered together and summarized in chapter 9 – implications for physics, for natural science, for Darwinian theory, neuroscience, quantum theory and mathematics (or at least the philosophy of mathematics), for social science and the humanities, for academic inquiry as a whole, and ultimately for our whole social world. Orthodox philosophy in the main does not have fruitful implications for other disciplines, or for life, and does not claim to have such implications. But philosophy devoted to trying to help solve aspects of the physical universe/human world problem can hardly avoid having such implications! We may even attempt to assess the relative merits of different approaches to solving the fundamental problem by comparing the fruitfulness of their implications for other disciplines and aspects of life.

A profitable way of thinking about the relationship between problems that are more and less fundamental is to represent all our problems in the form of a pyramid. At the apex of the pyramid we have the fundamental philosophical problem, the problem about *possibility*. As we descend the pyramid, more and more increasingly diverse, particular, specialized problems arise until, when we reach the base of the pyramid, we arrive at our actual, specific problems of life and research. The all-important point to appreciate is that we need an interplay, an interchange, in both directions, between more abstract and general problems, higher up, and more specific and particular problems, lower down. Thinking about our most fundamental *philosophical* problem needs to interact persistently with thinking about somewhat less general, more specific problems of living and problems of thought. There needs to be a constant interplay between thinking at different levels that goes in both directions. In thinking about our fundamental problem we need to attend to what is going on in physics, in neuroscience, in evolutionary biology, in history and literature, but also in the world – the problems people face in their lives. And thinking about specific problems that confront us, in life and thought, needs now and again to consider the broader context; our best ideas about how to solve our fundamental philosophical problem may have fruitful implications for our particular, immediate concerns.[1]

The second point I have to make has to do with the status of philosophical ideas that may emerge from trying to solve our fundamental philosophical problem. One reaction to the program I have indicated might be *horror*. Is the idea that the philosopher, sitting in his study, will come up with *solutions* to all our problems which the rest of us must just accept? (The philosopher, these days, is almost bound to be an academic, a professor in some university.) Such a state of affairs would amount to sheer intellectual tyranny – the academic philosopher ruling the world! The very idea is as ludicrous as it is obscene. If this is what professors of philosophy set out to do, they need to be, not listened to, but locked up and treated as power-mad lunatics!

It is of interest that the philosopher who many consider to be the greatest ever, namely Plato, did indeed have such power-mad aspirations. Plato thought that only philosophers could know the truth of things: only they could discern clearly such things as justice, reason, truth, knowledge, and what is good. Therefore, Plato held, they should be put in charge. The philosopher should become king.[2]

My view, however, is that philosophers should come up with, and can only come up with, *suggestions, possibilities, proposals, conjectures*. Philosophers need to come up with *arguments* too, designed to show that this or that *proposal* or *conjecture* really does solve the problems it is claimed to solve, and does not create even more serious unsolved problems. But even if these arguments are entirely valid, they cannot establish the truth of the conjecture in question if this conjecture is about substantial matters of fact. In the end, all our knowledge, even scientific knowledge, is conjectural in character. A proper task of philosophy is to put forward and critically assess conjectures intended to help solve our fundamental problem – conjectures that, we may hope, are true, and have fruitful implications for thought and life. Anyone may make a contribution to thought about our fundamental problem, and we should all ponder the problem, and its possible solutions, from time to time at least.[3]

The proper task of philosophy, in short, is to keep alive thinking about our fundamental problem; encourage everyone to think about it, now and again; try to improve attempts at solving aspects of the problem; and try to ensure that thinking about the fundamental problem interacts fruitfully, in both directions, with more specialized and particular problems of research and life. Philosophy pursued in this interdisciplinary spirit is rather different from most current academic philosophy, which conceives of itself as a specialized academic discipline alongside other specialized disciplines. We need a name for philosophy as done here. In the preface I suggested we call it *critical fundamentalism*.[4] I will have more to say about critical fundamentalism in chapter 9 and the appendix.

Enough of preliminaries! Let us begin our exploration of our fundamental problem, this great fissure in our thinking, this clash of continents.

In order for anyone to be aware of the human world/physical universe problem, it is necessary for something like the scientific vision of the universe to have emerged, at least as a possibility, as a view of things that just might be true. This first happened nearly 2,500 years ago, in ancient Greece, when Leucippus (fifth century BCE) and Democritus (460–370 BCE) invented atomism. Unfortunately, almost nothing is known of Leucippus, and little of Democritus. Their books were destroyed.[5] What we know of Democritus comes in the main from quotations from Aristotle (who opposed Democritus's atomism).

According to the atomism of Leucippus and Democritus, atoms are eternal, rigid, variously shaped, and devoid of perceptual qualities like colour, sound, and smell. Some are spherical, others are like needles, and others have hooks so that they hook together to form cohesive solids. All phenomena are the outcome of atoms in motion through the void.

Richard Feynman, a famous twentieth-century physicist, once said that if all scientific knowledge was destroyed and one had to capture what was most important in one sentence, that sentence should be "all things are made of atoms."[6] Leucippus and Democritus, in other words, discovered the most important nugget of scientific knowledge that there is. But this discovery came about in a most extraordinary way. An earlier Greek philosopher, Parmenides (late sixth–early fifth centuries BCE), became baffled by the very idea of change. He argued that it embodied a contradiction. If there is change, then that which initially does not exist – *nothing* – subsequently becomes something that does exist. But that means that, initially, the *nothing* exists – that which does not exist exists – a straight contradiction. The very idea of change is a contradiction. All change is impossible. Reality, Parmenides concluded, is an unchanging, homogeneous sphere, with nothing outside it, and all change and diversity are illusions.

Leucippus and Democritus, evidently, decided that this conclusion is absurd. Change and diversity are all too real features of the world. Therefore Parmenides's basic assumption must be false. The nothing – the void – must exist. It must surround Parmenides' unchanging, homogeneous sphere. Shrink this sphere down to a tiny size, populate the void with other such spheres, and one has atomism. Each atom is a tiny, Parmenidean universe, homogeneous and unchanging (internally). All change is simply relative motion of atoms.[7] Thus was born one of the most fruitful scientific ideas ever!

The nub of atomism, and the nub of one possible solution to the human world/physical universe problem, is contained in one of the statements of Democritus that has come down to us: "Colour exists by convention; sweet and sour exist by convention: atoms and the void alone exist in reality."[8] This sums up, in one sentence, the scientific view of the universe – even if scientific details about the nature of atoms and other matters need today a bit of elaboration. But can we really believe that the world we experience, colours, sounds and smells, and our inner sensations, feelings, and thoughts are all illusory, features that exist only "by convention," there being in reality nothing more in existence than impersonal, colourless physics?

Roughly two thousand years after Leucippus and Democritus, something like their vision of things emerged again as a viable option with the birth of modern science as a result of the work of Copernicus,[9] Kepler,[10] Galileo,[11] Descartes,[12] Huygens,[13] Hooke,[14] Boyle,[15] Newton,[16] and others.[17] Almost all those associated with the birth of modern science accepted some version of what I have called *the scientific vision of the universe.* This can be regarded as being composed of three basic ingredients.

1 Natural phenomena obey mathematically precise physical laws.
2 Everything is composed of atoms.
3 Colours, sounds, smells, tactile qualities, as we experience
   them, do not exist objectively; they are not real properties of
   things.

There was disagreement about some of the finer details. Descartes was perhaps the most radical in depriving physical entities of properties. For him, atoms possess only extension and motion: atoms are, for Descartes, indistinguishable from fragments of empty space. Newton, on the other hand, scornfully rejected any such view. For him, atoms are "solid, massy, hard, impenetrable, moveable Particles,"[18] certainly distinct from empty space. These particles attract and repel one another by means of forces that act at a distance – forces such as gravitation, electricity, and magnetism. However, Newton had grave doubts about the actual physical reality of forces. Even though he claimed to derive his law of gravitation from the phenomena by induction, he nevertheless declared, "That gravity should be innate, inherent, and essential to matter, so that one body may act upon another, at a distance through a vacuum, without the mediation of anything else ... is to me so great an absurdity, that I believe no man who has in philosophical matters a competent faculty of thinking can ever fall into it."[19] Newton may have believed that gravitation arose as a result of the moment-by-moment direct actions of God. Newton certainly believed God intervened to adjust the solar system from time to time to ensure its stability.[20] Despite these disagreements about the nature of the physical universe, there was much more widespread agreement among natural philosophers associated with the birth of modern science about the nonreality of sensory qualities as we perceive them.

Thus Galileo, in 1632, two thousand years after Democritus, expressed the point like this:

whenever I conceive any material or corporeal substance, I immediately feel the need to think of it as bounded, and as having this or that shape; as being large or small in relation to other things, and in some specific place at some specific time; as being in motion or at rest; as touching or not touching some other body; and in being one, or few, or many. From these conditions I cannot separate such a substance by any stretch of my imagination.[21] But that it must be white or red, bitter or sweet, noisy or silent, and of sweet or foul odour, my mind does not feel compelled to bring in as necessary accompaniments. Without the senses as our guides, reason or imagination unaided would probably never arrive at qualities like these. Hence I think that tastes, odours, colours, and so on are no more than mere names so far as the object in which we place them is concerned, and that they reside only in the consciousness. Hence if the living creature were removed, all of these qualities would be wiped away and annihilated.[22]

Galileo goes on to point out that if a feather tickles us, we hold that the tickling is in us, not in the feather. In a similar way, colours, sounds, and smells are a kind of tickling in us, and are not objective features of things external to us.

And Newton, for one, agrees. He writes,

if at any time I speak of light and rays as coloured or endued with colours, I would be understood to speak not philosophically and properly, but grossly, and accordingly to such conceptions as vulgar people in seeing all these experiments would be apt to frame. For the rays to speak properly are not coloured. In them there is nothing else than a certain power and disposition to stir up a sensation of this or that colour. For as sound in a bell or musical string, or other sounding body, is nothing but a trembling motion, and in the air nothing but that motion propagated from the object, and in the sensorium 'tis a sense of that motion under the form of sound; so colours in the object are nothing but a disposition to reflect this or that sort of rays more copiously than the rest; in the rays they are nothing but their dispositions to propagate this or that motion into the sensorium, and in the sensorium they are sensations of those motions under the forms of colours.[23]

Almost all scientists today would agree. Thus Semir Zeki, a present-day neuroscientist who has done much to unravel the neurology of colour perception, writes, "Ever since the time of Newton, physicists have emphasized that light itself, consisting of electromagnetic radiation, has no colour"; and Zeki goes on to quote a part of the above passage from Newton with approval.[24]

There is here an astonishing paradox. Almost all scientists, from the very few pioneer natural philosophers of the seventeenth century, via the ever-growing community of scientists through the eighteenth, nineteenth, and twentieth centuries down to the thousands upon thousands of scientists world-wide today, agree almost without discussion that colours, sounds, and other perceptual qualities do not really exist objectively out there in the world. But science, by common consent, is based on experiment and observation. And the most trivial observation one could make verifies that colours and sounds do exist. Open your eyes, look around, and, depending where you are, you will see green fields, red-brick houses, yellow sand, blue sky – assuming it is daytime and you have normal sight. Is not the theory that the world is devoid of colour and other perceptual qualities refuted by the most elementary observation conceivable? How can empirically based science ignore such an obvious refutation?

The solution to this paradox is to note that the scientific view of the world, when applied to processes associated with perception, cunningly undermines the very idea that perception can have any power whatsoever to verify the existence of perceptual qualities in the world. For note what occurs. Light of various wavelengths is reflected from the object perceived, enters the eye, and forms an image of the external object on the retina at the back of the eye.[25] Sensory cells react, and cause nerve cells to respond. These send signals along the optic nerve to the back of the brain, and it is only then, as a result of complex neurological processes occurring in the brain, that the miracle occurs and we have the experience of seeing. What we are directly aware of, in perception, is not the external object but our inner mental representation of the object. And we have every reason to suppose that this will be quite different from its external cause, the perceived object. Just think of the many transformations that are involved as we go from perceived object, a daffodil say, to mental "perception" of it. There is (1) the daffodil itself. Then there is (2) light absorbed and reflected by the daffodil. A minute fraction of the reflected light is (3) focused by the lens of the eye so that it falls as an image on the retina at the back of the eye. There, as a result, (4) complex chemical processes occur in light sensitive cells of the retina. These processes then (5) cause neurons of the optic nerve to fire, so that a wave of exchange of potassium and sodium ions across the membranes of these neurons travels from the eye to the brain. This in turn (6) causes complex neurological processes to occur in the back of the brain, progressively analyzing the stimuli. Finally, the miracle occurs, and these neurological processes (7) create or become *perceptual awareness of the daffodil*. This long chain of causal processes, involving at least seven major transformations, all but ensures that the final mental *visual experience of seeing the daffodil* must be radically different from the external *daffodil* itself. Daffodil; light; chemical processes in retina; neurological processes in optic nerve; neurological processes in brain; visual experience of seeing daffodil: each event in this chain of events is of a character profoundly different from the one that came before, and so the final event is bound to differ radically from the first one, and can hold few clues as to the nature of the first one – the daffodil out there in the world.

Let us call this *the argument from the causal account of perception*.[26] I take this argument to establish, if valid, two vital points. First, what we really see, what we really know about, in perception, is not the external object, the daffodil, but rather the final event in the above causal chain of events, our inner mental, visual representation of the daffodil. Second, we don't directly perceive objects external to us; and so our perception of objects, such as daffodils, may be systematically deceptive, so that we think we see daffodils to have properties, such as yellowness, which actually they don't possess at all.

The argument from the causal account of perception, if valid, leads remorselessly to something like the following picture. We are, as it were, locked inside our heads. We have a television screen that we take to depict what is going on around us, outside our heads. But we can never leave the privacy of our skull. We can never compare the images on the television screen with the real external objects that these images are supposed to represent. There is always the possibility that the images on the screen systematically misrepresent the external objects they are supposed to depict.

This argument from the causal account of perception cunningly uses the scientific view of the world, as I have said, to save it from observational refutation. The scientific view of the world itself implies that our senses are almost bound to lead us astray systematically about the real nature of things.

But the argument establishes more. It seems to provide overwhelming grounds for believing in *Cartesian dualism*.

Cartesian dualism is one of five major attempted solutions to our fundamental problem. It seeks to solve the great fissure, the clash of continents, by declaring that there are two worlds, two realms of existence: there is, on the one hand, the physical universe, composed exclusively of physical entities with physical properties; and on the other hand there is the world of Mind, the world of consciousness, that accommodates everything that the physical universe excludes and is quite different in character from anything physical. Our Mind contains our experiences, our thoughts, our feelings, our desires, everything we consciously experience. Minds are linked to living brains, and there may be a two-way interaction between brains and Minds.[27]

Cartesian dualism attempts to solve the human world/physical universe problem by sharply separating out the human world from the physical universe. The former is to be associated exclusively with this Cartesian entity, the conscious Mind.

Cartesian dualism may strike one as wildly implausible just because it postulates this weird, ghostly entity, the Mind, somehow entirely distinct from anything material or physical and yet, mysteriously, floating in some way within, or above, the brain. What possible grounds could we have for believing in such a fantastical, ghostly entity?

The argument from the causal analysis of perception provides us with such grounds. According to this argument, when you look at things in the world, what you are really, directly perceiving – what you really know about – are the visual experiences you have, your inner visual experiences of trees, fields, sky, people, buses, houses, or whatever your visual experiences may be composed of. You don't directly perceive the external objects, the trees, the fields, and so on. At best, you infer that that is what you are looking at. What you directly perceive, and most immediately know about, are your inner visual experiences of these external things.

There is one point, then, about which we can be absolutely certain. These inner visual experiences are utterly different from anything going on in our brain. Our brain is made up of soggy grey matter creased and folded, in turn made of billions of neurons, synaptic junctions, and glial cells. All that is utterly different from our inner visual experiences, composed of perceived vistas of green grass, the sight of people walking, a perceived dome of blue sky. Insofar as we know anything when we see (or hear, touch, smell, or taste), we know utterly and intimately the real nature of our inner perceptual experiences – according to the argument from the causal account of perception – and what we know tells us that these inner experiences are wholly different from all that there is in the brain. Mysteriously, furthermore, these inner experiences are wholly private to us. If anyone else opens up my skull and looks inside, without killing me or rendering me unconscious, they certainly won't come across anything that remotely resembles my inner experiences. My brain is a part of the public material world, the physical universe; my Mind is private to me and utterly distinct from the public material world.

Thus, to update slightly what I said earlier, the argument from the causal account of perception performs two functions. It saves the scientific view of the world from obvious observational refutation. And it provides a convincing argument for Cartesian dualism. It does these things, at least, just as long as the argument is *valid*. Whether the argument is valid or not will be examined in the next chapter.

The argument from the causal account of perception has played a quiet but key role in persuading many scientists and nonscientists, from the beginnings of modern science, that both the scientific view of the world and Cartesian dualism (or something like it) deserve to be accepted. It is striking that Galileo in the quoted passage does not – quite – appeal to the argument, although his remarks about tickling and the feather get close. Descartes, who first clearly enunciated what later came to be called Cartesian dualism, did not appeal to the argument in expounding and defending the view. Nevertheless, the logic of the situation is such, I suggest, that it is this *argument from the causal account of perception* that plays a key role in rendering acceptable both the scientific view of the world and the doctrine so closely linked to it, Cartesian dualism.

But Cartesian dualism presents us with horrendous problems.

First, this irredeemably private, ghostly Cartesian Mind has such weird properties that it is very difficult to believe it actually exists. Can we really believe there are all these Minds floating about in the world, utterly distinct from brains but nevertheless mysteriously linked to brains? When in evolution did they first emerge? How could a step in evolution, a mutation perhaps, abruptly create this entirely new kind of nonmaterial entity, the Cartesian Mind? It all seems like the most ludicrous spiritual nonsense.

Second, there is the problem of how Mind and brain interact, or are interrelated – the so-called mind-body problem. The brain must cause things to occur in the Mind, or we would not perceive anything at all. But does the Mind cause things to occur in the brain? If it does, then purely physical explanations of what goes on in the brain must be incomplete, or false. Those events caused by the Mind cannot be explained physically. This would amount to poltergeist-type events persistently occurring in the brain, events that are not as dramatic, but just as implausible, as scenes depicted in horror movies, when a disturbed child causes furniture to be hurled about the room by thought alone. On the other hand, if our Mind does not cause events to occur in the brain, then there can be no such thing as free will. We are bereft of the power to act. Our Mind is utterly impotent.

Third, there is the horrendous problem of how we can ever know anything about the external world whatsoever, if Cartesian dualism is true. For Cartesian dualism locks us up inside our Cartesian Mind. All we ever perceive are our inner perceptual experiences of things external to us, the flickering images on our internal television screen. How, then, can we possibly know that our inner perceptual representations of external objects resemble these external objects? We can never hold a daffodil in one hand, and our inner perceptual Cartesian mental representation of it in the other hand, to compare the two. Any such comparison can never be made. We are, according to Cartesian dualism, condemned to be stuck forever inside our skulls, inside our Cartesian Minds, staring at the flickering images on our internal TV screens.

John Locke (1632–1704) tried to solve this problem with his *representational theory of perception*, as it came to be called.[28] Physical objects external to us do really possess some properties, such as shape, size, and number. These Locke calls primary qualities. Our inner perceptual representations of these features of things do genuinely and accurately depict the real features of things external to us, the primary qualities. But all the other perceptual features we seem to experience – the colours, sounds, smells, tastes, and tactile qualities – do not accurately represent their external cause. Some combination of primary qualities corresponds to these perceptual experiences of colour, etc., very different from what we seem to see, hear, smell, taste, and feel. Locke called these combinations of primary qualities *secondary qualities.* According to Locke, then, we see clearly the nature of primary qualities in perception, but have only a massively delusive experience of the nature of secondary qualities.

It did not take long for a philosopher to come along and detect the fatal flaw in Locke's theory. That philosopher was Bishop Berkeley (1685–1753). He pointed out that there could be no reason whatsoever to distinguish primary qualities (which we can see accurately) and secondary qualities (which we wholly misrepresent). All we ever know are our inner perceptual experiences. Confined remorselessly to our Cartesian Minds, we can only know about the contents of our Cartesian Minds. We cannot know anything else at all. Thus Berkeley came to defend the *second* of the five attempted solutions to our fundamental problem: *idealism.* There are only perceptual experiences and ideas: the material world does not exist at all. As we can only ever experience our inner experiences, and can never experience anything material and external at all, we can have no evidence in support of the material world at all. And Berkeley summed it up in a succinct phrase: *esse est precipe – to exist is to be perceived.*[29]

One can argue that it is not just that we can have no *evidence* in support of the existence of a material world, no *reason* to believe in its existence: even more serious, all propositions about the material world must be *meaningless.* We can describe meaningfully what we have had experience of, our visual, auditory, and tactile experiences. And we can describe meaningfully what we can compare with these inner perceptual experiences. But we can say nothing meaningful whatsoever about that which cannot, even in principle, be compared with our inner experiences. And that means we can say nothing meaningful about a hypothetical external material world. For that would require that we can make the comparison between a perceptual experience, and what it is supposed to be the perception of, a bit of the material world, a daffodil for example. But it is just that comparison that is inherently impossible to perform. Hence, not only can we have no evidence or reason whatsoever to believe the external material world exists. The very hypothesis that it does exist is meaningless. We have no choice other than to adopt idealism.

There is, of course, something seriously fishy about this argument. We begin with the scientific vision of the universe. We are then led to adopt Cartesian dualism, which in turn leads us to conclude that there is only Mind, the physical universe vanishing from the scene. This argument is, at best, a *reductio ad absurdum.* It begins with the scientific vision of the universe and ends with the conclusion that there is no such thing as the material universe at all – a contradiction. The argument does not establish idealism; it is at most a refutation of the scientific view of the universe. It could be argued, however, that if we reject this view, then idealism remains as the only option.

Idealism solves our fundamental problem with drastic simplicity: eliminate the physical universe, and the problem disappears!

One might think, however, that idealism is such an absurdity that no one, other than Bishop Berkeley himself perhaps, could possibly take it seriously for a moment. Not the case at all. Berkeley's idealism, watered down and transformed in various ways, exercised a profound and far-reaching influence on subsequent philosophy, and on subsequent thought more generally.

It profoundly influenced David Hume.[30] His entire philosophy assumes that all our knowledge consists of *sense impressions* (what I have called perceptual experiences) and *ideas* – the latter pale echoes of combinations of the former. Hume goes on to argue that an idea, in order to be meaningful, must be such that it can be traced back to some combination of sense impressions. The idea that there exists a *necessary connection* between cause and effect cannot, for example, be traced back to sense impressions; hence, Hume argues, it is meaningless. Cause and effect may be constantly conjoined, but there is no objective *necessity* ensuring that if one occurs, the other will also occur *necessarily* (or if there is such an objective necessity, we cannot have an idea as to what it is).

Berkeley's idealist outlook profoundly influenced Immanuel Kant,[31] partly via Hume. Kant, like Hume, thought all our knowledge is built up from sense experience, but he also thought that experiences, in order to be conscious, had to exhibit a certain *order* or *coherence*, and that means that there are certain basic principles which we can be absolutely certain all conscious experiences will verify – because if they don't, they won't be conscious! Kant differed from Berkeley in holding that the real world, the world external to our Minds, does exist, but he also held that there is nothing meaningful that we can say about it, because it lies beyond all possible experience. All we can say is that it exists.

Hume and Kant, in turn, exercised a profound influence on subsequent philosophy and thought. Hume influenced John Stuart Mill,[32] Bertrand Russell,[33] Ernst Mach,[34] Albert Einstein,[35] the logical positivists and logical empiricists,[36] A.J. Ayer,[37] and a vast host of more modern philosophers at work in Britain, North America, and Australasia in so-called *analytic* philosophy. Analytic philosophy holds that the task of philosophy is to analyze language and concepts, an idea that goes back at least to Hume, as we have seen. Kant influenced a host of philosophers in Europe who took seriously the Kantian idea that there is this world of structured experience that needs to be studied by direct contemplation and thought alone, untouched by natural science. There emerged much obscure work in metaphysics, often Idealist, anti-rationalist, and indifferent to, if not hostile toward, natural science. Kant led to Fichte, Schelling,[38] Schleiermacher,[39] Hegel,[40] Schopenhauer,[41] Husserl,[42] and Heidegger.[43] This post-Kantian metaphysics even spread to Britain with the work of Green, Bradley, and McTaggart,[44] and to France with existentialism, structuralism, post-structuralism, and the work of Jean-Paul Sartre[45] (1905–1980), Maurice Merleau-Ponty,[46] Michel Foucault,[47] Jacques Derrida,[48] and many others belonging to the so-called *Continental* school of philosophy. And these two schools, analytic and Continental philosophy, broadly speaking, still dominate down to today (2017 at the time of writing).

Philosophy lost the plot. The story I have just sketched began well, with Descartes and Locke making a good, initial stab at solving philosophical aspects of the human world/physical universe problem. It should, however, have rapidly become apparent that Cartesian dualism creates more problems than it solves, and so a better attempt at the solution to the fundamental problem needs to be found. Initially, this did happen. Both Leibniz[49] and Spinoza[50] put forward alternatives to Cartesian dualism. But then the original problem – the human world/physical universe problem – got increasingly lost sight of. Instead of returning to it, philosophers for centuries, paradoxically and absurdly, continued to grapple with problems generated by Cartesian dualism *even though they rejected this very doctrine, the doctrine that created these problems in the first place.* What they failed lamentably to do was return to the original human world/ physical universe problem that Cartesian dualism fails to solve, try to get clearer about what the problem amounts to, and what alternative possible solutions there may be that do justice *both* to what seems to be of most value about our human world *and* what science seems to tell us about the universe. Very strikingly, granted the views of Berkeley, Hume, Kant, and many of their successors, one cannot even *state* the human world/physical universe problem properly, let alone put forward possible solutions for consideration. Berkeley eliminates one half of the problem: the physical universe. Hume renders it impossible to talk meaningfully about it, insofar as the physical universe lies beyond the reach of human experience. And Kant declares that the real world, the noumenal world as he called it, does exist but nothing meaningful can be said about it (apart from that it exists).

One very striking feature of this sorry tale of philosophy increasingly failing to come to grips with its basic problem is the glaring contrast between philosophy and science. Initially, these two enterprises were one. Modern science began, in the seventeenth century, as natural philosophy, a synthesis of what we today call natural science and philosophy. Today, we may declare Kepler, Galileo, Hooke, Boyle, Huygens, and Newton to be scientists, Francis Bacon, Descartes, Leibniz, Locke, and Spinoza philosophers, but that classification is something we project, anachronistically, into the past. At the time, they were all natural philosophers. But then the more scientific aspects of natural philosophy began to go from strength to strength. A cascade of discoveries were made in physics, chemistry, biology, astronomy, and geology, transforming our knowledge and understanding of the natural world, throughout the seventeenth, eighteenth, and nineteenth centuries. A gulf opened up between astonishingly successful natural science on the one hand, and increasingly unsuccessful philosophy on the other.[51] Philosophers failed to keep up with the avalanche of scientific discovery and progress. Instead, they shambled off into various kinds of increasingly irrelevant, obscure absurdities that had little or nothing to do with natural science.

The basic failure of philosophy, however, was the failure to keep alive awareness of the human world/physical universe problem – so that it would come to be generally understood, as science advanced, that this is our fundamental problem, and needs sustained attention, persistent efforts being required to improve attempted solutions in the light of scientific progress. If philosophy had been pursued in that spirit, from Descartes onward, natural philosophy would never have split apart into science and philosophy. Philosophy would have remained an integral and fundamental part of natural science.[52]

Nothing of the kind occurred. On the contrary, as philosophy developed, it became increasingly difficult, if not impossible, even to *state* the human world/physical universe problem within the context of philosophy, let alone develop better ideas as to how it is to be solved.

In recent decades, things have improved a bit. Philosophers have begun to explore aspects of the human world/physical universe problem, for example, J.J.C. Smart (1963), Thomas Nagel (1986), and David Chalmers (1996). Karl Popper has tackled urgent problems with their roots in the real world with exemplary clarity, integrity, and originality,[53] and has argued that this is what philosophy ought to do.[54] Academic philosophy has failed, however, to put our fundamental problem centre stage, so that every university would have an enduring Symposium that explores the problem, and explores interactions between the problem and more specialized research, to which everyone is invited. Academic philosophers have made no attempt to set up such a Symposium; even worse, they have not even had the idea that it is a basic responsibility of philosophy to do so.[55]

So far, I have considered two attempts at solving the fundamental philosophical problem: Cartesian dualism, and idealism, the second emerging from the first. Cartesian dualism creates horrendous problems, and idealism seems absurd. Are there any other ideas that are better?

Three further proposed solutions deserve special consideration.

The first is *materialism* or *physicalism*. Idealism tries to solve the problem by denying the existence of the physical universe. Physicalism tries to solve the problem by denying the existence of the human world – as something distinct from the physical. Everything, according to physicalism, is made up of basic physical entities, whatever exactly these may be. Everything that seems to be nonphysical – colours as we experience them, inner experiences, feelings and thoughts, persons, states of consciousness, actions consciously performed by people, the existence of that which is meaningful and of value: all this, insofar as it cannot, even in principle, be derived from physics, is a pure illusion and does not really exist. In the end, everything is just physical in character, and that is all there is.[56]

Physicalism implies that everything that cannot even in principle be derived from physics does not exist. Colours, sounds, smells, tastes, and tactile qualities, as we experience them; our inner experiences, thoughts and feelings as they appear to us; much of the content of what we think, say, and write; the meaning of works of art and music; actions that we perform of our own free will; the meaning and value of our lives; even perhaps our existence as persons: all these things, insofar as they cannot be derived from physics, do not exist, and our impression that they do exist is a massive illusion.

Even science itself becomes problematic, as science depends on there being theories, valid arguments, meaningful propositions, and it is difficult to see how there could be a purely physicalist account of these things. What a sentence asserts is not the same as the material manifestation of the sentence in the form of ink stains on the page, for example, or marks on a screen. The latter might be purely physical, but it is hard to see how this could be the case for the former, the content of the sentence, what the sentence asserts.

The second idea that deserves consideration is the *common sense view of the world*, sometimes called *naive realism*. This accepts that the world really is as it appears to us in ordinary life. The task of science is to predict observable phenomena, not undermine belief in the reality of what we observe. Unobservable theoretical entities postulated by physical theory – electrons, protons, quarks – are convenient fictions, not real entities of the material world. The whole of scientific theory must be interpreted to be about the observable, and thus cannot deny the reality of what we observe. And if the unobservable physical universe of physicalism does not exist, equally the Mind of Cartesian dualism doesn't exist either. We experience sensations and feelings, but that doesn't mean there is a Cartesian Mind floating around inside our head.[57]

But can we human beings really be the measure of all things in the way that naive realism seems to require? What of the world before any human beings were around to make observations, and when conditions were such that human beings could not have existed in any case? What of conditions now, where human beings cannot exist to make observations: the centre of the earth, the centre of the sun, the centre of a black hole? Real physical states of affairs and processes exist there, and yet they are in principle unobservable by human beings. And is physical theory really acceptable if reinterpreted to be about what can be observed by human beings only, and not about physical entities in principle unobservable? Is it, in addition, really unproblematic to associate physical processes going on inside our heads with our inner experiences, when these inner experiences seem so utterly different from anything to be found in the brain?

The third and final option to be considered is *the two-aspect view*, usually attributed to Spinoza.[58] This holds, not that there are two kinds of entity, the physical and the mental, but rather that there are two kinds of features or properties of things. Material things in the world, material processes – such as those associated with a forest fire, let us say, or those that go on in our brains – have two kinds of features: *physical* features, the exclusive concern of physics, and *mental* or *experiential* features, such as the colours and sounds of things in the world around us as we experience them, and the mental features of brain processes that go on inside our heads, our awareness of our inner states of consciousness, our inner experiences.

This view faces a host of problems too. How are we to explain and understand the existence of the experiential features of things, in addition to the physical? How are the interconnections, the correlations, between the two to be explained and understood? Why does the experiential exist at all? What do we really see and know about in perception? What are the defining characteristics of the *physical* and the *experiential*? How are these two kind of features to be distinguished? Are *experiential* features purely subjective, or do they have an objective existence too? Are colours, sounds, smells, etc., real, objective features of things in the world around us? Or are they features only of processes going on in our brains? If the latter, why do just brain processes have these mysterious, extra, experiential features?

It is a version of this two-aspect view that I defend in this book. I tackle these problems in the next chapter.

We have before us, then, five attempted solutions to the philosophical part of the human world/physical universe problem: Cartesian dualism; idealism; physicalism; naive realism; the two-aspect view. All face serious problems.

Many other ideas have been put forward.[59] Most people alive today probably see the world in religious terms. Like Isaac Newton, they believe that God is ultimately in charge of the physical universe, so our fundamental problem needs to be reformulated as the problem of our human world existing within the being and care of God. (This is the way Bishop Berkeley saw the matter.)

Any such religious view is faced, however, with a devastating objection. The idea that there is a God who is all-knowing, all-powerful, and all-loving faces the dreadful problem of an out and out contradiction. Given all the human suffering and death that has been caused, and continues to be caused, by natural phenomena, and thus by God, since God is ultimately in charge, one can only declare God to be a mass torturer and murderer to an extent that far outdoes the crimes of a mere Hitler or Stalin. The conjecture that an all- knowing, all-powerful God exists is decisively refuted by human experience. Such a God is not good, but a cosmic Monster.

Human suffering and death caused by natural phenomena is actually caused by something utterly impersonal, and thus incapable of knowing what it is doing: the physical universe. We could not forgive God His monstrous deeds if He existed, but we can forgive the physical universe because it is not capable of knowing what it does.[60]

Rational (that is, imaginative and critical) exploration of our fundamental problem would include consideration, not just of diverse attempts at solving the problem, but also of diverse ways in which the problem may be formulated – the merits and demerits of alternative formulations being open to discussion.[61]

Are there reasons for adopting the formulation of the fundamental problem given in this book? Yes, there are. In chapter 4 I expound a doctrine I call aim-oriented empiricism. This provides good reasons for taking what physics tells us about the universe very seriously indeed – and thus for adopting the version of the fundamental problem that I discuss in this book.

3

How Our Human World Can Exist in the Physical Universe

❧ *Outline of the two-aspect view* ❧

One of the intellectual diseases of the modern age is rampant spe-cialization.[1] This would not matter at all if there were a sufficient drive in the opposite direction – a drive to generalize, to encom-pass broader and broader vistas that stretch across all disciplinary boundaries. It is this that is lacking. This lack accounts for the failure to install the human world/physical universe problem as the central, fundamental problem of all thought in the university, encompassing all other more specialized problems of research and education.

Even within philosophy, there is a marked tendency to split the human world/ physical universe problem into a number of more specialized, distinct problems: problems in the philosophy of phys-ics, problems of perception, the mind-body problem, the problem of reductionism versus emergentism,[2] problems in the philosophy of biology and evolution, problems in the philosophy of psychology and other social sciences, problems of ethics; problems of political philosophy.

In order to solve the philosophical human world/physical universe problem, however, it is absolutely essential to resist this fashionable urge to chop the problem up into bits. This is because, in order to solve the problem, we need to bring together, to *integrate*, ideas from different aspects of the problem: ideas about what it is that phys-ics tells us about the universe, with ideas about the nature of the experiential, with ideas about what it is that we know about most directly in perception. We need to compare and contrast the very different ways in which physical phenomena and human actions can be explained and understood. It is absolutely essential that we can move about, from one aspect of the problem to another, in this way interconnecting disparate ideas. This we can do if we keep the fundamental problem before us, in all its generality. We cannot do it if we chop the problem up into isolated, specialized bits.

There is one confession that I ought, I think, to make, a sort of declaration of intellectual prejudice. Many who have thought about the problem have tried to soften it at the edges. They have sought to show that physics does not present us, after all, with such a harsh, alien, threatening view of the universe that seems to deny we have any value, any meaning, even any existence as persons. Others have sought to deny that there is this mysterious inner world of experience and consciousness that seems so at odds with anything going on in our brain. My inclination is to do the exact opposite to both blurring, softening tendencies. I seek to formulate the problem in the harshest, most extreme way possible, and then solve that version, in a way which does justice *both* to what science seems to be telling us about the universe and ourselves, *and* to the full richness and miraculousness of our human life on this earth. My hunch is that if we allow ourselves to conceive of ourselves fully as an integral part of the physical universe, we will also be able all the better to realize the full richness of what it is to be alive. We will not be crouching in fear, shielding our eyes, trying to keep terrifying knowledge of the nature of the universe at bay.

THE TWO-ASPECT VIEW

There is just one world, and we are a part of it. We can, however, distinguish two aspects to things, two kinds of features of things: the physical, and the human. The physical, very roughly, is what physics seeks to depict. The human is made up of all those features that are distinctive of our human world: the look, sound, feel, smell, and taste of things; the mental aspects of our inner experiences, our feelings, desires, and thoughts; what it is to *be* a certain kind of physical system (a conscious person); the human character of human actions and lives; the meaning and value of things; our friendships, quarrels, and loves; our dreams, our plans, decisions, deeds; our works of art, our literature, music, and science; our technology and architecture; our laws, traditions, and institutions.

But it is not just that two kinds of features of things can be distinguished, the physical and the human. Even more strikingly, things are intelligible, or comprehensible, in two very different kinds of way: physically and humanly. On the one hand, everything has (in principle) a physical explanation; everything is comprehensible physically. And on the other, some things, namely, ourselves, and some aspects of our human world, are intelligible or comprehensible humanly.

We are, in other words, doubly comprehensible. We are comprehensible physically (as physical systems); and, simultaneously, we are comprehensible humanly (as conscious persons, as persons acting in the world). The miracle of miracles is that we are comprehensible in both ways, simultaneously, the two kinds of comprehensibility intermeshing subtly and intricately, so that both can be valid at one and the same time.

How is this miracle of *double comprehensibility* to be understood? Via biology and evolution. Darwinian evolution, appropriately interpreted, enables us to understand how this miracle of double comprehensibility can have come to obtain. Biology is the umbilical cord that connects us to the physical universe (that is, it helps render intelligible the miracle of our double intelligibility).

The two-aspect view, as understood here, ought perhaps to be called *the double comprehensibility view.*[3]

I make no attempt to *prove*, or to argue for the truth of, this two-aspect, or duo comprehensibility, theory. All I do is try to show that, when developed a bit, it solves a host of problems (including problems of perception, the mind-body problem, and the problem of free will) and is thus a good candidate for the solution to at least an important part of the human world/physical universe problem.

There are problems aplenty. What are the defining characteristics of the *physical* and the *human* or *experiential*? How are these two kind of features to be distinguished? How are we to explain and understand the existence of the experiential features of things, in addition to the physical? How are the interconnections, the correlations, between the two to be explained and understood? Why does the experiential exist at all? What do we really see and know about in perception? Are *experiential* features purely subjective, or do they have an objective existence too? Are colours, sounds, smells, etc., real, objective features of things in the world around us? Or are they features only of processes going on in our brains? If the latter, why do brain processes have these mysterious, extra, experiential features? How are physical and human explanations to be understood? How can they both be validly applicable to the same things or processes? What ensures that one is not reducible to the other? I take these questions more or less in turn.[4]

THE PHYSICAL UNIVERSE

Physics seeks to depict only a highly selected aspect of all that there is – that aspect that determines, perhaps probabilistically, how instantaneous states of affairs evolve in time.[5] In other words, physics is concerned to depict only what may be termed the *causally efficacious* aspect of things.[6] The human, experiential features of things receive no mention within physics because these features are not causally efficacious. The *causally efficacious* features of our human world are depicted within physics (the molecular structure of things in our environment, the neurological processes going on in our brains), but not the *experiential* features of these things (the colours of things in our environment, our inner experiences, feelings, and thoughts).

That physics is concerned only with the causally efficacious aspect of things has one profoundly important consequence: the silence of physics about *noncausally efficacious* features provides no grounds whatsoever for holding that these features do not really, objectively exist. Insofar as colours, sounds, smells, tastes, and tactile qualities of things as we perceive them are not causally efficacious – that physics is silent about them – does not mean at all that they don't exist. And likewise for the experiential or mental aspects of processes going on inside our heads. If these aspects are not causally efficacious, then the fact that physics says nothing about them is no reason whatsoever for holding that they do not really exist (as some seem to suppose).[7]

The physical aspect of things is – I have suggested – that aspect that determines, perhaps probabilistically, the way instantaneous states of affairs evolve in time. But what exactly does this mean? It means this. There is some yet-to-be-discovered (perhaps never-to-be-discovered) physical theory that applies to *all* phenomena and, in principle, predicts how phenomena occur in time. Let us call this hypothetical theory T. Then, given T, and given a precise specification of the state of the universe at any given instant in time, T plus this specification, in principle, predicts subsequent states of the universe, when specified in the same terms.[8] Physical properties are those referred to by the specification of the instantaneous state of affairs. If T is probabilistic, not deterministic, then it predicts that a (probably very large) number of future states are possible at any given instant, and assigns a probability to each of these possible states, these probabilities all adding up to 1. Just one of these possibilities occurs; T can predict only the probability of its occurrence. In what follows I assume for the sake of simplicity that T is deterministic; we will consider again the possibility that T is probabilistic in chapter 5.

It is clear that T, in order to fulfill its predictive task, must be thoroughly comprehensive. It must apply to *everything* – everything that is causally efficacious, that is. If it misses out a kind of physical entity, or a kind of force, T's predictions will go disastrously astray, given that the neglected entity or force exists. But even though T can predict everything that occurs, that does not mean that it predicts *everything about* everything that occurs. It predicts only those facts about future states of affairs *that need to be specified for further future predictions* – the causally efficacious facts or features, in other words. Insofar as colours, sounds, smells, tastes, and tactile qualities as we perceive them, and our inner sensations, feelings, and thoughts, as we experience them, do not need to be referred to in order to further the predictive tasks of physics, they will not be referred to – although physical states of affairs and processes corresponding to them will be referred to. Experiential features play no role in physics, in short, because omitting all reference to them does not in any way impede the predictive tasks of physics.

It may seem a bit much that one could have, even in thought, a precise specification of the state of the entire universe at some instant. We can, however, characterize the comprehensiveness and completeness of T without appealing to a specification of the state of the entire universe. We can do it like this.

Consider any bit of the universe, taken a long way away from external forces, so that the bit in question forms an isolated system. We require that T, together with a precise specification of the state of the system at some instant, implies future states of the system *when specified in precisely the same way*.[9]

The comprehensiveness and completeness of T is guaranteed by the requirement that this has to be true of *all* possible isolated systems – *any* isolated bit of the universe.

In asserting that the universe is such that there *could exist* a yet-to-be-discovered (or possibly never-to-be-discovered) physical theory T, with the predictive powers just indicated, we thereby make a very powerful assertion about the nature of the universe. Let us call this doctrine *physicalism*. It is a component of the two-aspect view. We require, in addition that, insofar as there exist *nonphysical* properties and objects in the world, not included within physicalism, then, if these nonphysical properties or objects change, there must be physical changes as well. This denies the existence of Cartesian Minds, ghosts, spirits, and gods that change independently of physical changes. More substantial links between the physical and the nonphysical experiential and human will be discussed below.

Physicalism as I have characterized it so far is, in a sense, highly orthodox in that it presupposes a highly orthodox view of the aspirations of theoretical physics, namely, to discover T with the predictive powers indicated. In one crucial respect, however, this orthodox characterization of physicalism is profoundly unsatisfactory. There is no possibility of explaining *why* phenomena everywhere, for all time, conform precisely to the regularities stipulated by T. According to this version of physicalism, there is nothing that *exists* in the physical universe that determines necessarily that phenomena must always conform precisely to the predictions of T. And this mystery as to why phenomena everywhere observe precise laws can only deepen as physics advances, and the regularities specified by the best theories of physics become more and more wide-ranging and precise.

David Hume famously argued that there can only be *regularities* in the world; there cannot be *necessary connections* between successive states of affairs which might explain these regularities, a point I noted in the last chapter. But Hume was wrong. Necessary connections between successive states of affairs *are* possible. We cannot know for certain that they exist. But equally, we cannot know that they don't exist.[10]

Consider humble dispositional properties of our common-sense world: solidity, rigidity, inflammability, stickiness, transparency, solubility. All these properties determine how things change (or do not change) in certain ways, in certain conditions. If something is inflammable, then it bursts into flames if put into a fire. If it does not then, ipso facto, it is not inflammable.

Physical properties, like mass, electric charge, magnetic charge, even gravitational charge, are just like common-sense dispositional properties except that they are far more widely prevalent throughout the world, and specify absolutely precise changes in precisely specified conditions. Consider Newtonian gravitational charge, the power of massive objects to attract each other in accordance with

Newton's law of gravitation, $F = Gm_1m_2/d^2$. Here, G is a constant, m_1 and m_2 are the masses of two bodies at a distance d apart, and F is the attractive force that exists between them due to gravity. We can interpret Newton's law *essentialistically*, as attributing a *necessitating property* of gravitational charge to objects, equal to their mass. This is such that, if there are two bodies of mass m_1 and m_2, distance d apart then, *of necessity*, there is a force F of attraction between them, where $F = Gm_1m_2/d^2$. If such a force of precisely that strength does not exist then, ipso facto, the bodies do not possess the necessitating property of Newtonian gravitational charge. Newton's law ceases to be factual. It is what philosophers call "an analytic truth," like "All bachelors are unmarried." The law just makes explicit what it *means* to attribute Newtonian gravitational charge to a body, just as "All bachelors are unmarried" explicates what it means to say of a man that he is a bachelor. All the factual content of Newton's law is contained in the assertion "all bodies everywhere possess Newtonian gravitational charge, equal to their mass."

We may now add on Newton's law of force, $F = ma$, where m is mass as before, and a is acceleration, and interpret this essentialistically too, so that a body of mass m impressed by a force F of necessity accelerates in accordance with this equation. Given these two Newtonian necessitating properties, the one that necessitates acceleration in response to a force, and gravitational charge, then, given two bodies possessing gravitational charges equal to their masses m_1 and m_2, distance d apart, *of necessity* they will accelerate toward each other in accordance with these two laws. If they don't then, ipso facto, they don't possess these two Newtonian necessitating properties.

What all this enables us to do is to indicate how there could be *necessitating physical properties* in existence which provide an explanation why the regularities of T are observed by all phenomena. We interpret T *essentialistically*, as specifying *necessitating properties*. A physical universe made up entirely of entities that possess these necessitating properties must, as a result, obey the regularities of T. The *existence* of nothing but physical entities with these T-type necessitating properties suffices to ensure that the regularities of T are observed. If they are not then, ipso facto, entities with precisely those T-type necessitating properties do not exist – or something else physical exists in addition to them.

Deterministic physicalism can now be interpreted to assert the following. Consider an instantaneous state of the universe at any moment t. Consider, further, a precise, complete specification of the necessitating properties of things at time t, plus a specification of instantaneous changing states of affairs, such as relative position or velocity. Deterministic physicalism holds that such a specification at any time t implies specifications of subsequent states of affairs when specified in the same terms. Why are the regularities of T observed? Because what exists at any instant *necessarily determines* what exists subsequently in such a way that the regularities of T are observed.

The crucial requirement here is that the specification of what exists at time t, which implies logically what exists subsequently, *must not contain any factual assertion other than specifications of what exists at time t*. But, it may be objected, the specification of what exists at time t implicitly contains laws in the specification of necessitating properties. In the Newtonian case, the laws $F = Gm_1 m_2 /d^2$ and $F = ma$ are implicit in the specification of the corresponding necessitating properties, and so more than what exists at time t *is* included.

What this objection ignores is that these laws are interpreted to be *analytic truths*. They are not factual statements; they merely explicate what "Newtonian gravitational charge" and "Newtonian mass" *mean*. So they are not factual statements *in addition* to what exists at time t.

But is not this a disaster for this whole interpretation of physicalism, and the task of physics? How can theoretical physics be *empirical* and *factual* if all its laws are *analytic*? The answer is that the whole factual, empirical content of the theories of physics interpreted essentialistically resides in their assertion that the world is made up of such and such physical entities that possess such and such *necessitating physical properties*. The assertion that such and such entities with such and such necessitating properties *exist* is highly factual (and conjectural), and very far from being analytic.

We have here, then, a reinterpretation of the basic task of theoretical physics. It is, not to discover universally observed regularities or laws. Rather, it is to discover physical entities with universally possessed *necessitating physical properties* whose existence suffices to explain why corresponding regularities are universally observed.[11]

In addition, we have a reinterpretation of what it is to be a *physical property*, and what it is that *physicalism* asserts. A physical property is a *necessitating* property. And physicalism asserts that all phenomena occur in accordance with some yet-to-be-discovered comprehensive physical theory T, and they do so because they consist exclusively of entities that possess necessitating properties explicated by T when essentialistically interpreted.

Once it is recognized that necessitating properties are possible, it would be absurd to deny their existence while at the same time holding that phenomena conform to universal regularities or laws. For that would be to hold that, as far as what exists at this moment is concerned, *anything whatsoever might exist at the next moment*, it being utterly inexplicable as to why physical laws continue to be observed – *even though a perfectly sensible explanation does exist as to why these laws do continue to be observed*: it is due to the existence, at this moment, of entities with appropriate necessitating properties.

THE INCOMPLETENESS OF PHYSICS

Once it is clear that physics is concerned exclusively with the causally efficacious and, more specifically, with necessitating properties, it is clear that, despite its comprehensiveness, its capacity to be about *everything*, nevertheless physics will be entirely silent about vast domains of our human world. All sorts of aspects and features of our human world that we would ordinarily hold to exist just do not have the character of being *causally efficacious*: perceptual qualities; our inner experiences, feelings, and thoughts; the human meaning and value of things. All of this physics will remain silent about, even though it aspires to be about everything. In short, the moment it becomes clear that physics is *only* about the causally efficacious, it also becomes clear that all those features of things that are not associated with the causally efficacious will be omitted from physics. Physics is concerned only with a highly specialized *aspect* of all that there is.

But would this convince Democritus, Galileo, Newton, Zeki, J.J.C. Smart, and the host of modern scientists and philosophers who believe that there is nothing in existence in addition to the physical? Probably not. Here, however, are absolutely decisive grounds for holding that features of our human world must remain forever beyond the scope of physics, not so much because these features are too inexplicable to be captured by physics, but rather because they are features of a type of no interest to physics.

Consider again an isolated physical system, a tiny bit of the cosmos; and consider again the hypothetical physical theory T, applicable to all phenomena and capable in principle of predicting all physical phenomena. This time, however, suppose that the isolated system is a space capsule containing a person who looks at red shutters either side of the window of his capsule, thinks "what a tiresome shade of red," says for the sake of the voice recorder "next time I want blue shutters," and then inscribes in his diary "remember to ask for blue shutters for next space voyage." This is not a brilliant narrative, but it will do for our purposes.

T plus a precise specification of the physical state of the system at some instant logically implies specifications of the physical state of the system at future times.[12] (As I have already remarked, even if we had discovered T, we could not *in practice* predict future states because we would not be able to obtain sufficiently precise specifications of the system at the initial moment, and we would not be able to solve the equations of T to make the predictions. We can, nevertheless, consider what T predicts *in principle*.)

The all-important point to note is that the specification of the initial physical state of the capsule and its contents would say nothing about the redness of the shutters as seen by the cosmonaut, nothing about his inner visual sensation of redness as he experiences it, nothing about his thought, or the content of what he says or writes down in his notebook. All these human aspects of the situation would be left out. But the physical aspects of these human features would be included: the molecular structure of the dye covering the blinds which leads them to absorb and reflect light of such and such wavelengths; the light reflected by the blinds; the light that enters the eyes of the cosmonaut and there causes physical processes to occur in cells of the retinas of his eyes, in turn causing neurological processes to occur in his optic nerve and brain, in turn causing muscles to contract, air to be exhaled, vocal chords to vibrate which, in turn, send vibrations through the air and, as a result of other muscular contractions, marks to be made in a notebook. All the physical aspects of the human features of the situation are depicted and predicted, but the human features themselves are ignored. Physics ignores all the human features of the situation because these features are not required for the comprehensive, but also exclusive, narrow-minded predictive task of physics.

It deserves to be noted that all the human features of the situation
– colour, inner experience, thought, what is said and written – all
relate quite essentially to the human being, at least as a possibility.

Physics does not refer to human qualities of one kind or another
because it does not need to for the sake of its predictive tasks. But
of far greater significance, there is a decisive argument that shows
that physics *cannot* predict experiential qualities, even if scientists
wanted to. All physical properties and concepts, and all scientific
properties and concepts reducible in principle to physical ones, have
the following distinctive feature: one does not need to have any special kind of experience in order to understand them. One needs to
have *some* sensations, no doubt, in order to be conscious at all. But
in order to understand the physics of vision, for example, no special
kind of experience is required. Even though one is blind from birth,
one is not thereby debarred from understanding the physics of light
and vision just as well as a sighted person. The congenitally blind
or deaf person can understand wavelength, frequency, mass, energy,
and electric charge just as well as the person with sight and hear-
ing. All the predictive consequences of physics have this feature as
well: no special kind of experience is required in order to understand
them. But in order to understand what *redness* is, the visual property of a poppy, let us say, that those of us who are normally sighted
see, it is necessary to have had oneself a very specific experience at
some stage in one's life: the visual experience of redness. Those blind
from birth who have had no such experience cannot know what
redness is. They cannot know what "Poppies are red" *means*. And
that means that physics cannot predict "This poppy is red," however
complete a physical specification of the poppy, and processes occurring around the poppy, is provided. Physics cannot predict any fact
that is such that its statement can only be understood by persons
who have had some special kind of experience in the past. Facts
about perceptual qualities of things (if facts they be) are, however,
all of this type: they all do require one to have had some special kind
of experience in order to understand the statements that assert the
facts. Therefore, physics, and any science reducible to physics, however comprehensive, cannot predict perceptual qualities – or inner
experiences of them, we may add.[13]

But, it may be objected, is it not possible to extend the physical theory, T let us say, by adding on postulates that link physical

states of affairs and experiential qualities that are associated with them? This extended theory, T* say, would be able to predict experiential qualities.

There is, however, a fatal objection to this idea. Correlations between physical and experiential properties are incredibly complex. For example, a specific hue of redness does not correlate with one specific wavelength of light. Light of infinitely many different mixtures of wavelengths corresponds to the same perceived hue of redness. Furthermore, the precise colour we see is affected by kinds and levels of illumination, and what colours surround it. Thus the postulate linking physical states of affairs and a specific hue of redness is incredibly complex. Furthermore, there will be a vast number of these incredibly complex postulates, to take into account all the great variety of different sorts of perceptual and other experiences that we can have. And if we take into account experiences by other sentient beings, actual and possible, on our planet, and on other planets perhaps too, the list of postulates grows ever longer – and most of these postulates become incomprehensible to us in any case (because we can't have the experiences required to understand them).

What all this means is that the extended theory, T*, capable of predicting experiential qualities, is inevitably so extraordinarily complex, being made up of endlessly many incredibly complex postulates, that it is utterly nonexplanatory. By contrast, T, we may suppose, being a purely physical theory, like Newtonian theory, classical electrodynamics, quantum theory, or Einstein's theory of general relativity, is an astonishingly simple, unified theory, and therefore is *explanatory*. This is a theme that I will take up in the next chapter, where I will justify the claim that accepted physical theories must be unified, and so explanatory, and I will explicate what it is for a theory to be unified. Here, we may, very reasonably, assume that a basic task of science is to explain; only simple, unified theories are explanatory; and furthermore the extended theory T*, consisting as it must do of endlessly many horrendously complex postulates, must be wholly unacceptably nonexplanatory.

This, then, is the nub of the reason why physics ignores the experiential, the human. If it is taken into account, the wonderfully explanatory theories of physics *become so complex that they cease to be explanatory*. Ignoring the experiential, the human, is the price we pay to have the marvellously explanatory theories that we do have in physics. There is here, in other words, an *explanation* as to why physics must be silent about the experiential. Physics concentrates on the causally efficacious, comprehensible skeleton of the world so that it can predict and explain everything that goes on; it both can and must ignore the multitudinous experiential flesh of the world – the world of our experience.[14]

In brief, physics omits all references to colours, sounds, and smells as we experience them, not because they do not exist, but because (1) physics *can* omit all reference to them without this sabotaging its basic predictive and explanatory tasks, and (2) physics *must* omit all reference to them if physical theory is to be explanatory.

DO PERCEPTUAL QUALITIES REALLY EXIST OBJECTIVELY IN THE WORLD?

The argument so far establishes decisively that the silence of physics about perceptual qualities provides no grounds whatsoever for holding that these qualities don't objectively exist. I have not said anything so far, however, in support of the thesis that colours, sounds, smells, tastes, and tactile qualities, as we perceive them, really do exist objectively out there in the world. What reasons do we have for believing that poppies are red, grass is green, and daffodils are yellow?

Much depends on whether we hold that *the argument from the causal account of perception*, expounded in the last chapter, is valid. If it is valid, we can have no reason to believe that poppies really are red, just as we see them to be. But if the argument is invalid, we may come to a quite different conclusion.

The argument, remember, appeals to the long chain of physical processes that obtain between perceived object and inner experience, and comes to the conclusion that all we really know about in perception is the last event, the inner visual experience, in this long chain of events. We may, however, hold exactly the opposite view. What we really know about, in perception, is just what we ordinarily suppose we know: what we see, hear, and touch in the environment around us. In stark opposition to the conclusion of the argument from the causal account of perception, we may hold that all that we know about our inner perceptual experiences is derived entirely from our more fundamental knowledge of perceptual features of things external to us.

I am blindfolded. A portion of my skull is removed, and a probe stimulates the visual part of my brain. Suddenly I seem to see a yellow daffodil. I have the visual experience of seeing a yellow daffodil.

I definitely know that something is happening to me, something has come into existence. But what do I know about it? All I know can be put like this: *something is going on inside me that is like what goes on when my eyes are open and I really am seeing a yellow daffodil.*[15] In other words, I ordinarily know very, very little about my inner perceptual experiences, and what I do know is derived from my knowledge of the perceptual properties of things external to me – in this case the visual properties of a yellow daffodil.

We have before us two diametrically opposed views about what it is that we most directly, fundamentally *see* in perception. There is what we may call *internalism*: what we directly, most fundamentally see is our inner perceptual experiences. And there is the opposite view *externalism*: we most directly, fundamentally see what we ordinarily suppose we see, things external to us.

What view we adopt has dramatic consequences for the mind-brain problem. If we adopt internalism, we are obliged to hold, as we saw in the last chapter, that our inner experiences are fundamentally distinct from anything going on in the brain. We are pushed remorselessly toward some version of Cartesian Dualism. But if we adopt externalism, the outcome is quite different. According to this view, we hardly know anything about the real nature of our inner experiences, and certainly not enough to know that they cannot be brain processes. Indeed what we know fits in perfectly with the conjecture that they are brain processes. "What is going on in me is like what goes on when I really see a daffodil" fits in perfectly with the hypothesis that what is going on me is a certain kind of brain process that normally occurs when I really see a daffodil. The tiny bit we know about the nature of our inner perceptual experiences fits in perfectly with the hypothesis that these inner perceptual experiences are brain processes.

Accept internalism, and we are confronted by a major mind-brain problem. Accept externalism, and the mind-brain problem all but disappears – the *philosophical* part of the problem, that is.

How, then, do we choose between internalism and externalism?

If things in our environment possess only *physical* properties, we would have to reject externalism. For in that case, we would be obliged to hold that we do not really see, and know about, the real features of things around us. The perceived yellow daffodil is not real; it is an illusion. We have seen, however, that the silence of physics about perceptual qualities provides no grounds whatsoever for holding that these perceptual qualities don't really exist. That physics says nothing about the perceived yellowness of the daffodil doesn't mean that the daffodil isn't really yellow. So the silence of physics about perceptual qualities of things around us provides no grounds for rejecting externalism.

The argument from the causal account of perception, however, if valid, does provide strong grounds for accepting internalism and rejecting externalism. For that argument pushes us toward accepting that what we really know about in perception is the last event in the long chain of events, namely, the inner perceptual experience.

But is the argument valid? What do we really know about, fundamentally, in perception – the external perceived object or the inner perceptual experience of it? How do we decide what it is that we most fundamentally and directly *see* in perception?

The answer, I suggest, is that we really *see* what we really *know about* in perception. At once the argument from the causal account of perception is faced by the following challenge: granted that there does exist this long chain of events between daffodil and inner perceptual experience when I see the daffodil, what *reason* can there be for holding that what I really *know* about is the last event in this chain? Why should it not be that what I really know about is what we ordinarily suppose we know about, namely, the daffodil? The mere existence of the long chain of events between daffodil and my brain, my inner experience, does not in itself provide *any grounds whatsoever* for holding that what I really know about is my inner experience. Additional assumptions are needed to make this plausible. What might these additional assumptions be?

One assumption might be that we can only really *know* what we are intimately in contact with. I am intimately in contact with my inner experience, not the daffodil, so it's the former that I really know about, and so really *see*. But why should it be the case that we only really know about what we are intimately in contact with? Perhaps, on the contrary, the nature of our inner being (and processes that occur therein) is, as far as ordinary knowledge goes, a profound mystery. It is too close, as it were, for clear inspection.

Another, related assumption lurking implicitly in the way we think about perception may be a thoroughly naive view that might be called the *gaze* theory of perception. Once upon a time we thought we saw objects by sending out a gaze from the eyes. It is relevant that thinkers before Kepler did indeed tend to think of perception along

these lines. We think of perception on analogy with reaching out a
hand to touch an object. And of course seeing does involve muscular control of the eyes, in that we direct and focus our eyes. And
we experience the gazes of others when they look at us. Then we
learn about science, and realize, perhaps with a shock, that nothing
is emitted from the eyes; it is all the other way round. What I really
see, know, intimately touch, cannot be the daffodil, nor the (upside
down) image of the daffodil on my retina, nor the brain processes in
my brain: it must be my inner perceptual experience. But this whole
line of thought depends on adopting the fallacious *gaze* theory of
perception in the first place. Reject it, as we must, and the whole line
of argument collapses. We are left with no reason whatsoever for
holding that what we do not really know about, and so see, is the
daffodil. We do not need to send out a *gaze* to touch the daffodil to
know about it in perception, and so *see* it.

Another additional assumption that might be made is that what
we really *know about* in perception is what we cannot be mistaken
about, what we know *with absolute certainty*. I cannot know for
certain that the daffodil I seem to see really does exist. It might be
some kind of illusion, or a hallucination. But I cannot doubt that
I have the visual experience of seeing the daffodil: that is beyond
doubt. Hence, that is what I really know, and really *see*. But again,
the assumption deserves to be rejected. Why should what we really
know about in perception be beyond all doubt? Furthermore, this
argument from certainty does not, in any way, refute the thesis that
all I know about my inner visual sensation is "it is like what goes on
inside me when I see a daffodil." It does not rebut externalism.

There is a fourth consideration which may make the existence of
the causal chain of events associated with perception seem powerful
grounds for holding that what we *really see* are our inner perceptual
experiences and not things external to us. Invoke the causal chain
of events involved in perception – from light absorbed and reflected
at the surface of an external object, via chemical processes occurring
in the retina, to neurological processes going on in the brain – and
one thereby automatically invokes physics, since physics is what is
required to describe and explain this causal chain in full generality. As
an immediate consequence, all perceptual properties, such as colours,
seem to disappear from the external world. We have, however, only
limited scientific knowledge and understanding of our incredibly
complex brains; inevitably, there is the temptation to suppose that

in this region of our ignorance something as yet not understood and mysterious happens, and brain processes cause our inner perceptual experiences to occur, we experience colours and sounds which we, mistakenly, project outward onto things in the world around us.

But there is a double fallacy here. First, as we have seen, the silence of physics about colours and sounds in the world around us provides no reasons for thinking that these perceptual qualities don't exist. If they do exist, physics would not mention them (since they are not required for physical prediction, and cannot be included if we are to have physical explanation). Second, the reasons for physics to be silent about experiential qualities in the world around us are precisely also reasons for physics to be silent about the experiential aspects of our inner experiences. Once we enter into the world of physical descriptions and explanations, we will never encounter either the yellowness of daffodils or the inner perceptual experience of seeing yellow daffodils: instead we encounter electromagnetic waves of various wavelengths being absorbed and reflected by the molecules that go to make up the surfaces of the daffodil's petals, and neurological processes going on in our brains described as physical processes. If we hold that colours and sounds don't really exist in the world around us, then we should also hold that the extra-physical, experiential aspects of our brain processes, our states of awareness, don't really exist either. The arguments for the nonexistence of the one are as good – or as bad – as those for the nonexistence of the other. The complexity of the brain does not provide an honourable shelter to resist the import of this argument.

All the arguments exploiting the causal account of perception in favour of internalism and against externalism collapse. Both the internalist and the externalist accounts of perception are, it seems, viable. How do we choose? Internalism faces two major problems that externalism avoids. (1) If what we really see, and know about, in perception, are our inner perceptual experiences, how can we know anything about the external world? (2) If what we really know about are our inner perceptual experiences, then we know they are utterly different from anything going on in the brain; they must be distinct from the brain: we are confronted by the fully fledged mind-brain problem. Externalism avoids both problems. It holds: (1) What we know about in perception, most directly and fundamentally, *is* the perceptual character of things around us. (2) What I know about my inner perceptual experience of the daffodil – namely, that it is the sort of thing that occurs whenever I really see a daffodil – is so limited that it does not conflict at all with the conjecture that it is a particular kind of brain process. Indeed, what I know accords with the hypothesis that it is a brain process. The philosophical part of the mind-brain problem dissolves. The problem only arose in the first place because (a) the silence of physics about perceptual qualities was taken to be decisive grounds for holding that these qualities don't really exist out there in the world; and (b) the causal account of perception was mistakenly taken to provide grounds for holding that what we really know about, and so see, in perception is the last event in the chain of events, namely, the inner perceptual experience.[16]

All the arguments for internalism and against externalism – especially those that stem from the causal account of perception – collapse. Internalism creates severe problems which externalism avoids, without introducing any new problems of its own. It's a no brainer, as they say. We should reject the internalist account of perception, and accept the externalist account.

There is a good evolutionary reason why we and other mammals see what is in our environment and not what is inside our heads: animals that see only what is inside their heads would not be good at surviving.

SOME QUESTIONS

Does this mean that perceptual properties – colours, sounds, and so on – really do objectively exist as properties of things in our environment? Yes and no.

There are two quite different distinctions between objective and subjective.[17] The first has to do with existence: let us call it the objective$_E$/subjective$_E$ distinction, "$_E$" standing for "existence." A thing or property is objective$_E$ if it really does exist out there in the world; it is subjective$_E$ if it appears to exist but does not really do so. In terms of this first distinction, colours and the other perceptual qualities are objective$_E$. They really do exist out there in the world.

The second distinction has to do with whether a thing or property is, or is not, entirely independent of human experience and physiology. It has to do with whether it is utterly *impersonal*, or quite essentially related to *persons* in some way. Let us call this distinction the objective$_I$/subjective$_I$ distinction, "$_I$" standing for "impersonal." A thing or property is objective$_I$ if it is utterly impersonal, so that it is not related in any way to human experience or physiology; it is subjective$_I$ if it is related in some essential way to human experience or physiology – or perhaps to the experience or physiology of other sentient or conscious beings.

Colours and other perceptual properties are subjective$_I$. In order to discover what colours are – in order to know what they are – as we perceive them, you have to be a conscious being who has human visual experiences of colour, which in turn means that you have to have a physiology sufficiently similar in the relevant respects for it to be possible for you to have these experiences. If you come from another planet and have sense organs and a brain different from our human brains so that you cannot have experiences like ours, then you cannot know what the colours, sounds, etc., that we perceive, *are* – just as congenitally blind or deaf humans cannot. Thus colours, etc., are subjective$_I$. But that colours, etc., are subjective$_I$ does not mean that they do not exist. It does not mean that they are not objective in the first sense – objective$_E$ in other words. Perceptual qualities are objective$_E$ but subjective$_I$. They really do exist out there in the world (objective$_E$), but they are such that they relate specifically to human experience and physiology (subjective$_I$).

It is crucially important to distinguish these two different ways of drawing a distinction between the objective and the subjective. If we do not, we will be obliged to conclude, with Galileo for example, that the fact that perceptual qualities are subjective in one obvious sense (subjective$_I$ in other words) must mean that they do not really exist *objectively* in any sense. Make the above distinction, and it is entirely obvious that perceptual qualities can be subjective$_I$ *and* objective$_E$ – so that they really do exist out there in the world!

Some may argue that it is ridiculous to hold that the yellow quality of the daffodil that we see (or seem to see) really is a property of the daffodil itself, when almost everything that has to do with this perceived yellowness resides within us – within our eyes, our optic nerves and brain. This is a good argument for holding yellowness to be subjective$_I$, but it is not a good argument for holding it to be subjective$_E$. In order to become aware of the yellowness of the daffodil, the property that exists objectively$_E$ (but not objectively$_I$) out there in the world, it is essential to possess a human eye, optic nerve, and brain, and have them in good working order. Yellowness just is that kind of objective$_E$ property – very different, admittedly, from any property of physics.

We have every reason to believe that there are sentient beings on earth – bats, dogs, and other mammals – that experience qualities that we humans know nothing of. And it is reasonable to suppose that there are sentient, and even conscious, beings on other planets who experience qualities we know nothing of. Even if we are alone in the universe, still, presumably, other creatures with experiences different from ours are *possible*. We are thus led to hold that things in our environment have all kinds of perceptual qualities about which we can know nothing. The world is a richer place than we might at first suppose.

What, then, are these perceptual qualities, these colours, sounds, smells, tastes, tactile qualities as we experience them? They are just what we perceive, and know about, when we really do experience them, in standard conditions, and no more. Redness is not the disposition to cause the experience of redness in us. It is just what we see, and know – those of us who are not colour blind – and nothing more.

But what of our inner experiences? In experiencing the visual sensation of a yellow daffodil I know only "Something is going on inside me that is like what goes on when I really do perceive a daffodil that actually exists." The minuscule bit that I do know about my inner perceptual experiences is entirely compatible with the conjecture that these inner experiences are brain processes; indeed, the little that I do know fits in perfectly with the hypothesis that they are brain processes. But does this mean that inner experiences are *no more* than brain processes as described by physics, or by neuroscience?

It does not. When I declare, "What is going on inside me now is what goes on when I really see a yellow daffodil," my declaration goes beyond anything that can be predicted by physics because it refers to a *yellow* daffodil. A person cured of congenital blindness, and seeing and having inner visual sensations for the first time, learns something entirely new: what it is to experience colour, visual sensations. She learns what the *mental* or, as I have called them, the *apperceptual* properties[18] of certain brain processes are. Just as things in our environment have *perceptual* properties in addition to, and not reducible to, their physical properties, so too processes going on inside our heads – *head processes* we may call them – have mental or apperceptual properties in addition to their physical or neuroscientific properties.[19]

But what is the mental property of a brain or head process? As a first approximation we may say: it is what we are aware of when it occurs inside our heads – just that, and no more. Just as we *perceive* things external to us, we can, in a sense, *apperceive* processes inside our brains: the one is, in a way, the obverse of the other. One big difference between perception and apperception, of course, is that many of us can perceive the same yellow daffodil, but only I can apperceive the mental aspect of the brain processes that *are* my perception of the daffodil.

According to this head process view, sentient brains are unique among objects in the universe in alone having *three* aspects: physical, perceptual, and mental. There are the physical aspects of my head processes – the neurological processes going on in my brain. There are the perceptual aspects – normally hidden from view, but which would become visible if my skull were to be opened up. And there are the mental aspects of some of the head processes going on inside my head – aspects I alone experience as I see, feel, imagine, think, become aware.

Can we ever know whether another person has similar inner experiences to ours? According to the two-aspect view, we can. If another person is to experience what I experience when I see yellow, then that other person must have occur in his brain a brain process sufficiently similar in the relevant respects to the one that occurs in my brain when I see yellow, and which *is* my visual sensation of yellow. We require, furthermore, that our two brains are, structurally and functionally, sufficiently similar, and the two brain processes in question occur in the two brains in ways that are related to the rest of the respective brain in a sufficiently similar way. Each brain process must occur in that part of the brain associated with perception, and with colour perception.

What does "sufficiently similar" mean here? The truth is that we don't at present know enough about the brain to be able to answer this question. As we grow, and grow old, our brains change; what occurs in our brains when we see yellow changes. And yet, over time, we seem to see colours in the same way (unless we become colour blind, or blind). It is reasonable to suppose that the same sensation of yellow corresponds to a vast number of brain processes different in detail: a different number of neurons involved, firing in somewhat different ways. No two human brains are exactly alike – not even the brains of identical twins. But despite these neurological differences, we may, nevertheless, be able to experience exactly the same kind of sensations.

We may take the view that what matters, from the standpoint of what is experienced, is not what *stuff* a brain is made of, but rather the structural and functional features of the brain, its *control* aspects as I would prefer to say. If it is physically possible to have a brain in a body that functions like a human brain but is made of *microchips* rather than *neurons*, then we should take the view that the microchip person has inner experiences and states of consciousness essentially similar to a human being.

It deserves to be noted that this is not the same thing as *behaviourism* – the view that a being is conscious if it behaves as if conscious. One could imagine a vast computer that has, in it, a model of a conscious brain, and is able to calculate, in real time, processes going on inside the brain – if it existed. There is also a robot with eyes and ears, in radio communication with the computer. The computer receives signals from the robot reporting on what the senses of the robot detect. The computer then, very rapidly, works out how the brain of the robot would respond – if such a brain existed – and sends radio signals to the robot which prompt the robot to act *as if in response to what the robot has perceived.* The robot behaves, we may suppose, exactly as if it is a conscious being. Nevertheless, the robot is not conscious. No head processes occur anywhere required for consciousness. In particular, consciousness is not located in the computer. The computer calculates what processes would go on inside the robot's brain if the brain existed, *but no such brain does exist*, not even inside the computer. Processes going on inside the computer involved in calculating what the brain would do, what brain processes would occur, *if the brain existed*, are very different from the brain processes themselves, if they existed. A model of a brain is not a brain. A computer that calculates how a hypothetical brain would act is not thereby exhibiting brain activity. It is thus possible, in principle, to have a robot behaving as if conscious and yet not being conscious. And that suffices to establish that the "head process theory" – as we may call the account of the relationship between consciousness and the brain that I have just indicated – is not the same as behaviourism.

This account of the mental aspect of brain processes needs to be extended to take into account emotions, desires, imaginings, and thoughts. I do this in chapter 5. The broad idea, then, is that head processes have two aspects: the mental aspect (what we experience) and the physical or neuroscientific aspect (neurological processes going on in the brain). The relationship between the molecular structure of the daffodil petals (or light being absorbed and reflected by the petals) and the yellow colour of the daffodil is somewhat similar to the relationship between neurological processes going on in the brain and the visual experience of seeing the yellow daffodil. And just as a physical description of the daffodil, however comprehensive, is powerless to predict its yellow colour, for the reasons we have explored, so a physical description of brain processes, however comprehensive, would be powerless to predict the mental or apperceptual features of these processes – the features of the perceptual experience, in other words. The mental features of brain processes are, in a sense, no more mysterious than the perceptual properties of daffodils, poppies, hillsides, and ocean waves.

The philosophical part of the mind-brain problem is, in large part, generated by the false view that perceptual qualities of things external to us do not really exist out there in the world around us; reinforced by the false *argument from the causal account of perception*, it leads to the view that what we really know about in perception is, not the externally perceived object, but our inner perceptual experience, our inner mental representation of it. At once there is a horrendous problem of how this inner experience, this mental representation, can be related to neurological processes going on in the brain. Accept that perceptual qualities as we perceive them do exist around us in the world, accept that the argument for the causal account of perception is invalid, what we know about and directly perceive are things external us, not our inner experiences, and at once the philosophical mind-brain problem is transformed. We do not know enough about our inner experiences to know that they have properties – mental properties – that clash with, or pose a problem for, these inner experiences being neurological processes. That physical processes going on inside my head should have mental features of which I am aware is no more mysterious than that the physical daffodil has perceptual properties in addition to its physical ones.

Are perceptual and physical properties mutually exclusive? No, there is a sense in which they overlap. I *see* or *feel* that a football is roughly spherical, and the roughly spherical feature of the football is a physical property as well. I *feel* that a 20 kilo bag is heavy, or a lawn-roller is massive; weight and mass are physical properties.

Perceptual and physical properties overlap, and the domain of the overlap corresponds, very roughly, to what Locke called *secondary qualities* (concatenations of primary qualities that correspond to perceptual qualities we experience).

There would seem to be much less overlap when it comes to the mental and physical properties of head processes, but even here there is some. I am aware, let us suppose, that my inner experiences – my head processes – are changing in some way: there is a corresponding change in the neurological aspects of my head processes. Every experience, thought, and feeling, however gossamer and fleeting, *is* also some neurological process. A change in the former means a change in the latter.

Perceptual properties of things exist external to us, and mental aspects of brain processes exist within us. But science is, it seems, powerless to explain the existence of this vast domain of the experiential. How is this utterly mysterious domain of the experiential, floating somehow inside the physical universe, to be explained and understood?

The first thing to say in response to this question is that the experiential can *seem* profoundly mysterious just because it cannot be explained scientifically. So utterly inexplicable is the experiential – so it can seem – that it eludes entirely even our best kind of explanation, namely, scientific explanation. But this, as we have seen, is not a good reason for finding perceptual and mental features of things and processes inherently mysterious and inexplicable. There is a perfectly good reason *why* science (that part of science in principle reducible to physics) cannot predict and explain the perceptual and mental. Physics does not need to refer to the perceptual and mental to carry through its predictive and explanatory tasks; and if physical theory is extended to include the experiential, the resulting (extended) theory ceases to be explanatory. It is a straightforward, entirely understandable feature of our world that there cannot be a scientific explanation of the experiential. The failure of science to explain the experiential does not, therefore, render the latter mysterious. The experiential features of things we experience are utterly familiar to us – indeed the most mundanely familiar aspects of the world that there are.

But what about correlations between physical and experiential features of things – or human features, more broadly? How are these to be explained?

Some human/physical correlations are purely conventional and historical, such as correlations between what a sentence *means* or *asserts*, and its physical shape as written down on a piece of paper or represented on a computer screen. Other correlations are extraordinarily complex, and likely to depend, to some extent, on historical accidents, such as correlations between perceived colours, and physical states of affairs corresponding to perceived colours. Yet other correlations, even if extraordinarily complex, may be much more significant and illuminating, such as correlations between kind of brain process and kind of inner experience – say the inner visual experience of redness. How can correlations that we may conjecture to hold between brain processes and inner sensations of colour, sound, smell, taste, and feel be explained? Or can there be no such explanation because there can be no *scientific* explanation?

Philosophers, psychologists, and neuroscientists have long been baffled by this question. No one has been able to come up even with a *possible* explanation for such correlations. However, some years ago, I did think of a possible explanation.[20] Suppose our inner sensory experiences – visual, auditory, tactile, olfactory – are tiny patches of sensation in a vast virtual "space" of all possible sensations to be had by all possible sentient creatures whatsoever, this vast "space" being such that sensations vary smoothly as one goes through the space, so that the closer together two points are in the space, so more nearly the two corresponding sensations resemble one another. And consider another vast virtual space of all possible brain processes that correspond to, or *are*, sensations of one kind or another, brain processes being depicted in such a way that one kind of brain process corresponds to one kind of sensation. Suppose, further, that these two "spaces" can be put into one-to-one correspondence in *one way only* so as to preserve smoothness in both spaces, brain processes changing smoothly as one goes through the "space" of sentient brain processes, and corresponding sensations varying smoothly as well in the "space" of all possible sensations. If all this is the case – and it might be for all we know – then a kind of explanation *can* be given as to why *this* particular sensation – the visual sensation of redness, for example – corresponds to *this* particular kind of brain process. If the sensation was correlated with another kind of brain process, then smoothness would be violated, either in the "space" of all possible sensations, or in the "space" of all possible sentient brain processes.

All this argument establishes is that it is *possible* that there is an explanation for the way sensations and brain processes are correlated with one another. But that seemed to me to be important. Up to that moment, no one had been able to think of even a *possible* explanation. Once an explanation has been discovered *as a possibility*, the way is opened up for the development of an *actual* explanation.

Two features of my possible explanation are important, and are likely to be preserved in any actual explanation. First, my possible explanation appeals to a kind of *order* in the way sensations and brain processes are correlated. And second, it appeals to *all possible sensations* of all possible sentient creatures, not just to our actual sensations. Genuine explanations always fit what is to be explained into some big, coherent, patterned structure of possibilities.

UNDERSTANDING THE HUMAN WORLD

The emphasis of the discussion so far has been on *physics*: what it seeks to depict; how it predicts and explains; why its silence about essential features of our human world doesn't mean at all that these features don't really exist, or are inherently inexplicable. But I have said nothing, so far, about how our human world is to be explained and understood, in its own terms. I now make good that omission.

When it comes to people, a kind of explanation and understanding becomes relevant that differs profoundly from *scientific explanation*. If I want to understand another person *as a person* I need to know what it is to *be* that other person with his or her desires, fears, feelings, beliefs, view of the world, plans, skills, problems, relationships, pattern of activities, environment, values, self-understanding, and understanding of the world. I need to be able to imagine that I am that other person, desiring, feeling, believing, experiencing what that other person desires, feels, etc. I need to have the kind of understanding of the other person that I have of myself.

And I need more. It is likely to be true of all of us that our own self-knowledge and self-understanding has its limits, its deceptions, its illusions, its distortions, its areas of ignorance.[21] In order to understand another person *as a person* adequately, I need to know not just how that person understands himself or herself, but also that understanding *corrected* and *amplified*, all limitations, deceptions, illusions, distortions, areas of ignorance, and fallacies removed and corrected. The goal is what might be called *God-like understanding*.

I shall call this kind of understanding that people have of each other, more or less adequately, *personalistic understanding*. In the past I have called it *person-to-person understanding* to emphasize that, ideally, it is a kind of understanding that two people have of each other.[22] An essential feature of personalistic understanding is that it brings oneself into the picture, and involves imaginatively extending one's own experiences so that they become a simulacrum of the experiences of the person to be understood.

Something very similar to what I have in mind is often called *empathic understanding*, and psychologists and neuroscientists often refer to it as *theory of mind* and *folk psychology*. What I mean by *personalistic understanding* differs, in important respects, from what others mean by these other terms, as I shall explain in what follows, so I stick to my terminology.

All human life is aim-pursuing. Even when we are only idly day-dreaming, we are still pursuing aims, in our imagination. Our actual aims may differ from those we suppose we have. Our aims can be extraordinarily complex and varied, from the specific and immediate – to raise an arm, to close a door – to the long-term, vague, and aspirational: to become a success in one's chosen career, to find happiness, to do well for one's children. In order to acquire a good personalistic understanding of another person we need to discover what that person's complex hierarchy of goals in life are, how and why they are sought, how they are interrelated, what strategies, what repertoire of actions, are likely to be deployed in the attempt to achieve them, *both* what the goals are and what is in fact likely to be done in pursuit of them, *and* what the goals ought to be and what ought to be done in pursuit of them. We need to be able to enact in our imagination what the other person would do, feel, think, in a variety of situations, in pursuit of his or her goals in life.

Personalistic explanation and understanding is an enriched form of a much more widely applicable kind of explanation and understanding, namely, *purposive explanation*. This is applicable to anything that pursues goals, and it seeks to explain the actions of the thing in question as being designed to help achieve the goal in the given environment. But purposive explanations do not appeal to sentience or consciousness. Purposive explanations apply equally to nonsentient purposive things, such as bacteria, insects, self-guided rockets, and thermostats, and to sentient and conscious beings, such as foxes, rabbits, and people.

Darwin's theory of evolution tells us that all living things pursue the aims of survival and reproductive success. Plants pursue these aims, in the main, by means of growth. Purposive explanations thus apply to all living things. It is a basic task of evolutionary biology and the study of animal behaviour to explain characteristic actions of animals as being conducive to attainment of the basic goals: survival and reproductive success. Purposive explanations thus have an important role to play in biology. But, as I have already indicated, purposive explanations are also applicable to goal-pursuing devices that we have created: self-guiding rockets, robots, even thermostats.

The thermostat can be regarded as the *atom* of purposiveness. It has a very basic aim: to keep the room at some definite temperature, 18° centigrade, let us say. If the room gets warmer, a metal rod (in one kind of primitive thermostat) expands and shuts off the heating. If the room gets colder, the rod contracts and turns the heater on. The thermostat, in short, contains a negative feedback mechanism, and it is this which enables the thermostat to pursue, and attain, its aim.

All goal pursuing things, whether artifacts created by us, plants, nonsentient animals, sentient animals, or human beings, are able to pursue and attain goals in the real world because they possess negative feedback mechanisms, in the case of many living things feedback mechanisms of extraordinary complexity to match the complexity of the goals and actions of the living things in question. The guiding control systems of animals are, of course, the *brains* of these animals. Brains guide animals to act in their ever-changing environment so as to attain diverse goals – food, drink, escape from predators, shelter, mates, sleep, sustenance and safety of offspring – that are required to achieve the overall goals of survival and reproductive success. Brains consist of hierarchical structures of control systems. From the lowest to the highest, one might have neurological systems that control a muscle; a limb; characteristic actions of a group of limbs, such as running, leaping, sitting, lying down; an overall task, such as hunting, caring for young, finding a mate and mating, digging a burrow; choosing what task to pursue, when to pursue it, when to drop it for another kind of action (as when a rabbit, nibbling grass, gets a whiff of fox and runs for its life).

Purposive explanations may declare that the thing in question – robot, guided missile, chess-playing computer program – is "solving such and such a problem," "thinking what to do next," "deciding to swerve to the right to put the flight back on course," or "trying to overcome such and such an obstacle." Purposive explanations may, in other words, employ descriptive and explanatory vocabulary that comes from personalistic explanations; the meaning of this vocabulary is, however, stripped of any suggestion of sentience or consciousness. The chess-playing computer "thinks" about its next move on analogy with what a human chess player would be doing: processes are going on in the computer that need to occur before the computer is able to make its move, but there is no suggestion that the computer really does consciously *think* about what to do next, as a human chess player would.

All living things are doubly comprehensible: comprehensible *physically* and *purposively*. Sentient animals and conscious human beings are trebly comprehensible: comprehensible *physically*, *purposively*, and *personalistically* – the latter being reduced to the purposive when consciousness and sentience are excluded.

Neither personalistic, nor even purposive, explanations are reducible to physical explanations. We already know that personalistic explanations are not reducible to physical explanations. Personalistic explanations refer to perceptual qualities, inner perceptual experiences, conscious thoughts, feelings, and desires, none of which is reducible to the physical. That purposive explanations are not reducible to physical explanations is perhaps a bit more contentious. We can, however, argue that purposive descriptions and explanations include references to goal-pursuing, success and failure, problem-solving, thinking, deciding, perceiving, even acting for a reason (when one goal is pursued as a step toward realizing another, more distant goal). All these terms are stripped of any hint of consciousness or sentience. Nevertheless, they do not figure in any purely physical description or explanation, and it seems impossible to capture what they mean in purely physical terms.[23]

According to the version of the two-aspect view being defended here, however, purposive and personalistic explanations, though not *reducible* to physical explanations, are nevertheless *compatible* with physical explanations.[24] Everything we do, think, experience, and are is compatible with physicalism.[25]

This assertion may well be greeted with horror. If everything we do, think, and are is compatible with physicalism, does not this render personalistic explanations redundant? Are not the *real* explanations for what goes on in connection with human life purely *physical* explanations? Are not human desires, decisions, intentions, motives, all entirely redundant, the real reasons for our thoughts and our actions being purely physical? If physicalism holds sway, how can we have even a ghost of free will? Is not our whole life ruled remorselessly by physics? How can we even exist – since to exist as a person requires, as a minimum, that one has some power to act, even if only internally, in one's imagination, in what one does in thought? If everything we experience, think, and do is determined by physics, do we not become less than puppets to the physical universe, our whole life and existence nothing more than a gigantic illusion? Is not our entire human world no more than a local smudge of the experiential in this vast physical universe, without significance, our every flicker of thought, feeling, and·deed remorselessly determined by physics?

These crucial questions will be tackled in chapter 5. But before I do that, I must first confront the possibility that the threat to the meaning, the value, the mere *existence* of our human world that comes from the physical universe is even grimmer, harsher, more alarming, than what has been said so far might suggest. Not only does physicalism need to be interpreted in a much stronger, harsher way; we must, it seems, hold that this metaphysical thesis is a key component of current scientific knowledge.

In what follows, the version of the two-aspect view that I have expounded and defended in this chapter will be called *experiential physicalism*. This doctrine asserts that the universe is physically comprehensible; it is such that some yet-to-be-discovered unified physical theory of everything is true. The experiential exists in addition to the physical, and is not reducible to the physical for the reasons I have indicated.

PROBLEMS OF THE MINIMALIST TWO-ASPECT VIEW

Many contemporary philosophers defend versions of the two-aspect view[26] that differ radically from the version I have expounded here, experiential physicalism, in holding that the *only* physical processes that have nonphysical experiential aspects associated with them are those that occur in sentient or conscious brains. These versions of the two-aspect view hold that everything external to us is, in reality, devoid of the perceptual qualities we seem to experience – the colours, sounds, smells, tastes, and tactile qualities of things.[27]

These *minimalist* versions of the two-aspect view create insoluble problems that do not face the full-blooded version of experiential physicalism I have expounded here; as a result, they fail to do what experiential physicalism succeeds in doing, namely, solve an important part of the philosophical mind-brain problem.

The first problem that faces the minimalist version of the two-aspect view can be put like this: why should it be that, of all the vast diversity of physical processes that occur throughout the universe, the *only* ones that have nonphysical, experiential features or properties associated with them are processes that occur in sentient or conscious brains? What on earth can be so special, so distinctive, about physical processes occurring in sentient brains that causes them *alone* to have nonphysical features or properties associated with them?

The second problem arises from the first. How is it possible, even in principle, to understand how the minute, incremental changes involved in evolution can have abruptly created an entirely new kind of property, of which there was not a trace before, namely, a nonphysical, experiential property? At one moment, there is no nonphysical, experiential property on earth – it is all just physics; at the next moment, as a result of a minute evolutionary change, the mutation of a gene perhaps, there abruptly does exist an entirely novel kind of property in the world – a nonphysical, experiential property. It seems inconceivable that such a monumental, abrupt change – the creation, one might say, of a whole new category of being – could occur as a result of a minute step in Darwinian evolution.

There is no plausible solution to these two problems. Those who uphold the minimalist version of the two-aspect view are well aware of the profoundly problematic character of the view, and some are prepared to resort to desperate measures in an attempt to resolve these difficulties. Thus, Nagel argues that the implication must be that there is something profoundly inadequate in our whole scientific view of the world.[28] Others, such as Daniel Dennett, struck by the appalling implausibility of the experiential features, the so-called qualia or "raw feels" of the minimalist two-aspect view, are led, in effect, to deny that any such nonphysical inner experiences exist at all.[29] Still others, such as Chalmers and Galen Strawson, in an attempt to distribute the mental more widely throughout the universe (and thus solve the two problems), flirt with the idea of panpsychism: every physical entity, even the electron or the proton, has some kind of proto mental aspect as well as its physical aspect which, when billions of these particles are organized into a sentient brain, result in the mental experiences of the sentient creature.[30] But any such panpsychism view faces horrendous problems, as even its proponents tend to acknowledge.[31]

The full-blooded version of experiential physicalism expounded here does not face these difficulties. According to this view, familiar nonphysical, perceptual features exist throughout the universe whether there are sentient creatures around to experience them or not. When animals first experience inner sensations, it is not the case that a nonphysical, experiential feature abruptly comes to exist in a world that was devoid of any such feature before. Indeed, if we hold onto J.J.C. Smart's characterization of what it is to experience a visual sensation, we can perhaps begin to see how "seeing the yellow daffodil" might emerge very gradually, from something that is initially so dim as to scarcely exist to something vivid and intense as experienced, let us say, by William Wordsworth, or by you or me.[32]

What is the mistake that has led philosophers to uphold the minimalist version of the two-aspect view, and thus run into all these difficulties? The mistake is to fail to appreciate that physics seeks to depict, not *everything* about everything, but only a highly restricted, specialized *aspect* of everything, the causally efficacious aspect. Once this point is fully appreciated, it is clear that the silence of physics about the perceptual features of things – the redness of a tomato, the clang of a bell – provides no reason to think that these perceptual features do not really exist out there in the world. Fail to appreciate the point about the restricted character of physics, and at once the silence of physics about the perceptual does carry the implication that the perceptual does not exist.

There is an additional problem that faces versions of the two-aspect view that fail to acknowledge the highly restricted character of physics. If the physical is implicitly assumed to encompass everything about everything, it becomes baffling as to why there should be any nonphysical features of things at all. Acknowledge that physics is about only the highly specialized, causally efficacious aspect of everything, and this problem does not arise. It becomes understandable that other sorts of nonphysical features of things should exist as well: what things look like, sound like, feel like, smell like, taste like, and what it is to have such and such a physical process occur in one's own brain.[33]

The above mistake about physics is allied to a more basic mistake: the failure to put the mind-brain problem into the broader context of the human world/physical universe problem[34] – the context of our fundamental problem, in other words. It is the failure to pursue philosophy as critical fundamentalism!

SUMMARY

Key elements of the solution to the philosophical physical universe/ human world problem that I have proposed so far are the following. Physics is about a highly selected *aspect* of all that there is, the *causally efficacious* aspect (that which, at any instant, determines necessarily – if perhaps probabilistically – what occurs next). Physics does not need to refer to the experiential in order to carry through its predictive and explanatory tasks, and it *cannot* predict existential qualities such as colours as we see them, or mental features of our conscious experiences. Furthermore, physical theory cannot be extended to include the experiential: to do so would be to destroy the unity, the explanatory character, of physical theory. The silence of physics about the experiential thus provides no grounds whatsoever for holding it does not exist – and this applies just as much to perceptual qualities of things external to us as it does to mental qualities of brain processes inside our heads. That some brain processes have mental features we are aware of is thus no more mysterious than that the physical daffodil has perceptual features we are aware of, such as its yellow colour. Thus, the failure of physics to predict and explain the experiential does not mean that there is something inherently mysterious about the experiential which renders it impervious to scientific explanation. The reasons for the failure of physics to predict and explain the experiential are entirely clear. There is, furthermore, a different kind of *personalistic* explanation that renders people comprehensible *as persons*, a kind of explanation that is compatible with but not reducible to physical explanation. The experiential, necessarily ignored by physics, becomes comprehensible granted personalistic explanation. There is, furthermore, a possible explanation as to why the two aspects of processes going on inside our heads, the neurological and the mental, are correlated in the way that they are. All this solves an important part of the philosophical mind-body problem, the *hard* problem as it is sometimes called.[35] A crucial element of this solution is that the mind-body problem must be put back into the context of the broader, more fundamental physical universe/human world problem. Perceptual qualities of things external to us are just as much involved as are mental qualities of brain processes within us. And the nature of the *physical* is just as much an issue as the nature of the *experiential*. What it means to say of a physical theory that it is unified and thus explanatory, and what reasons there are for accepting unified theories in physics (to be discussed in the next chapter) are key components of the solution to the problem.

4

Is the Universe Physically Comprehensible?

⋙ Argument for aim-oriented empiricism ⋘

So far, in attempting to solve the philosophical part of the human world/physical universe problem, I have argued for the two-aspect view and, as an integral part of that, physicalism. Physicalism, as understood so far, is the doctrine that the universe is such that there is a yet-to-be-discovered physical theory, T, which is true and in principle predicts and explains all physical phenomena.[1]

But how do we know that physicalism is true? Or, more modestly and better, what reasons do we have for holding that physicalism is a conjecture worthy of acceptance? Almost all scientists and philosophers would hold that physicalism may be suggested by modern science but is very far from being a part of current scientific knowledge. How can it be? Physicalism is a *metaphysical* thesis; that is, it is neither falsifiable nor verifiable empirically, and so cannot be a component of scientific knowledge.[2]

This judgment depends crucially on a certain view of science being correct – a view so orthodox that almost everyone, scientist and nonscientist alike, takes it unthinkingly for granted. But this orthodox conception of science is untenable, and that changes everything. The upshot is that we need to adopt a new conception of science. This holds that physicalism *is* a part of current scientific knowledge, indeed an especially central, secure part. Furthermore, it is physicalism interpreted in an especially substantial, precise, and severe way that becomes a basic tenet of current scientific knowledge.

All in all, our fundamental problem, our human world/physical universe problem, will have become even harsher and more serious by the end of this chapter!

STANDARD EMPIRICISM

What is this orthodox view of science – so orthodox that everyone, scientists and nonscientists, takes it unthinkingly for granted? It is the view that in science only *evidence* may decide what theories are accepted and rejected. Most proponents of this view accept that, in deciding whether or not to accept a theory, scientists may legitimately be influenced by how simple, unified, or explanatory the theory is, but this influence must not operate in such a way that scientists in effect, surreptitiously perhaps, assume that the universe itself is simple, unified, or comprehensible. The absolutely crucial point is this: *in science, no proposition about the world can be accepted as a part of scientific knowledge independently of evidence – let alone in violation of evidence.*

I call this doctrine about science *standard empiricism*. It is taken for granted, as I have said, by scientists and nonscientists alike, and by almost all philosophers of science.[3] If acceptable, standard empiricism establishes decisively that physicalism, an unfalsifiable, metaphysical doctrine, cannot conceivably be regarded as a part of current scientific knowledge. But standard empiricism is not acceptable. An essentially simple argument shows decisively that it is untenable, and must be rejected. Here, in outline, is the argument.

REFUTATION OF STANDARD EMPIRICISM

Physics only ever accepts theories that are *both* sufficiently empirically successful *and* sufficiently *unified*. (In order to be unified, a theory must make the same assertion about all the phenomena to which it applies. A disunified theory, by contrast, makes *different* assertions about ranges of phenomena to which it applies. It might be called a *patchwork quilt* theory.) The second requirement of being *unified* is as important as the first. It even persistently overrides the first. Given any accepted, unified physical theory, endlessly many *disunified* rivals can be formulated especially doctored to fit the facts even better, and thus be even more empirically successful. These empirically more successful rivals are never considered for a moment, precisely because they are all horribly *disunified*.[4]

But this persistent preference for unified theories over empirically more successful disunified rivals means that physics makes a big, although possibly implicit, assumption about the nature of the universe: it is such that all disunified theories are false, however empirically successful they may be. This contradicts standard empiricism. For standard empiricism holds that science must make *no assumption about the world independent of evidence* (whether implicit or explicit). Standard empiricism is contradicted by what actually goes on in physics. It is contradicted by the fact that physics cannot help but make a big assumption about the nature of the universe in persistently accepting *unified* theories only, and persistently *ignoring* endlessly many empirically more successful rival theories merely because they are *disunified*.

Suppose physicists only accepted theories that postulate atoms, and persistently rejected theories that postulate different basic physical entities such as fields – even though many field theories can easily be, and have been, formulated that are even more empirically successful than the atomic theories. In this case the implication would surely be quite clear. Physicists would in effect be assuming that the world is made up of atoms, all other possibilities being ruled out. The atomic assumption would be built into the way the physics community accepts and rejects theories – built into the implicit *methods* of the community, methods which include: reject all theories that postulate entities other than atoms, whatever their empirical success might be. The physics community would accept, implicitly or explicitly, the assumption: the universe is such that no nonatomic theory is true.

Just the same holds for a physics community that rejects all disunified rivals to accepted theories, even though these rivals would be even more empirically successful if they were considered. Such a community in effect accepts the assumption: the universe is such that no disunified theory is true. The universe is such, in other words, that it has some kind of underlying physical unity. And that is starkly at odds with standard empiricism.

What, we may ask, does it mean to say of a theory that it is unified? Philosophers of science have not done too well in trying to answer this question.[5] Even Einstein was baffled by it.[6] What makes the issue problematic is, in part, that one and the same theory may be formulated in endlessly many different ways, some simple and unified, others complex and disunified. In order to solve the problem, the first step to concentrate on is, not the formulation of the theory, but what the theory says about the actual and possible phenomena to which it apples, the *physical content* of the theory in other words. The solution to the problem, in a nutshell, then amounts to this: A

physical theory is disunified to degree N if what the theory asserts
about all the possible phenomena to which the theory applies splits
into N domains, the physical content being the same throughout any
one domain, but different from all the others. For unity, we require
that N = 1.[7]

It is important to note that it is not just that physics *as a matter of
fact* assumes that the universe is such that all disunified theories are
false. Physics *must* make some such assumption. Evidence is always
hopelessly insufficient to decide what theory should be accepted.
However empirically *successful* a theory may be in physics, endlessly
many rival theories can always be concocted that are, not just *equally*
successful, but actually *more* successful empirically. Something other
than empirical considerations *must* be invoked to exclude all these
empirically more successful rivals, and this extra-empirical consideration is the demand that a theory, in order to be acceptable, must be
unified. And in persistently demanding unity of theories qualified to
be accepted, even when this clashes with empirical considerations,
physics thereby makes a big, persistent assumption about the nature
of the universe. And that means standard empiricism, as characterized above, is untenable.

Crucial to this refutation of standard empiricism is the claim that
whenever a theory is accepted in physics, there are always endlessly
many empirically more successful but *disunified* rival theories that are
all always ignored. Is this really the case?

Let us consider a specific physical theory: Newtonian theory. In
order to keep things as simple as possible, let us take this to consist of the two laws we encountered in the last chapter. There is first
Newton's law of gravitation, $F = Gm_1m_2/d^2$, which specifies how the
force of gravitation, F, between two bodies varies with variation in
the masses, m_1 and m_2, of the bodies and the distance d between them
(G is a constant). Second, there is Newton's force law, $F = ma$, which
specifies the acceleration, a, of a body of mass m that is subjected to
a force F. For a given mass, the greater the force, the greater the acceleration. If the force is zero, the acceleration is zero too, and the body
continues in a state of uniform motion in a straight line (as long as no
force is imposed on it).

Given these two laws, and the masses and instantaneous positions and velocities of bodies interacting with one another by
gravitation only, Newtonian theory (in principle) predicts the way
the bodies move in the future.[8] Thus, Newtonian theory can be

used to predict future positions of the planets of the solar system for centuries into the future.

We can now easily concoct endlessly many *disunified* rivals that are all just as empirically successful as Newtonian theory, as follows. All we need do is modify Newtonian theory *in any way we please* just for phenomena *not yet observed*. For example, we can modify Newtonian theory as far as the future is concerned. One such theory asserts: everything occurs as Newtonian theory says it does up to the last moment of 2050; after that moment, the law of gravitation becomes abruptly an inverse cube law: $F = Gm_1m_2/d^3$. Or, indeed, we can replace "d^3" by "d^N," where N is any number greater than 2. Or we can stipulate that, on the first moment after 2050, gravitation becomes a *repulsive* force, we all fly into the air, and there are, again, endlessly many repulsive force laws that we may specify. Just for the one date, 2050, there are infinitely many disunified rivals to Newtonian theory just as empirically successful, so far at least. All these rival laws are *disunified* because they make different assertions before and after the crucial date 2050. Doubtless, when 2050 arrives, they will all be refuted, but there are infinitely many more analogous disunified rivals that specify a dramatic change in the law of gravitation at still future dates – 2075, 2095, and so on.

There are many other ways in which we can concoct disunified rivals just as empirically successful as Newtonian theory. All we need to do is specify phenomena to which Newtonian theory applies which have not yet been observed, and modify Newtonian theory for these unobserved phenomena in any way we please. One such disunified rival to Newtonian theory asserts: everything occurs as Newtonian theory predicts except for gold spheres of mass greater than 1,000 tons adrift in outer space, in which case the law of gravitation becomes $F = Gm_1m_2/d$.[32] Another such disunified rival theory asserts: everything occurs as Newtonian theory predicts except for any two objects in a box made of gold, silver, platinum, and uranium in such and such proportions, in which case gravitation becomes repulsive such that $F = - Gm_1m_2/d$.[42] (Here, the proportions need to be specified so that no such box has, as yet, been made, and the minus sign in the equation represents that the force is repulsive.)[9]

Equally empirically successful rivals to Newtonian theory can be concocted by modifying, for as-yet unobserved phenomena, not just the law of gravitation, but the force law as well, so that it becomes $F = ma^2$, or $F = ma^N$, where N is any number greater than one.

So far, I have indicated potentially infinitely many *disunified* rivals to Newton's theory – all blatantly ignored in scientific practice – that are *just as empirically successful* as Newton's theory. I now indicate how we can easily concoct at least one disunified rival that is empirically *more successful* than Newtonian theory.

Given any accepted theory in physics – Newton's, Einstein's, or modern quantum theories developed by many theoretical physicists – it is invariably the case that the theory is empirically successful for phenomena A, cannot predict phenomena B because the equations cannot as yet be solved, meets with problems for phenomena C (and is ostensibly refuted), and does not predict phenomena D because these phenomena lie outside the scope of the theory: see Figure 4.1. We can always concoct a rival theory, T*, which is empirically more successful than T, as follows. T* asserts that, for phenomena A, everything occurs as T asserts; for phenomena B, C, and D, phenomena occur in accordance with empirically established laws, L_B, L_C, and L_D. T* successfully predicts everything that T successfully predicts (in A); T* successfully predicts phenomena that ostensibly refute T (in C); and T* successfully predicts phenomena that T fails to predict (in B and D). T* is clearly empirically more successful than T – and yet T* would never be considered in scientific practice for a moment, because of its horrible disunity. It is in part an arbitrary collection of many empirical laws, perhaps hundreds or such laws.

All this applies to Newtonian theory. It successfully predicts a vast range of phenomena (in A). It is refuted by many phenomena, for example, the motion of the planet Mercury around the sun, and motions of bodies close to the velocity of light, or in intense gravitational fields. There are phenomena that cannot be precisely predicted by Newtonian theory because the equations of the theory cannot be solved: there is no precise solution to the equations for systems of three bodies interacting by means of gravitation (in B). And there are phenomena about which Newtonian theory makes no prediction, for example, chemical phenomena (in D). We may then readily concoct a horribly disunified rival to Newtonian theory that successfully predicts phenomena in A, B, C, and D, and is thus more successful empirically than Newtonian theory.

We can now put these two results together to concoct endlessly many rivals, all of which are more successful empirically than Newtonian theory. All we need do is take any disunified rival to Newton which is just as empirically successful as Newtonian theory, and modify it

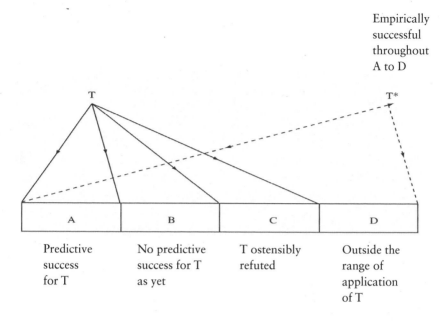

Figure 4.1 Empirically successful, disunified rival theories

further, in the way just indicated – see figure 4.1 – to create a horribly disunified rival to Newton that is even more successful empirically than Newtonian theory. And we can repeat this procedure for all the disunified rivals to Newton, thus creating endlessly many empirically more successful rivals to Newton.

Physics persistently ignores all these endlessly many empirically more successful rivals on the grounds that they are all horribly *disunified*. In doing that, physics thereby assumes that the universe is such that all horribly disunified theories are false. And that contradicts standard empiricism, which holds that science makes, and can make, no assumption about the nature of the universe independent of the evidence – let alone, as here, in a sense, against the evidence!

This refutation of standard empiricism is decisive. Nevertheless, there may seem to be a powerful reason for rejecting it and holding on to standard empiricism (which is what most philosophers of science do[10]). If the above refutation is valid, that means science accepts, as a part of knowledge, a big metaphysical assumption about the nature of the universe. But it would seem to be impossible to establish that such an assumption is *true*, or even *probable*. It would be a mere conjecture, which seems unacceptable. Scientific knowledge cannot, it would seem, be composed of mere *conjectures*.[11]

But that attitude profoundly misses the point. It is precisely because the assumption *is* a mere conjecture that it is vital that it be explicitly acknowledged within science, so that it can be critically assessed, so that alternatives can be developed and assessed, in the hope that the specific assumption that is made can be improved. Pretending science accepts no such conjecture damages science. Whatever conjecture is accepted, whether implicit or explicit, will inevitably exercise an enormous influence over physics, in influencing both *acceptance* of theories and the direction in which new theories are sought. It is important, for progress in physics, that a good choice of metaphysical conjecture is made, one that reflects reasonably well the way the universe actually is. But this is a conjecture about the ultimate nature of the universe – that of which we are most ignorant. And it is a mere conjecture, lacking any very good reason to suppose that it is true. We are almost bound to get it wrong, in other words, and getting it seriously wrong would block scientific progress. Indeed, this has already happened. Before the scientific revolution, in the sixteenth and seventeenth centuries, the prevailing view was that gods, demons, spirits, or God governed the natural world. Attempts to improve knowledge, taking some such view as that for granted, did not meet with much success – because this kind of view is seriously at odds with the nature of the world around us. Only when we abandoned the idea that the world is *purposive* in character, and adopted, with Kepler and Galileo, the idea that natural phenomena have some kind of mathematical structure, did modern science take off. Since then, we have changed the metaphysical ideas of science a number of times. In the seventeenth century, the view associated with the new natural philosophy was that the world is made up of tiny, hard corpuscles that interact by contact. This gave way to the idea that it is made up of point-atoms with mass, surrounded by a rigid, spherically symmetrical field of force, alternatively repulsive and attractive as one moves away from the point-particle. This transmuted into the view that the universe is made up of a self-interacting, unified field, particles being merely especially intense regions of the field. Today, we have string theory: everything is made up of tiny, closed quantum strings in a space-time of ten or eleven dimensions (all but three of the spatial dimensions being curled up into a tiny ball, and so not noticed).[12]

It is vital, for scientific progress, that we make a good choice of metaphysical conjecture, and yet we are almost bound to get it wrong, and we have, many times in the past, clearly got it wrong, sometimes to the serious detriment of scientific progress. Here, above all, we need to consider possibilities with all the attention and care of which we are capable. We cannot do this if we cling to standard empiricism and deny that physics makes any metaphysical assumption at all about the nature of the universe.

The crucial question becomes: How can we give ourselves the best chance of *improving* the metaphysical conjecture accepted by physics, especially, if possible, in the light of improving scientific knowledge and understanding? Any choice we make has to meet two contradictory conditions. On the one hand we want a conjecture that is as *specific* as possible, to give the greatest guidance for the construction and assessment of physical theories. On the other, we want a conjecture that is as *unspecific* as possible, to give ourselves the best chances of picking a conjecture that is *true*. Other things being equal, the more specific the conjecture, the less the chances are of it being true. The less you say, the greater the chances that what you say is true.

How can these contradictory conditions both be met? We can do it by accepting, not *one* conjecture, but a *hierarchy* of conjectures. At the top of the hierarchy, we have a conjecture so unspecific that it is almost bound to be true. As we descend the hierarchy, the conjectures become increasingly specific, increasingly substantial until, at the bottom of the hierarchy, we have a conjecture so specific it is almost bound to be *false*. In this way, we create a framework of relatively unspecific, unproblematic, stable conjectures (and associated methods), high up in the hierarchy, within which much more specific and problematic conjectures (and associated methods) low down in the hierarchy can be critically assessed, developed, and *improved*: see figure 4.2. I call this hierarchical conception of science *aim-oriented empiricism*.

AIM-ORIENTED EMPIRICISM

Here, then, is an indication of what each conjecture asserts at each level, and a brief account of why this is the best conjecture to accept, at this level. No attempt is made to establish that any of these conjectures is true, not even to any degree of probability. All that is argued is that these are the best conjectures to *accept*, at each level, either because accepting the assumption can only help, and cannot hinder, the pursuit of knowledge of the truth, or because the conjecture is associated with or is implicit in what seem to be our most empirically successful research programs devoted to the pursuit of knowledge, or because the conjecture provides the greatest hope of empirical progress if accepted. The arguments are all, in other words, *pragmatic*, but only in a very narrow sense of that word. Accepting the conjectures in question is either required for progress in knowledge of empirical truth to be possible at all, or gives us the best hope of such progress.[13]

These arguments emerge from a revision of Karl Popper's solution to the problem of skepticism. The problem of skepticism is: How can there be any knowledge at all? The traditional approach to this problem, stemming from Descartes, takes skepticism to be the enemy of knowledge. In order to defeat this enemy, the task becomes to identify that part of our knowledge that seems most secure, most immune to doubt, and then build up the rest of our knowledge from that solid foundation. Philosophy, traditionally, identifies two possible foundations: either *reason*, or *experience*. Popper's approach is almost exactly the opposite of this traditional approach. For Popper, skepticism is the *friend* of knowledge, the means by which knowledge is acquired. We acquire knowledge by subjecting what we take to be knowledge to ferocious skeptical attack. What survives this skeptical attack is what we take to be knowledge – for the moment at least, until something better turns up.

Popper's approach needs to be revised, however. It is not enough to be ferociously skeptical, dogmatically skeptical, as one might say. We need to be a bit more skeptical than that: we need to be skeptical of skepticism itself. The whole point of skepticism is to promote the growth of knowledge. Skepticism is only rational insofar as it does promote the growth of knowledge – or at least holds out the promise or possibility of doing that. If skepticism holds out no hope of promoting knowledge – if it can only undermine the growth of knowledge – then it has become irrational, and can be rationally, justifiably, ignored. Skeptical rejection of the five metaphysical conjectures at levels 7 to 3, depicted in figure 4.2, is to be resisted on the grounds that accepting these conjectures, provisionally, as a part of our knowledge, promises to promote the growth of knowledge.

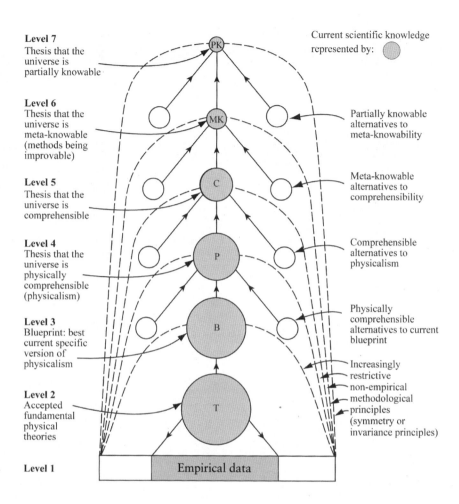

Level 7
Thesis that the universe is partially knowable

Level 6
Thesis that the universe is meta-knowable (methods being improvable)

Level 5
Thesis that the universe is comprehensible

Level 4
Thesis that the universe is physically comprehensible (physicalism)

Level 3
Blueprint: best current specific version of physicalism

Level 2
Accepted fundamental physical theories

Level 1

Current scientific knowledge represented by:

Partially knowable alternatives to meta-knowability

Meta-knowable alternatives to comprehensibility

Comprehensible alternatives to physicalism

Physically comprehensible alternatives to current blueprint

Increasingly restrictive non-empirical methodological principles (symmetry or invariance principles)

Empirical data

Figure 4.2 Aim-oriented empiricism

Level 7. Partial Knowability: The universe is such that we possess and can acquire some knowledge of our immediate environment as a basis for action.

We have every reason to be skeptical of this conjecture. At least, we have no good reason to believe it to be true, or probably true, as far as the future is concerned. But if it is false, the acquisition of knowledge of our environment, and life itself, become impossible. Accepting the conjecture as a part of our scientific knowledge cannot undermine the pursuit of knowledge in any circumstances whatsoever, and may well assist that pursuit. Therefore, we should accept the conjecture as a secure part of our scientific knowledge.

Level 6. Meta-knowability: The universe is such that there is some rationally discoverable assumption about it that, if accepted, makes it possible to improve methods for the improvement of knowledge. Not only is the universe such that we can acquire knowledge; it is such that we can acquire knowledge about how to acquire knowledge.[14]

The idea of a "rationally discoverable" assumption is somewhat problematic. I take it to mean, at least, that the assumption in question must not be one among infinitely many analogous, equally viable assumptions.

Again, we have every reason to be skeptical of this conjecture, and no good reason to believe it to be true, as far as the future is concerned. Nevertheless, accepting the conjecture can only help, and cannot do much to harm the pursuit of knowledge, whatever the universe may be like. If the conjecture is true, then the universe is such that we can put forward some conjecture about it that, if taken as a basic assumption we make in our attempts to improve knowledge, will enable us to improve our methods for improving knowledge. It provides the means for us to learn how to learn. If, on the other hand, the conjecture is false, then all our attempts to improve methods for the improvement of knowledge will fail. But we can discover whether or not it is possible for us to improve our methods for improving our knowledge only by trying. It is worthwhile to make the attempt even though we have no guarantee of success. Thus, accepting the conjecture of meta-knowability does not harm, and may well help, the pursuit of knowledge. It leads us to do what we should do, in any case. The conjecture deserves to be accepted as a secure item of scientific knowledge.

Level 5. Comprehensibility: The universe is comprehensible in some way or other, there being *something*, or an aspect of something (kind of physical entity, God, society of gods, cosmic purpose, cosmic program, or whatever) that runs through all phenomena, and in terms of which all phenomena can, in principle, be explained and understood.

This conjecture of cosmological comprehensibility is exactly the kind of conjecture that meta-knowability licenses us to accept. It requires us, however, to consider various versions of the conjecture and favour that version that seems to stimulate the greatest growth in empirical knowledge at levels 2 and 1 (see figure 4.2). It is exactly this that we need to do if we are to put into practice the basic idea of meta-knowability, namely, learn how to learn, improve basic ideas and associated methods in the light of improving knowledge (at levels 2 and 1). The historical record reveals that humanity has found it extraordinarily difficult to put this elementary idea of meta-knowability into practice. Almost all – perhaps all – societies and cultures accept a cosmological view that holds that the universe is (more or less) comprehensible in some way or other, but almost all have upheld their view dogmatically, and have failed to develop and explore alternatives, even though the accepted view is not especially fruitful from the standpoint of assisting the growth of knowledge.

Level 4. Physical Comprehensibility (Physicalism): The universe is physically comprehensible, everything being made up of just one kind of physical entity (or perhaps just one entity), all change and diversity being capable, in principle, of being explained in terms of this one kind of entity. This conjecture asserts that the universe is such that some yet-to-be-discovered physical "theory of everything" (in the jargon of theoretical physicists) is both true and *unified*.

It was only when versions of physicalism were adopted in the seventeenth century by Kepler, Galileo, and others that the comprehensibility conjecture began to be immensely fruitful for the growth of empirical knowledge (at levels 2 and 1). It was the explicit or implicit acceptance of physicalism, tied to the vigorous exploitation of the methods of empiricism – observation and experimentation – that led to modern science, and to the astonishing successes of modern science.

As before, we have every reason to be skeptical of the truth of physicalism, especially in view of the very substantial, specific assertion it makes about the nature of the universe and the problems it poses for the way we ordinarily conceive of the world – and conceive of ourselves as having some free will, and living lives of some meaning and value. No other conjecture, however, at this level, offers anything remotely like the promise that physicalism does for the task of acquiring empirical knowledge and understanding at levels 2 and 1.

Some historians and philosophers of science have denied that any-thing theoretical persists through scientific revolutions.[15] Actually, all theoretical revolutions in physics exemplify the persisting idea that there is some kind of underlying unity of physical law in the universe. These revolutions are all great achievements of theoretical *unification*. Thus Newton unifies Galileo's terrestrial laws of motion and Kepler's astronomical laws of motion. James Clerk Maxwell's theory of elec-trodynamics unifies the electric and magnetic forces into the one force of electromagnetism. It unifies optical theory and electromagnetism by revealing that light is just waves in the electromagnetic field. And it further unifies gamma rays, X-rays, infrared rays, ultraviolet rays, and radio waves by revealing that all these are waves in the electromagnetic field, of different wavelengths. Special relativity brings greater unity to Maxwell's theory,[16] unifies energy and mass by means of $E = mc^2$, and partially unifies space and time to form space-time. General relativ-ity unifies gravitation and space-time by absorbing gravitation into a richer conception of space-time. The theory of elements and chemical compounds initiated by Lavoisier brings astonishing unification to chemistry, in reducing millions of different sorts of elementary sub-stances to around one hundred elements. Quantum theory and the theory of atomic structure bring massive unification to atomic theory, properties of matter, interactions between matter and light. Instead of nearly 100 elements plus electromagnetic radiation, the theory pos-tulates just four entities: the electron, proton, neutron, and photon. Instead of a multiplicity of laws concerning the chemical and physical properties of matter, there is Schrödinger's equation. Quantum elec-trodynamics unifies quantum theory, special relativity, and classical electrodynamics. The electro-weak theory of Weinberg and Salam par-tially unifies the electromagnetic and weak forces. The quark theory of Gell-Mann and Zweig brings greater unity to the theory of fundamen-tal particles: a large number of hadrons – particles like protons and neutrons – are reduced to just six quarks. Quantum chromodynam-ics brings further unification to the theory of fundamental particles by providing a quantum theory of the strong force. The standard model, the current quantum theory of fundamental particles and the forces between them, partially unifies the electromagnetic, weak, and strong force.[17] All theoretical revolutions in physics without exception embody the discovery of greater unity in nature. The whole enterprise of theoretical physics, from Kepler and Galileo down to today, cries out to be interpreted as the progressive discovery of unity in nature, the level 4 conjecture of physicalism. As I have put it elsewhere, "Far from obliterating the idea that there is a persisting theoretical idea in physics, revolutions do just the opposite in that they all themselves actually exemplify the persisting idea of underlying unity!"[18]

Physicalism is a metaphysical thesis; it is not empirically testable, and so cannot be said to be empirically successful. It can be said, however, to be empirically *fruitful*. Let me explain. A body of scientific work, a research program, stretching over decades or even centuries, may accept, explicitly or implicitly, a *metaphysical conjecture* which it seeks to capture in the form of a true, testable theory. In order to be the *metaphysical conjecture* of such and such a research program, the conjecture must influence both (a) the direction in which those who work in the program seek new theories, and (b) what theories are *accepted* and *rejected*. Such a *metaphysical conjecture* is empirically *fruitful* if the research program with which it is associated (i) progressively develops theories that draw closer and closer to capturing the basic *metaphysical conjecture* as a testable theory, and (ii) these theories meet with ever-greater empirical success.

What the above reveals is that physicalism has been an astonishingly empirically *fruitful* metaphysical conjecture for theoretical physics from Copernicus onward. Physicalism influences both (a) the discovery and (b) the acceptance of theories in physics; and successive physical theories (i) have drawn closer and closer to capturing physicalism as a testable theory, and (ii) have met with ever greater empirical success.

No other version of the level 5 thesis of comprehensibility has been remotely as empirically *fruitful* as physicalism. The level 6 thesis of meta-knowability tells us that physicalism is the conjecture to accept, at level 4.

But what of rival versions of physicalism, it may be asked, which assert that there is only partial unity in nature – for example, versions that assert that there are *two* or *four* different kinds of fundamental physical entity, and not just *one*? Are not these partially unified versions of physicalism just as empirically *fruitful* as perfectly unified physicalism, in that the whole research program of theoretical physics can, equally well, be interpreted as seeking to capture some such partially unified version of physicalism?

That may well be, but these partially unified versions of physicalism fail to accord with the level 6 conjecture of meta-knowability. A version of physicalism that postulates two kinds of basic entity is one among infinitely many analogous, equally viable conjectures, in that, keeping one kind of entity fixed, we may vary the other kind in endlessly many different ways. Meta-knowability excludes these ad hoc variants of perfectly unified physicalism.

There are two further arguments for accepting perfectly unified physicalism at level 4 as providing the best help with progress in scientific knowledge at levels 2 and 1 – or at least providing the best *promise* of such help.

First, as the universe becomes such that it is depicted by increasingly *disunified* versions of physicalism, so the more remote become the chances that theoretical physics will meet with ultimate success. Granted that we are engaged in the task of trying to discover the ultimate nature of the universe, we might as well assume that the universe is such that our enterprise can meet with success. Even if the universe is such that some disunified version of physicalism is true, our best hope of achieving success may still be to adopt the simplest possible conjecture – that is, assume underlying unity – and get as far as we can in this quest.

Second, in considering what metaphysical conjecture ought to be accepted at level 4, we need to consider what is implicit in those current methods of physics that influence what theories are to be accepted on nonempirical grounds – having to do with the simplicity, unity, or explanatory character of the theories in question. There can be no doubt that, as far as nonempirical considerations are concerned, the more nearly a new fundamental physical theory is perfectly unified, so the more acceptable it will be held to be. Furthermore, failure of a theory to be unified is taken to be grounds for holding the theory to be false even in the absence of empirical difficulties. For example, high energy physics in the 1960s kept discovering more and more different hadrons (fundamental particles similar to protons and neutrons), and was judged to be in a state of crisis as the number rose to over one hundred. Again, even though the standard model (the current quantum field theory of fundamental particles and forces) does not face serious empirical problems, it is nevertheless regarded by most physicists as unlikely to be correct just because of its serious lack of unity. In adopting such nonempirical criteria for acceptability, physicists thereby implicitly assume that the best conjecture as to where the truth lies is in the direction of physicalism in the strongest, most unified sense. Intellectual rigour requires that this implicit assumption – or conjecture – be made explicit so that it can be critically assessed and, we may hope, improved. Theoretical physics with physicalism in the strongest sense explicitly acknowledged as a part of conjectural knowledge is more rigorous than physics without this being acknowledged because physics pursued in the former way is able to subject nonempirical methods to critical appraisal as the strongest version of physicalism is critically appraised, whereas physics pursued in the latter way is not able to do this as well. Because the strongest version of physicalism makes more definite, substantial claims than any rival version of physicalism, it is more open to critical appraisal than rival versions.

Level 3. Best Blueprint: By "blueprint" I mean the best available more or less specific metaphysical conjecture as to how the universe is physically comprehensible, a conjecture that asserts that everything is composed of some more or less specific kind of physical entity, it being in principle possible to explain all change and diversity in terms of this kind of entity. Entities considered at one time or another in the history of physics include (as I have already mentioned): rigid corpuscles; point-particles surrounded by a rigid, spherically symmetrical field of force; self-interacting field; quantum strings. The blueprint accepted at any stage in the development of physics is almost bound to be false – as the historical record of previously accepted blueprints indicates. Precisely because it is all but impossible to pin down a blueprint that is *true*, it is vital, for the sake of theoretical physics, that the effort is made to formulate that blueprint that does the best justice to (a) physicalism at level 4, and (b) accepted physical theories at level 2. Modifications of the accepted blueprint need to be developed and critically assessed, in an attempt to arrive at a blueprint that (i) accords better with physicalism, and (ii) when made precise, leads to the discovery of a new physical theory, at level 2, that both unifies pre-existing physical theories, and meets with greater empirical success, thus constituting an advance in theoretical knowledge and understanding.

Level 2. Fundamental Physical Theory: Here we have fundamental physical theories of physics, sufficiently empirically successful, and sufficiently in accord with the best blueprint at level 3, or physicalism at level 4, to be accepted as a part of theoretical scientific knowledge. At present, there are two such theories: Einstein's general theory of relativity, and the so-called standard model, the current quantum theory of fundamental particles and the forces between them.

Level 1. Evidence: This, in the main, consists of experimental results, repeatable phenomena, and thus, in effect, low-level empirical laws.

A new theory in physics, in order to be accepted as constituting an advance, must satisfy two conditions. It must be more empirically successful than predecessor theories (or meet with sufficient empirical success if there is no predecessor theory). And it must enhance the overall unity of the totality of fundamental physical theory when it replaces its predecessor theories (or empirical laws if there is no predecessor theory). It must, in other words, produce a better accord between theory at level 2, and *both* evidence at level 1 and best blueprint at level 3 – or, at least, physicalism at level 4.

It is extraordinarily difficult to meet these two requirements simultaneously. Since Newton in the seventeenth century, only eight physical theories have been put forward that met both requirements.

What does this argument for aim-oriented empiricism establish? It provides us with a new conception of natural science, one that makes sense of the way theories are discovered and accepted. It establishes that we must interpret science as accepting a hierarchy of metaphysical conjectures about the nature of the universe that concern its knowability and comprehensibility – conjectures that must be regarded as increasingly secure items of scientific knowledge as we go up the hierarchy. Elsewhere, I have shown in some detail that aim-oriented empiricism does what standard empiricism notoriously fails to do: solve the problem of induction.[19] This is a decisive argument in support of aim-oriented empiricism, and against standard empiricism. There is no argument, however, to establish the *truth*, or *probable truth*, of any of these metaphysical conjectures. These conjectures are accepted either because their truth is required for the pursuit of knowledge or science to be possible at all, or because of the role they play in the astonishing (apparent) empirical success of science. Put briefly, these conjectures are either *required* or *extraordinarily fruitful* for scientific progress. But they might still be false.

How seriously, then, do we take the truth of these conjectures – in particular, the one that matters, the level 4 thesis of physicalism? Physicalism is a basic item of scientific knowledge. Even though it is a metaphysical thesis, and thus not empirically verifiable or falsifiable, nevertheless it is extraordinarily fruitful empirically, in the sense indicated above. But it remains a conjecture.[20]

Perhaps an analogy can be drawn with the epistemological situation we find ourselves in. Suppose you wake up to find yourself in a strange, pitch black room. You have no idea where you are, or what kind of room you are in. It might be a bedroom, a dining room, a garage, a kitchen, an indoor swimming pool. You fumble around, find what might be a diving board, and jump off. You hit a hard floor: you do not seem to be in an indoor swimming pool. You grope around seeking a bed, or an armchair, and do not find either: you do not seem to be in a bedroom or sitting room. It occurs to you that you might be in a kitchen. Suddenly, everything seems to make sense. Here is the stove, here the sink, here the draining board, here the fridge, here the pots and pans, here the vegetables. You find you can even turn on the stove and cook yourself a meal, even though the room continues to be pitch black and you have not verified with your sight that you are in a kitchen.

Somewhat analogously, here we are in this strange, unknown universe. There are various possibilities. It might be governed by spirits, demons, gods, or one supreme being, God. It might be dominated by some overall cosmic purpose, to which everything that occurs contributes. Events might occur in accordance with some cosmic program. Or physicalism might be true: the universe might be physically comprehensible. As in the case of the pitch black room, so it is in this case too: if one of the possibilities begins to promote the growth of empirical knowledge in such a way that empirically testable theories that accord with that possibility – that conjecture – meet with ever greater empirical success, then that is the best grounds we can have for taking that conjecture seriously, more seriously than any of its rivals. Just as the kitchen hypothesis led to specific empirical success (a meal), so physicalism has led to empirical success – the astonishing, apparently ever accelerating empirical success of modern science, and the vast array of associated technology that has made the modern world possible.

CONCLUSION

The upshot of the argument of this chapter is that our fundamental problem – the human world/physical universe problem – as formulated in chapter 1, is very much more serious than one might at first suppose.

Our problem arises, in the form we have been considering, insofar as we take *physicalism* seriously, the doctrine that everything is made up of one kind of physical entity – perhaps just one entity – the physical properties of which determine (perhaps probabilistically) the way events unfold as time passes. Physicalism asserts that the universe is physically comprehensible: everything that occurs has in principle (but not in practice) the same physical explanation. In other words, physicalism asserts that the universe is such that a physical theory can be formulated (if we are clever enough to discover it) that, in principle, predicts and explains the way all physical phenomena occur.

If physicalism is true, we are at once confronted by the problem of this book: How can *we* exist? How can the world as we experience it exist? How can consciousness, free will, meaning, and value exist?

But what grounds do we have to suppose that physicalism is true?

Physicalism may seem to be suggested by modern physics. It is, however, a *metaphysical* doctrine. That is, it cannot be empirically verified or falsified. That means, according to orthodox conceptions of science – versions of standard empiricism – that physicalism is not a part of scientific knowledge. Physicalism is a mere *philosophical* doctrine, suggested by modern physics perhaps, but not a part of scientific knowledge and therefore not to be taken too seriously.

Unfortunately, this orthodox conception of science of standard empiricism is untenable, as we have seen. We need a new conception of science, aim-oriented empiricism, that recognizes that metaphysical doctrines concerning the knowability and comprehensibility of the universe are an integral part of scientific knowledge. In particular, physicalism is a key component of scientific knowledge.

This means that our fundamental problem – the human world/ physical universe problem – is very serious indeed. That which creates the problem – physicalism – cannot be dismissed as a mere *philosophical* doctrine. Physicalism is a central component of current scientific knowledge. Our fundamental problem cannot be evaded; it ought not to be ignored. It cannot be left to academic philosophers to worry about. The problem deserves to be given centre stage in education and in our intellectual deliberations. We all need to ponder, now and again, how our lives can make sense and be of value if the universe really is as physicalism says it is.

The argument that standard empiricism is untenable and that, in order to make sense of science, we need to adopt aim-oriented empiricism instead, has another major implication for a basic theme of this book: the whole relationship between science and philosophy needs to be transformed.[21] Accept standard empiricism, and it looks as if empirically untestable philosophy is more or less irrelevant as far as science is concerned – a view that corresponds to the attitudes of many scientists. Reject standard empiricism and accept aim-oriented empiricism, and philosophy becomes a vital part of science itself. The metaphysical theses of aim-oriented empiricism concerning the knowability and comprehensibility of the universe are empirically untestable *philosophical* theses; but they are also vital components of physics and of natural science. The fundamental lesson of the argument for aim-oriented empiricism is that the scientific quest to understand what kind of universe this is cannot be dissociated from philosophical speculation about what kind of universe this is.[22] Some kind of provisional answer has to be given in order to make science possible at all. As this answer is almost bound to be false, it is vital to keep alive fundamental philosophical thinking about what kind of universe this is, and to keep such philosophical thought in close contact with testable physics so that each may influence the other. The hierarchical framework of aim-oriented empiricism shows how this is to be done. Whereas standard empiricism splits off philosophy of science from science, aim-oriented empiricism, on the contrary, demands that philosophy of science – philosophical exploration of aims and methods of science – be done in a way that is in two-way contact with science itself. It is this contact that makes it possible for there to be explicit positive feedback between improving scientific knowledge and improving aims and methods of science – improving knowledge about how to improve knowledge, in other words. Science adapts its nature to what it finds out about the nature of the universe!

5

How Can There Be Free Will
If Physicalism Is True?

Purposive action; fundamental requirement for free will; treble comprehensibility; improbability of free will

THE PROBLEM

Physics is about only a highly selected aspect of things – the causally efficacious aspect, that aspect that determines (perhaps probabilistically) the way events unfold. Physics makes no mention of the experiential – how things look, feel, smell, or sound, or how it is to *be* a bit of the physical universe (this body, this brain) – first, because none of this is needed to predict and explain any physical phenomena, and second, because, if physical theory is extended to include all this experiential stuff, the theory would become so horrendously complex it would cease to be explanatory. Omitting all reference to the experiential is the price that must be paid to have the marvellously explanatory theories of physics that we do have – Newtonian theory, James Clerk Maxwell's theory of the electromagnetic field, Einstein's theory of general relativity, quantum theory, quantum electrodynamics, and the so-called "standard model," the current best theory we have of fundamental particles and the forces between them. The physical universe is just that aspect, that slice, of all that exists, that we must pick out if we are to explain and understand why events occur as they do. Physics is about the explanatory skeleton of the world with all the experiential flesh omitted.

This is what I argued for in chapter 3. If correct, the argument goes some way toward enabling us to understand how our human world, imbued with sensory qualities, consciousness, meaning, and value can exist in the physical universe. The silence of physics about the experiential provides no grounds whatsoever for holding that the experiential does not really exist. *Experiential physicalism* is the doctrine that emerges from this argument.

But much more than this is required to show how it is possible for our human world to exist embedded in the physical universe. There is still the grave problem of showing how it is possible that *we* exist in the physical universe. We persons are not merely passively experiencing beings – vessels for passing sensations of sights and sounds and smells. We *do* things in this world, we *act*, we initiate actions and are responsible for what we do. It is of the very essence of what we are that we act. Even our thinking, our imagining, our inner world of consciousness, our very identity as a conscious being is a kind of action, the product of inner imaginary action. Bereft of the capacity to *do*, to *act*, we are nothing, we cease to exist altogether.

But if physicalism is true, then everything that occurs – or at least the physical aspect of all that occurs – is capable (in principle) of being explained and understood in purely physical terms. Everything that we do, say, think, feel, all our deeds throughout our life from the most momentous to the smallest flicker of an eyelid is the inexorable outcome of prior physical states of the universe. Our entire life is just the outcome of fundamental physical entities – electrons, quarks, superstrings, or whatever – interacting with one another in accordance with precise physical law. We may feel we exist and act; our life certainly seems charged with human significance, with experience, emotion, struggle, plans, intentions, deeds that sometimes succeed and sometimes fail. But all this is, it seems, a hollow charade. Behind the scenes, impersonal physics determines everything that goes on, everything we think, decide, and do, permitting us merely the illusion that we are in charge of our actions. Physics triumphs, and human action turns out to be mere shadow play, a mockery.

This problem has become all the more serious as a result of the argument of the last chapter. If standard empiricism is tenable, physicalism is no more than a somewhat dubious metaphysical doctrine, suggested perhaps by physics but definitely not a part of scientific knowledge. But standard empiricism must be rejected; aim-oriented empiricism must be accepted in its stead. At once, physicalism becomes as secure an item of scientific knowledge as anything theoretical in science can be. The problem of how we can have free will – how we can exist as acting beings in the universe – becomes serious indeed.

We have here a much more severe problem than the one tackled in chapters 2 and 3. There, the task was to see how the experiential could be accommodated alongside the physical. The solution, I argued, is to appreciate that physics is only about that which determines how events unfold as they do, physics thus being silent about everything that does *not* determine how events unfold, and hence being silent about the *experiential* aspect of things. This solution concedes that the physical is solely and entirely responsible for the way events occur. It is at once clear that this solution, this line of thought, cannot solve our present problem. For what is at issue is *our* capacity to make things happen. We must be, it would seem, in direct competition with physics, with that which determines necessarily how events occur. Physics cannot be solely responsible for what goes on. We must be responsible for at least some of what happens – namely, what we do, what we create, even what we think, what we imagine and decide. Some power, some responsibility for making things happen, must be wrested from physics, it seems, if we are not to be merely the puppets of physics, our existence as acting beings an illusion.

Philosophers tend to formulate this as the problem of how (or whether) there can be free will if determinism holds, determinism being the claim that every event is strictly determined by prior states of affairs. But this traditional formulation is inadequate in a number of respects.[1]

First, the problem is generated not by determinism but by physics, or rather by the truth of physicalism.[2] Physicalism is not at all the same thing as determinism. Determinism is both too broad and too narrow. Determinism might be true, every event might be strictly determined by prior states of affairs, and yet physicalism might be false, and the universe might not be physically comprehensible. The true theory-of-everything of this universe, capable of predicting events, might be grotesquely complicated and disunified, and thus nonexplanatory. On the other hand, physicalism may be true, the universe may well be physically comprehensible, and yet determinism may be false. The true physical theory-of-everything may be probabilistic, not deterministic – capable only of predicting events in probabilistic fashion. Determinism neither implies, nor is implied by, physicalism.

Second, the traditional formulation of the problem is inadequate in suggesting that what is at issue is free will. Much more than that is at stake. It is our very existence as acting persons that is under threat. We exist as persons only if we *do* things in this world, initiate *actions*. If the physical is solely and entirely responsible for everything that goes on, including of course everything going on in our minds and brains, then we can be responsible, it seems, for nothing. We do not exist. Our existence is an illusion.

In the end, the problem is simple and stark. Granted physicalism – granted that physics is responsible for everything that happens – there can be no room for us too. We can do nothing. Everything we seem to do is really physics, acting through us. We persons, and all other conscious and sentient beings, shrivel and die before the unchallengeable might of physical necessity. We are mere puppets of the physical universe.

A rather different kind of reservation about the traditional formulation of the problem may have to do with putting all the emphasis on the freedom of the *will*. What is this "will" that we require to be free? Does "willed action" arise only when we consciously intend an action, our intention initiating and controlling the action, and not when we act spontaneously, instinctively, in response to feelings and desires? Might we not be most ourselves, acting most freely, even most creatively and generously, when we act in a wholly instinctive, spontaneous, unpremeditated, and thoughtless way? A person who never gives in to impulse, to instinct, but always acts in a premeditated, willed way, might in reality be a very unfree person, imprisoned in a set of prescribed actions, never free to be himself or herself spontaneously, without constraint.[3]

Posing the problem as the freedom of the *will* suggests that the problem has to do with the *will* becoming impotent, or being subverted in various ways, by means of brainwashing, post-hypnotic suggestion, domination, obsessive desire, or, more radically, by means of the relentless unfolding of physical processes in the brain in accordance with physical law. But are there not other ways in which free will – the power to be responsible for what one does – may be undermined? One may be deceived about relevant matters of fact; one may deceive oneself about the nature of one's feelings, desires, beliefs, goals, actions; one may dogmatically hold onto beliefs that ought to have been rejected long ago. Self-deception, pig-headed prejudice, sheer stupidity, may undermine our capacity to be responsible for actions just as effectively, so it would seem, as traditional subversions of the will.

Another way in which traditional formulations of the problem can be inadequate is that they do not emphasize that free will can involve questions about *value*. A young man decides to join a circus and become a clown. Is this a free decision, a manifestation of free will, or is it the outcome of a fantasy, or the result of being overly influenced by a member of the circus? The answer that is given may depend on judgments of value: the value of life in a circus, the extent to which the desire for such a life comes from what is genuinely of value in the young man's personality; an expression of what is best in his makeup. The decision that a desire is *your* desire may involve decisions about value: this desire comes from what is best, of most value, in your personality.

The traditional formulation of the free will problem may be judged inadequate in an even more radical way. We may hold that the proper, fundamental problem is: "How can there be *wisdom* in a physicalistic universe?" Wisdom, here, is to be interpreted as the capacity, active endeavour, and desire to realize what is of value in life, for oneself and others, wisdom in this sense including knowledge, technological know-how, and understanding, but much else besides. "Realize" here means both "apprehend" or "experience," *and* "create" or "make real."[4] Insofar as free will is something that it is of value to possess, we may take it that wisdom implies free will, but free will does not imply wisdom. We may well freely act very unwisely. Wisdom is something that it is of greater value to possess than mere free will since, in having wisdom, we have free will, and in addition we have the capacity to realize what is of value to us in life, which we do not necessarily possess if we merely possess free will. The wisdom/physicalism problem is, we may hold, both more fundamental, and more important to solve, than the free will/physicalism problem. The former problem includes the latter problem, so that the solution to the former will also provide the solution to the latter. And, we may argue, it is more important to solve the former problem. What matters is that we can live wisely in this physicalistic universe. Living in such a way that we can successfully exercise free will is important, too, but not as important as being able to live wisely.

Formulating the free will/physicalism problem as the wisdom/physicalism problem has two further benefits. First, the wisdom version of the problem brings to the fore that what is of *value* plays a crucial role. This is not always obvious given the free will version of the problem.[5] Second, the wisdom version of the problem makes clear that the problem has to do with the existence of the capacity successfully to pursue a goal – the goal of realizing what is of value in life. This, I shall argue, is indeed the proper way to conceive of the problem. The free will version of the problem does not make this clear at all. In discussing free will, no goal is presupposed.

Despite what I have just said, for most of this chapter I will respect tradition and tackle the problem of how we can have *free will* in a physicalistic universe. Only at the end of the chapter will I say something about the more fundamental problem of how we can have wisdom in a physicalistic universe.

I have one other reservation about the usual formulation of the problem. Just as the traditional problem of knowledge needs to be formulated not as "How can we acquire knowledge?" but rather "How can we improve knowledge?," so too the free will problem needs to be formulated not as "How can we have free will?" but rather as "How can we improve, or enhance, our free will?" This point will, I hope, emerge out of our discussion of the traditional problem.

Any tackling of a serious problem is likely to lead to the transformation of the problem in question as one proceeds. This is especially true of philosophical problems, and above all of the free will/physicalism problem.[6]

INTERNAL AND EXTERNAL THEORIES OF PERCEPTION

In tackling this problem, it is a matter of profound importance whether we adopt the internalist theory of perception indicated in chapter 3, and Cartesian dualism so closely associated with it, or the externalist theory, which permits us to hold that our inner experiences, our states of consciousness, are brain processes.[7] If we uphold Cartesian dualism, we have had it. Reconciling our existence with the universe being physically comprehensible is impossible. In order for our conscious intentions to affect what goes on in our brains, and what our bodies do, it is necessary for these nonphysical mental states or events to influence physical processes occurring in our brains, which means that some physical processes are not fully explicable physically (which in turn means that physicalism is false). But if, on the other hand we hold the brain process theory, indicated in chapter 3, allied to externalism, there is at least a glimmer of hope. For then conscious intentions that initiate and guide our actions *are* themselves physical processes, and these physical processes can be a part of the cause of our actions without any physical laws being violated at all. There is just the faintest hint that "free will," and our existence as acting persons, might be compatible with physicalism.

In the end this vital point is extremely simple. If Cartesian dualism is true, then we – our conscious selves – are entirely distinct and separate from the physical universe. If my Cartesian conscious self is to be able to make my physical body act, then it must interact with physical processes going on in my body – physical processes going in my brain, we may presume – thus violating the sole determination of physics. But if Cartesian dualism is false, the brain process theory is true, and all my conscious states, intentions, decisions to act are themselves *brain processes, physical processes*, then it becomes possible that my conscious intentions to act cause and guide my actions *without any physical laws being violated at all*, everything occurring in accordance with the as-yet-undiscovered physical theory of everything, T. In initiating action I have all the power at my command of the physical universe. I am myself, in part, a bit of the physical universe.

But there is still the mystery, of course, of how it can be possible for me to be in charge of my thoughts and deeds *even though the physical processes that are these thoughts and deeds unfold in a precisely determined way in accordance with the laws of physics*. I may be in part a bit of physics, but nevertheless I am doomed, it seems, to think and act precisely as mere physics dictates. How can I and physics *both*, simultaneously, be in charge, be responsible for what occurs? How is dual control, dual determination, possible?

In order to explore this question, let us assume that Cartesian dualism and the "internalist" theory of perception are false. We directly perceive things external to us, and our inner experiences are brain processes. Or rather, to state the last point more carefully, processes going on inside our heads – "head processes" as we may call them – have both a physical aspect and an experiential aspect. Head processes are neurological processes going on in our brains; but some of them are also conscious inner experiences, thoughts, feelings, desires, decisions to act, sensory experiences, imaginings – all the contents of our rich inner life. That head processes have an experiential aspect and a physical aspect is somewhat analogous to the way honeysuckle, let us say, has an experiential aspect – its colour, its smell – as well as a physical aspect. Or, to give another example, it is somewhat analogous to the way this very sentence has an experiential or human aspect – its meaning, what it asserts – and a physical aspect.

I shall argue that we can – we do – have free will, even though we live in a physicalistic universe, because our bodies and brains are so constituted to marshal all the force, the power, of physical causality to work in our interest. The physicalistic universe becomes our servant, even our slave. It does our bidding, even to the extent of slavishly ensuring that our thoughts, desires, feelings, cogitations, plans, motives and reasons for action, decisions, and impulses to act – all these are *our* thoughts, *our* desires, *our* feelings, *our* cogitations, etc. Within the massive constraints of our power to act, we are the gods of the physicalistic universe, gods able to command physics to obey and serve our will.

There is, however, an apparently devastating objection to this idea that we can have free will even though (experiential) physicalism is true. If *deterministic* physicalism is true, then everything we think and do, our entire life, indeed the whole of human history, is fixed and determined by the physical state of the universe shortly after the big bang, long before life of any kind began. How can there be any free will whatsoever, if this is the case?[8]

In what follows, I shall argue, in effect, that even granted deterministic physicalism, some degree of free will is possible, even though, admittedly, a pretty meagre degree, a pretty thin, weak kind of free will. It can be argued that, once we exist, our decisions to act play a crucial role in producing our actions, and without these decisions, our actions would not have occurred: to that extent, at least, we can have free will.

It may well be the case, however, that *probabilistic* physicalism is true. Quantum theory is by far the most successful physical theory, on empirical grounds, ever proposed, and quantum theory makes probabilistic predictions. Unfortunately, this does not provide decisive grounds for favouring probabilism. Quantum theory is a deeply unsatisfactory theory, despite its immense empirical success, because it is only about the results of performing measurements, and does not tell us what goes on physically in the absence of measurement. As a result, quantum theory is ambiguous on the crucial question of whether quantum phenomena themselves are deterministic or probabilistic. Some interpretations of quantum theory say one thing, some say the opposite. A strong case can be made out, however, for the view that quantum theory is trying to tell us that nature is fundamentally probabilistic, so that a decent version of quantum theory would specify precisely when probabilistic events occur in nature.[9] Future developments in physics may well support probabilistic physicalism.

If probabilistic physicalism is true, our actions are not precisely determined by the physical state of the universe before life began. At that time, our very existence and our actions were likely to have been wildly, gigantically, absurdly improbable. The mere fact that our actions are not precisely determined before we came into existence – or indeed before any life came into existence – makes free will possible in a much richer, stronger sense than the very meagre kind of free will that might be possible granted determinism.

Some philosophers have argued that probabilism provides less scope for free will than determinism does. They argue that if probabilism holds then, on occasions, when we decide to do something, a probabilistic event may intervene in our brain, and we find ourselves doing something quite different – not exactly an enhancement of free will. If determinism holds, that need never occur. But this line of argument is wrong on two counts. First, probabilism does not mean that it is inevitable that probabilistic events intervene in our brain to produce actions different from what we intended. Second, the argument ignores the fact that probabilistic physicalism provides scope for a much more substantial kind of free will to exist than deterministic physicalism does, just because the latter implies that the whole of human history is fixed by the state of the universe before life began, whereas the former carries no such implication. In addition, probabilism holds that there are many, possibly infinitely many, possible futures, some wildly improbable futures being brought about by our actions, whereas deterministic physicalism implies that the future is precisely determined by the present (and the past). This crucial difference allows us to have free will in a much stronger sense in a probabilistic universe with an open future than in a deterministic universe with a fixed future.[10]

One important point that this discussion reveals is that having free will is not an all or nothing affair. It is a matter of degree. This is recognized in law courts, which appreciate that there can be degrees of responsibility for a criminal act, depending on such things as the extent to which the balance of the mind was disturbed, or the person acted out of high passion or cool, deliberate calculation. Thus, the proper question to ask is not: Is free will compatible with physicalism, yes or no? It is rather: How worthwhile a version of free will can we have if we live in a physicalistic universe? Some degree or kind of free will is possible, no doubt, granted (experiential) physicalism. The question is: Is it a sufficiently full-blooded, worthwhile kind of free will to be regarded as authentic free will?[11]

PURPOSE IN A PHYSICALISTIC UNIVERSE

One point deserves to be appreciated straight away. There is no problem whatsoever in understanding how it is possible for there to be things able to pursue goals – purposive beings in other words – in a fully physicalistic universe, even one that is *deterministic*. The problem of how this is possible is solved by the feedback mechanism – the unit of control. Devices, from thermostats to guided missiles and robots, are able to pursue goals even though acting wholly in accordance with deterministic physical laws, because they incorporate feedback mechanisms in their bodily structure.[12]

One of the simplest examples of a feedback mechanism is the thermostat (as we saw briefly in chapter 3). This consists of a heater, a thermometer, and a switch. The aim of the thermostat, let us suppose, is to keep the room at the temperature of 20° centigrade. It achieves this by switching the heater off if the temperature rises above 20° C, and switching it on if it falls below 20° C.

We can imagine this being done as follows. As the temperature of the room falls below 20° C, the metal strip, of which the thermometer is composed, shrinks in length and, as a result, makes contact with an electric circuit that turns the heater on. The room heats up as a result, the metal strip expands, and this breaks the electric circuit, which turns the heater off. The outcome is that the thermostat acts so as successfully to attain the goal of keeping the room more or less at 20° C.

We have here the most elementary kind of negative feedback mechanism in action conceivable – the atom of control. It can be elaborated in various ways. First, instead of the action being the discrete one of ON/OFF, the action may rather be to increase or decrease something smoothly, for example, to turn the heater up by degrees or down, or to steer a rocket to the left or to the right to a greater or lesser extent. The action of the primitive ON/OFF thermostat could be represented by an arrow that points at one or other of two positions, ON and OFF. The action of a purposive device which acts continuously can be represented by an arrow which points at some point on a line, and moves to the left or right smoothly, along the line.

This latter continuously operating feedback mechanism can be elaborated by increasing the number of dimensions of continuous variability, from one, to two, three, ... to 10,000, to N, where N is any number equal to or greater than one. A guided missile might, for example, have a three-dimensional feedback mechanism for control system, guiding the missile to change its direction upward or downward, to the left or right, and to change its speed to go faster or slower. More complex control systems might consist of a number, M, of distinct control systems, each performing distinct control tasks, and a master control system that decides which of these M control systems is to operate at any given moment. One can even imagine a control system consisting of a hierarchy of control systems. At the base of the hierarchy, there is a vast number of control systems. As one goes up the hierarchy, the number of control systems decreases until, at the top, there is just one master control system activating and controlling all the others. It is possible that the brains of animals and humans are hierarchical control systems of this type. I formulate the intention to go downstairs and put the kettle on for a cup of tea – and think no more of the matter, acting more or less on autopilot, my thoughts elsewhere. This is the master control system activating subsidiary control systems to do its bidding. Control systems lower down in the hierarchy (in my brain) then guide my body to get up, walk out of the room, go downstairs into the kitchen, pick up the kettle, fill it from the tap, put it on the stove, and light it. These midway control systems activate control systems still lower down in the hierarchy (in my brain) to move my legs, arms, and hands appropriately so that these actions are performed; and further control systems, still lower down in the hierarchy, of which I am entirely unaware, control individual muscles in my legs, arms, and hands so that the sequence of actions is performed. And this hierarchical structure of control, which might be true of me, might also be true of a monkey swinging from branch to branch in the forest, or of a fox out hunting for rabbits or mice.

This hierarchical hypothesis may or may not be true.[13] The crucial point is that there is no problem whatsoever in understanding in principle how purposive action is possible in a physicalistic universe – even complex purposive action of the kind that mammals, and even humans, perform in life. We are still profoundly ignorant of the way mammalian brains, and human brains, produce the complex purposive actions that they do produce. But purposive action in a physicalistic universe does not in itself pose a problem of principle. The key to the solution of this problem is the feedback mechanism. It is worth noting that, for the feedback mechanism to work properly, to produce the purposive action that it is designed to produce, it is essential that deterministic physical laws, on which the feedback mechanism depends, continue to operate. To return to the atom of control, the thermostat, if, as the temperature falls, the metal strip began to *expand* (and not shrink), this would play havoc with the capacity of the thermostat to achieve its goal and control the temperature of the room. Far from purposive action, produced by control systems (based on elaborations of the feedback mechanism) being *in conflict* with physicalism, it is all the other way round: purposive action of this type actually requires physicalism to be true – at least as far as the workings of the control system of the purposive actor is concerned.[14]

The problem of how purposive action is possible granted physicalism is solved. But that does not solve the rather more serious problem of how free will is possible granted physicalism.

FREE WILL IN A PHYSICALISTIC UNIVERSE

That we can pursue goals more or less successfully even though we live in a physicalistic universe is not, in principle, a problem. We can conjecture that our brains are control systems of just the kind to enable us to do this – as indicated in the last section. Furthermore, we can understand, in principle, how it is possible for us to pursue, more or less successfully, the kind of complex goals that we do pursue even though (experiential) physicalism is true. We can conjecture that our brains have the kind of complex hierarchical structure indicated in the last section. Consciousness is, let us suppose, the master control system.[15] I decide to stop work, get up, leave the house, and visit a friend: the decision *is* the initiation of neurological processes in the master control system of my brain (consciousness) which, in turn, initiate further neurological processes, control systems lower down in the hierarchy which control specific actions (getting up from my chair, walking across the room, opening the door), which in turn initiate further neurological processes, control systems lower down still in the hierarchy which control the movement of specific limbs. These in turn initiate further neurological processes, control systems even lower down in the hierarchy, which control the contraction of specific muscles.

But if everything that occurs in this hierarchical control system – my brain – does so in accordance with precise physical law, how can I have free will? In particular, how does adding *consciousness* to some of these control processes create free will if, despite that, everything proceeds remorselessly in accordance with physical law? How can physics be the *servant*, even the *slave*, of consciousness, and not its master? How can consciousness have any role to play whatsoever, if everything proceeds in accordance with physical law?

A first step toward answering this question is provided by the following requirement for free will:

Fundamental Requirement for Perfect Free Will: The control structure of the brain is such that control (or mental) aspects of head processes[16] are correlated with the neurological or physical aspects in such a way that the physical aspect of any head process interacts physically (i.e., causally) with the rest of the brain, the body, and the environment in just the way required for the control aspect to *be* the control item that it is[17] – and crucially, in just the way required for the person in question to be in control of his actions and decisions to act, thus having perfect free will.

My desires, thoughts, feelings, imaginings, decisions to act, beliefs, values, intentions, perceptions, states of awareness, motives, plans, hopes, and fears have to evolve, interact with one another, and play a role in what I do in quite specific ways if they are to be *my* desires, thoughts, etc., coherent elements of my experiences, my conscious life and actions. Thus my desire to visit my friend, in order to be a desire, must prompt me to visit my friend – even if it does not compel me so to act. Furthermore, in order to be *my* desire (as opposed to a desire foisted onto me in some way, by manipulation, post-hypnotic suggestion, or brainwashing), it must emerge out of my life appropriately, and must fit appropriately into the pattern of my activities, priorities, and other desires. Again, my belief that my friend will be found at home must influence my actions in specific ways in order to be this belief. It cannot influence me to look for him in a local cafe. And in order to be *my* belief it must have been acquired in a certain way (as a result of a text, for example, and not as a result of brainwashing), and it must cohere appropriately with other beliefs of mine. And the same goes for all the other elements of my conscious life and experience. These elements must interact with one another and must have been acquired in quite specific ways, and must play quite specific roles in what I do – or might do in such and such circumstances – if they are to be the constituents that they purport to be of my conscious life: thoughts, feelings, imaginings, decisions to act, values, intentions, perceptions, states of awareness, motives, plans, hopes, and fears.

Furthermore, if I were to comply with *the requirement for perfect free will*, then I would always be in control of my actions and my thoughts and decisions to act. I would never act out of feelings or motives of which I was unaware – subjecting a friend to a cruel remark, for example, because I felt humiliated for reasons that had nothing to do with my friend. I would never give in to uncontrollable impulses to act in ways that I would later regret or deplore. Conflicting motives or desires would be resolved in the best possible way. My ability to discover relevant facts about the world around me, and about my own inner emotional and motivational state, would be as good as it possibly could be. I would never deceive myself, or be deceived by others, about my actions, or about the context in which I acted.

Needless to say, I personally fail hopelessly to meet these extraordinarily demanding *requirements for perfect free will* in my day-to-day life. And no doubt all human beings fall short of having *perfect free will* in this sense. The crucial point is that there does not seem to be anything inherent in experiential physicalism that makes it impossible for there to be a being with perfect free will in the above sense in a physicalistic universe. It is, of course, wildly implausible that the brain, its structure, state, and function, the body of which it forms a part, and the environment in which it is located should be so astonishingly organized and interconnected that physical processes occurring in the brain in accordance with physical law should unfold in just the way required to be the thoughts, feelings, perceptions, desires, and decisions to act of the person in question, evolving in just the way required for the person to meet in her actions *the requirement for perfect free will*. But wild implausibility is not impossibility. Perfect free will in a world in which experiential physicalism is true is wildly implausible but not, it seems, outright impossible. And if perfect free will is possible then, very significantly, the much more modest degree of free will that we human beings believe we possess would seem to be possible as well. And as for the wild implausibility of free will, an explanation for it will be given in a moment.

The above requirement for free will specifies, in rather general terms, what must be the case if there is to be dual control – the brain, body, and environment of the person in question being so delicately and intricately structured and organized that physical processes occurring in the brain that control the body to act as it does are also the thoughts, feelings, desires, imaginings, and decision to act of the person perfectly in control of her inner and outer deeds, both her inner imaginings and her outer, bodily actions. The might of the physical universe is commandeered, as it were, to serve the interests of the person.

But does meeting the above *requirement for free will* suffice to ensure that the person in question has genuine free will? It may be objected that, if experiential physicalism is true, then even a person meeting the above *requirement for perfect free will* would still not have real free will. I now consider one or two arguments in support of this claim.

To begin with, it may be objected that for real free will we require that it is our conscious decisions to act that directly produce our actions. But, given the above account, this does not happen. It is not *conscious decisions to act* that bring about a person's actions, but rather *physical processes occurring in that person's brain*. That means there is only at most a simulacrum of free will, not the authentic article.

The reply to this objection is that, according to experiential physicalism, the conscious decision to act *is* the physical processes occurring in the brain. The two are one and the same thing. They are contingently identical – that is, the identity is a matter of *fact*, not of *logic* or *necessity*. So, to that extent, my conscious decision to get up from my chair and walk across the room *is* the cause of my actions (leaving aside all that which does not change), in that this conscious decision *is* (contingently identical to) physical processes occurring in my brain that cause my body to rise from my chair and walk across the room.[18]

But can *conscious decisions to act* be contingently identical to *brain processes*? As I have already noted in chapter 3,[19] a famous argument due to Saul Kripke claims to establish that whenever one kind of phenomenon, such as light, heat, or consciousness is explained in terms of another, such as electromagnetic waves, motion of molecules, or brain processes, so that the one kind of phenomenon is identical to the other, then the identity is necessary, not contingent.[20] If Kripke's argument were valid, that would destroy the account I have just given of how our conscious decisions to act can cause our actions. For that account requires that consciousness is *contingently identical* to brain processes, not *necessarily identical*. The account of free will just given collapses.[21] Fortunately, Kripke's argument is not valid, as I have shown in some detail elsewhere.[22] We can declare that some head processes have two aspects or properties: experiential aspects (sentience and consciousness) and neurological or physical aspects, just as a leaf can have perceptual aspects or properties (its greenness and texture), as well as physical aspects or properties (its molecular structure). The green leaf is contingently identical to the physical object with such and such molecular structure. And equally, the conscious decision to act is contingently identical to the (relevant) brain process.

It may be objected, again, that the above account provides at best only a simulacrum of free will because, for authentic free will, it must be the case that it is the *conscious* aspect of processes going on inside our heads that guides or controls what we do, and what we think and decide to do. But according to the above account, the *conscious* aspect of our head processes can play no role whatsoever in influencing what we do or think; everything is determined by physics, by the *physical* aspect of our head processes. *What I am aware of plays no role in determining what I do, and what does determine what I do I am entirely unaware of.* Thus, even if physical features of neurological processes are such that they lead to those processes evolving and interacting with one another, and with sensory organs and muscles of the body, so that the requirements of consciousness are miraculously observed – conscious thoughts following one another in a way which makes perfect sense, conscious decisions to act invariably resulting in the intended act being performed, and so on – nevertheless it is the *physics* that is doing all this, not the *consciousness*. Physics becoming the slave of consciousness, so that it does its every bidding, its every whim, is not enough for authentic, full-blooded free will. *That* requires that consciousness itself play a role.

There are two things wrong with this argument. First, to echo what I have already said, since my *conscious decision to perform some action* – such as walk across the room – is (contingently) identical to *those brain processes that cause and control my actions* (both being aspects of one and the same thing, namely, head processes going on inside my head), my conscious decision does cause and control my actions. It is quite wrong to say that conscious decisions play no role in causing and controlling what we do.

But second, and much more significantly, what is wrong with the above argument is that the mental or conscious aspects of our head processes *do* play a crucial role in guiding or controlling our actions. What is it exactly that we are aware of in being aware of our inner experiences, our sensations, thoughts, feelings, desires, imaginings, intentions, decisions to act? My answer is that we are aware of the *control* aspects of brain processes going on inside our skulls. What I am aware of about what is going on inside me when I see a red rose is the control aspect of the brain process that is my perception of the red rose – that aspect which informs me that there is a red rose before me, and therefore how I need to act to take its existence into account. In becoming aware of hunger, of a desire to eat, I am aware of the control aspect of the relevant brain process: its capacity to prompt me to go and get something to eat. And more generally, in being aware of feelings, thoughts, motives, desires, intentions, imaginings, decisions to act, I am aware of the control aspects of the relevant brain processes – the role that these processes have in influencing or guiding my actions – and my inner imagined activities, my thoughts. In imagining that I get up from the chair I am sitting in to greet a friend, I arrange for neurological processes to occur in my brain that are analogous, from a control standpoint, to neurological processes that would occur in my brain (and I would make occur) were I actually to get up and greet my friend. And when I do get up to greet my friend, I arrange for precisely those neurological processes to occur in my brain required to cause my muscles to contract in consort so as to result in me rising and greeting my friend – but what I know about are the control aspects of these brain processes, not the neurological or physical aspects. We have, in other words, incredibly detailed and precise knowledge of neurological processes occurring in our brain, and an incredible capacity to generate within our brain precisely those neurological processes that need to occur if we are to act as we intend, but what we know about these processes is the control aspect, not the neurological or physical aspect. The latter kind of knowledge, indeed, would be useless from the standpoint of enabling us to find our way around in the world and act as we intend to act. What we need to know, from the standpoint of action, is the control aspect of our head processes.

I have called this view *experiential functionalism*.[23] Here I shall call it *experiential controllism* (better terminology). It is not equivalent to orthodox functionalism – the view that the mental aspect of a brain process is no more than the function it has in producing behaviour.[24] It does not assert that the mental is reducible to the functional and so, ultimately, in principle, to the physical. This is explicitly denied. In having certain kinds of brain processes occur in our own brains (specified in control or functional terms), we learn things about the world, about the realm of possible experience, which we could learn in no other way, such as what it is for something to be blue or red (perceptually), or what it is to experience the visual sensation of blue or red.

Experiential controllism generalizes, and adds content to, the externalist theory of perception, discussed in chapter 3.[25] In declaring, after J.J.C. Smart,[26] that what I know about my inner visual sensation associated with seeing a red rose is merely "this is the sort of thing that occurs in me whenever I do see a red rose," the intention was to show that we ordinarily know very little about the nature of our inner experiences, and thus not enough to exclude the thesis that they are brain processes. Experiential controllism adds content to this. What we know about our inner perceptual experiences is the control aspect of these processes: what we know is what these inner processes tell us about the world around us, as captured in the above Smartian phrase. This is to be generalized. What we ordinarily know about our head processes – insofar as we know anything – is the control aspect of these processes. We have an extraordinarily detailed and precise knowledge of some of our head processes, and an extraordinarily detailed, precise, and powerful capacity to create just the head processes in our brains that we require – but specified, not in neurological or physical terms, but in control terms.[27]

How does this view of what the mental features of brain processes are help rebut the above objection to the *fundamental requirement for free will*, namely, it procures only a simulacrum of free will because it cannot give any role for the mental aspects of brain processes in producing or controlling action (everything being determined by physics)?

Here is the answer. The aspect of brain processes that we are aware of is their *control* aspect, and this is *the* feature that produces, controls, guides our actions – and our inner actions, our imaginings, and thoughts. That these brain processes possess these control features is due, ultimately, to the physical character and structure of these processes, the physical character and structure of the rest of the brain, the body, and the environment, and the manner in which these processes came to be. These physical features and structures underpin the control or mental features; they provide something like a causal explanation as to why any given brain process has the control feature that it does have.[28] But they are not identical to the control feature itself. That this is so is indicated by the following consideration. Knowledge of the neurological or physical aspects of processes going on in our heads would be useless. What we require is what we have: knowledge of the control aspects of head processes, and the capacity to generate those brain processes, construed in control terms, which cause us to do what we intend. Being aware of the mental – that is, the control – aspects of our brain processes is just what we need to be aware of in order to find our way around in the world, and do what we want to do.

What we are aware of in being aware of our perceptions, desires, feelings, thoughts, imaginings, motives, beliefs, intentions, decisions to act – the mental aspect of brain processes, that is, or the control aspect – is just the aspect that it is absolutely essential for us to be aware of if we are going to be able to control our thoughts, decisions to act, and actions: if, in other words, we are going to have authentic free will. The mental aspect of brain processes, far from being impotent and redundant from the standpoint of free will, is absolutely essential for possession of free will.

In the end, the point can be put quite simply like this. If we are to be in control, we need to be aware of – we need to know about – the control aspects of our brain processes. According to *experiential controllism* – as we may call the view I am expounding – it is just this control aspect that we are aware of in being aware of the mental aspects of our brain processes. The aspect of our brain processes that we are conscious of – the mental aspect – is, on this view, clearly absolutely essential for free will. And consciousness itself has a crucial role in initiating and controlling action, even if authentically free, spontaneous action can, on occasions, come from the unconscious, taking us almost by surprise.

There is, however, an apparently fatal objection to this attempt to provide *consciousness* with a role in producing and guiding action. Consider a hypothetical person, just like me, with a brain just like mine, but entirely bereft of any inner experiences, consciousness, or states of awareness whatsoever. This hypothetical person behaves as if conscious, but he is no more conscious than a robot, guided missile, or thermostat. Philosophers call such hypothetical beings *philosophical zombies.* The specific zombie under consideration, my zombie twin, is able to perform all the actions I can perform that would ordinarily be said to be possible only if one is acting consciously and freely – laugh, tell jokes, engage in reasonably intelligible conversation, write philosophy – but in the case of the zombie, all this is produced by the brain, by physics, alone, without any hint of consciousness. If experiential physicalism is correct, such a zombie must be a possibility. For, given experiential physicalism, the experiential cannot, even in principle, be derived from the physical. It must therefore be possible for there to be a person with a body and brain just like mine, acting like me, but devoid of any inner experience or consciousness. The thesis that such a being exists does not involve a contradiction. It is thus logically possible. And the mere *possibility* of such a zombie establishes that consciousness plays no role in producing and guiding my actions. If my zombie twin can act in a way which is just as if he is conscious, then my actions too are produced by the successive physical states of my brain, my consciousness having no role to play whatsoever. Free will, granted experiential physicalism, is impossible.

The crucial assumption of this argument is that my zombie twin is *possible*. That it is logically possible, granted experiential physicalism, must, I think, be conceded. Consciousness, the experiential, cannot, according to experiential physicalism, be derived from physics. Nothing about consciousness can be derived from a purely physical specification of a person's brain, however detailed and comprehensive it may be. Therefore, there can be no logical contradiction involved in specifying a brain in physical terms that produces apparently conscious actions but is deprived of any hint of consciousness or sentience.

A case can be made out, however, for holding that my zombie twin is not *in fact* possible, even if it is *logically* possible (in the sense that it does not involve a logical contradiction).

What is the experiential aspect of a neurological process occurring, let us suppose, in someone else's brain? It is, I suggest, what it is to have that neurological process occur in one's own brain, granted that one's brain is sufficiently similar to the other person's brain in relevant respects. We can, in principle, find out whether others experience what we experience when we see a rainbow, hear a trumpet sound, or smell violets. We can find out what neurological processes *are* these sensations, and we can then arrange for sufficiently similar neurological processes to occur in our brain.

This is, I submit, the natural way to think of the experiential aspect of neurological processes, granted experiential physicalism.[29] Granted this view, it is at once clear that it is not *in fact* possible for my zombie twin to exist. If neurological processes go on inside his skull that are similar to mine, then he will, as a matter of fact, have inner experiences and states of consciousness that are similar to mine. Ostensibly conscious and free actions produced by beings with brains like those of us who are conscious must in fact be beings who are conscious like us. To act as if conscious and free, you must in fact be conscious.[30] The above zombie argument is rebutted. Free will is still possible, it seems, granted experiential physicalism.

There is, however, yet another argument against this idea. It may be objected that the *real* explanation for what occurs when we deliberate and act is the *fundamental physical explanation*. This explanation refers to fundamental physical entities and forces – electrons, quarks, electromagnetism, the weak and strong forces, and gravitation – and employs fundamental physical theory (ultimately, the true, unified theory-of-everything), but makes no mention whatsoever of desires, thoughts, feelings, motives, reasons, plans, intentions, or decisions to act. Everything human disappears, and we are left merely with physical states of affairs evolving in accordance with fundamental physical law. Explanations of human actions in terms of desires, intentions, beliefs, motives, etc., may have a certain practical utility but, ultimately, such explanations are superfluous and impotent. The real explanation of what occurs is the *physical* explanation.

In order to rebut this objection, we need to consider in a little more detail the different ways in which phenomena associated with human life, human action, can be explained and understood. This is the task of the next section.

TREBLE COMPREHENSIBILITY: PHYSICAL, PURPOSIVE, AND PERSONALISTIC

We human beings, and other sentient creatures, possess the extraordinary feature that we are comprehensible in three different ways. We are trebly comprehensible.[31] Our multiple comprehensibility is in itself almost incomprehensible. We are mysteriously, inexplicably over-endowed with comprehensibility. It is such a striking, wildly improbable feature that it cries out for an explanation. The explanation comes from our past, from history, and from evolution, as I shall indicate below. (This means we are, in a sense, comprehensible in a fourth way – *historically* – a kind of comprehensibility that can render intelligible the combined presence of the other three.)

What are these three different ways in which we are comprehensible? First, we are comprehensible *physically*. Whatever else we may be, we are at least very complex physical systems interacting physically with our environment: all this is physically comprehensible; it can in principle (not in practice) be predicted and explained physically.[32] Second, we are comprehensible *purposively*. Again, whatever else we may be, we are at least beings that act in order to achieve goals – like all living things, robots, guided missiles, and other goal-seeking entities. Our actions can be explained and understood as being designed to achieve goals. And finally, we are comprehensible *personalistically*. We can be understood as conscious, or at least sentient, beings, our actions being consciously intended.

In seeking to understand another person, or even an animal, *personalistically*, I seek to understand the other as I understand myself. I imagine I am that other person (that other sentient being), with that other person's situation, experiences, desires, thoughts, feelings, perceptions, beliefs, plans, intentions, goals, skills, foibles, relationships, ambitions, hopes, and fears. I put myself, imaginatively, into the other person's shoes, and discover, as the other person, what I would feel, think, experience, desire, plan, imagine, hope for, fear, and do. What I call *personalistic* understanding is sometimes called *empathic* understanding, and the capacity to understand others in this way is often called by psychologists and others *theory of mind*, or *folk psychology*. There are, however, important differences between *personalistic* understanding and these other notions, as I will explain in a moment.

Purposive explanations apply to all goal-pursuing things: robots, guided missiles, thermostats, insects, dogs, cats, and people. They explain what these things do as actions designed to achieve goals. Crucially, however, everything *experiential* is omitted. No distinction is made between purposive things that do, and do not, have inner experiences. People are treated as if they are robots, or philosophical zombies. Purposive explanations are personalistic explanations with everything experiential deleted. Purposive explanations may make use of experientially denuded versions of personalistic concepts, such as "belief," desire," "perception," "motive," "feeling," "thought," "plan," "decision," and so on.[33] In every case, the experientially denuded concept refers to processes going on in the "brain" of the purposive thing that have a role in producing – initiating, controlling, and guiding – action designed to achieve goals that are analogous to the sentient and conscious processes that would be producing comparable actions in sentient or conscious beings, mammals, or persons.

Given any personalistic explanation of actions of a person or sentient animal, there corresponds a purposive explanation of the same actions, but the reverse is not true. No conscious being could be nothing more than a thermostat. The way of life of a thermostat is simply too spare, too impoverished, to accommodate consciousness – or even sentience.

Personalistic understanding adds to a corresponding purposive understanding in enabling one to know and understand what it would be like to *be* the other person (or sentient animal), seeing, feeling, thinking, desiring, hoping, and fearing what the other sees, feels, thinks, etc.

Personalistic understanding cannot be reduced to physical understanding, as we saw in chapter 3. Personalistic understanding cannot be reduced to purposive understanding either, essentially for the same reason. Any given nugget of personalistic explanation and understanding of a human action has, corresponding to it, a nugget of purposive explanation and understanding that differs only in that the experiential aspect is entirely excluded. For that reason, the former cannot be reduced to the latter.

Can purposive explanations be reduced to physical explanations? No. Purposive explanations appeal to actions performed to attain goals; such explanations appeal to success and failure, to motives and reasons for actions, to intentions, plans, even to feelings – all to be understood nonexperientially. None of these notions, or purposive facts or phenomena, has any role in fundamental physics, and we have no reason to suppose that such purposive facts or phenomena could be *derived* from any purely physical depiction of facts couched in fundamental physical terms. Furthermore, a purposive being might pursue a goal which cannot be depicted in physical terms because such a depiction *contradicts* fundamental physical laws: in this case, purposive explanations, appealing to this goal, could not be derived from physical explanations. An example might be the goal a person could have to discover a potion which, when drunk, renders one invisible.

What bearing does all this have on the crucial point, raised at the end of the last section, that the *real* explanation of human action is the *fundamental physical* explanation, that which refers to physical entities and forces, and says not a word about human intentions, decisions, motives, or consciousness and therefore makes it impossible that there should be any such thing as free will? The answer can be put like this. If all personalistic explanations were in principle reducible to physical explanations, then it might be legitimate to say that the real explanation for human action is the physical one, and there can be no such thing as free will. But personalistic explanations are *not* reducible to physical explanations. I decide to put my name forward as a candidate for a member of parliament in a general election in the United Kingdom. There is, let us suppose, in principle a physical explanation of everything physical that occurs in connection with my decision and subsequent actions. Physical processes inside my head and body, physical movements of my body, sounds I make, marks I make on bits of paper, and so on: all these things are, in principle, explainable physically. But this physical description and explanation of physical events and processes associated with my actions, however precise and comprehensive, cannot of itself imply descriptions of my thoughts, feelings, desires, intentions, decisions, motives – and my human actions, my deeds. Vibrations of molecules of the air are precisely specified, but not the meaning, the content, of what I say when I declare, "Yes, I wish to put my name forward to become an MP." Ink marks I make on a piece of paper are specified, not the content of what I write. There is a whole human dimension of what goes on – my inner thoughts and experiences, what I and others perceive and understand, what I say, write, and communicate with others, my actions imbued with human significance – all this escapes physics entirely, however precise and complete, even though purely *physical* aspects of these things are included. Above all, the freedom-ascribing, personalistic explanation for my action is not even in principle derivable from the physical explanation of all the physical phenomena associated with my action. And it is this that ensures that one cannot hold that the *real* explanation is the physical one, and the personalistic explanation is redundant. Both are valid simultaneously, and neither is reducible to the other.[34]

Personalistic explanations make sense of things in a way that differs profoundly from the way physics makes sense of things. From true personalistic explanations of human actions we come to understand what it would be for oneself to be what the other is, do what the other does. We come to appreciate the feelings, the desires, the intentions, motives, beliefs, hopes and fears of the other. We know *why* the other acted as he or she did, in the sense of what the motive, the reason, for the act was, what goal was being sought. The explanation makes human sense of the act. All this is very different from what a physical explanation supplies. The true, ultimate physical explanation of a phenomenon or event would consist of the following two elements: (1) the true fundamental physical theory, and (2) a true specification of the physical state of the initial state of affairs. The explanation derives a physical description of the outcome state of affairs from (1) and (2). Physical explanations, in other words, reveal that successive physical states of affairs follow one another in time in accordance with fundamental physical law.

Both kinds of explanation, personalistic and physical, explain by revealing that what occurs accords with a pattern in phenomena, but very different kinds of pattern are depicted. In the case of physical explanations, it is the pattern of phenomena unfolding in time in accordance with universal physical law; in the case of personalistic explanation, it is the pattern of conscious goal-seeking action in response to perceived needs and desires. The personalistic pattern is, as it were, superimposed on, but compatible with and backed up by, the physical pattern (plus the intricate structure of our brains and bodies, and the appropriate character of our environment).

Both explanations require a wide range of what may be called "conditional possible states of affairs" to be true. The physical explanation requires that the basic physical laws are true. This means that, for the physical explanation to be true, we require that infinitely many conditional statements must be true of the form "If the initial state of affairs had been different in such and such ways, then the outcome would have been different in such and such ways." In order for a personalistic explanation to be true, we require conditional statements to be true of the form "If the context had been a bit different, in such and such ways, then the person would have acted a bit differently in such and such ways, in order to attain his or her goal in these new circumstances" (or perhaps in order to attain a modified or different goal). Thus, if the personalistic explanation for my decision to put my name forward to become an MP is that I hope thereby to be of service to my fellow human beings, we require, for this explanation to be true, that I would act differently if I could be convinced that becoming an MP will not enable me to benefit my fellow human beings, or that I would be of much greater service to my fellow human beings if I took up campaigning on behalf of the destitute. True explanations do not just depict patterns in actual phenomena; in addition, they depict patterns in possible phenomena, in phenomena that would occur if circumstances were different.

Even if personalistic explanations are not reducible, even in principle, to physical explanations, there is a sense, nevertheless, in which personalistic explanations are *encompassed* by physical explanations. Whenever there is a human deed open to personalistic explanation, everything physical that occurs is in principle open to being explained physically, and furthermore endless variants of this physical explanation apply to phenomena about which personalistic explanations are silent. Physical explanations are all encompassing, whereas personalistic explanations are not. Does this not suffice to establish that the *real* explanation for what goes on in connection with human action is the physical one?

No. We human beings are just a minuscule fragment of the physical universe, so of course, personalistic explanations apply only to a minuscule fragment of what there is, whereas physical explanations have unlimited scope (given the physical comprehensibility of the universe). The limited scope of personalistic explanations does not deprive them of authenticity or reality.

It may be argued, however, that personalistic explanations do not have the intellectual status and power of physical explanations, and thus cannot be regarded as equally authentic or real. Personalistic explanations are (a) subjective, (b) personal, (c) emotional and evaluative (and thus nonfactual), (d) intuitive (and thus nonrational), (e) nonpredictive, (f) untestable, and (g) unscientific. Physical explanations, by contrast, are (a) objective, (b) impersonal, (c) factual, (d) rational, (e) predictive, (f) testable, and (g) scientific. In every respect, (a) to (g), physical explanations have greater intellectual standing, validity, authenticity, and power than personalistic explanations. The two simply do not stand comparison. The real explanation for what goes on is the physical one. Personalistic explanations can only at best provide the illusion of authenticity. And that means there is no such thing as free will.

My reply to this objection must be deferred until chapter 7, where I will defend the authenticity of personalistic explanations against this attack.

It may be asked: But how does the above overcome the objection that experiential physicalism must deny the reality of free will – it must be a version of epiphenomenalism[35] – because, despite all the stuff about "control," nevertheless the *mental* aspects of brain processes have no causal efficacy whatsoever, and thus can have no role whatsoever in causing other brain processes, or bodily movements, to occur? My answer can be summed up like this. First, mental events and processes *do* have causal efficacy, because they are contingently identical to brain processes – ultimately, to physical processes. Second, in asking what the causal efficacy of the *mental* aspect of a brain process can be we are asking the wrong question. Insofar as a feature of a brain process is a *nonphysical, mental* one, it is, ipso facto, noncausal. To ask for the causal efficacy of the purely mental aspect of a head process is to ask for the blatantly impossible. But the fact that *mental* aspects of head processes have no causal role does not mean that they have no role whatsoever in producing human action. They play a crucial role in true personalistic explanations of human actions, and such explanations really do explain how and why people do what they do. Furthermore, as we have seen, such personalistic explanations of human actions are not reducible to physical explanations. Mental aspects of head processes play a vital role in producing human actions, not via their role in physical or causal explanations, but via their role in true personalistic explanations.

The *physical* aspects of brain processes play a crucial role in producing human action because of their *causal* features or, as we may equivalently say, because these physical features play a crucial role in the true *physical explanation* of the human action in question.[36] At once we have a more general requirement for an aspect of a head process to play a significant role in human action: this aspect must have a vital role in *true, intellectually authentic explanations* of the actions in question. For mental aspects of head processes to have a significant role in human actions, we require that these mental aspects play an important role in some kind of *true, intellectually authentic explanations* of the human actions in question that do not reduce to *physical explanations*.

Just this requirement is satisfied, I have argued, within the framework of experiential physicalism. We do indeed, all the time, give *personalistic explanations* of human actions, couched in terms of mental aspects of head processes and states such as feelings, desires, perceptions, thoughts, intentions, decisions; these *personalistic explanations* may well be *true* and *intellectually authentic*; they are most certainly *not reducible to physics*. These personalistic explanations, in appealing to the *mental* aspect of head processes or states, appeal to their *control* aspect – the role that the feeling, desire, or perception plays in controlling *action*. It is because mental aspects of head processes have such a significant role to play in potential true personalistic explanations of human action that these mental, or control, features have a significant role to play in human action itself.

And this is just how we would ordinarily conceive of the matter. If I am to act freely, then what matters, surely, is that there is, potentially, a true (personalistic) intellectually authentic explanation of what I do that (a) refers to my reasons for acting as I do, my relevant feelings, desires, beliefs, and so on, (b) describes me as acting freely, but (c) is not reducible to a physical explanation of what I do. If (a), (b), and (c) are satisfied, that ought to suffice for me to be acting freely.

In attributing mental processes and states to a person, we thereby imply that certain sorts of actions may be the outcome. A person who is feeling angry may begin to act in an angry fashion; a person full of joy may begin to jump for joy. Both mental and physical aspects of head processes and states have implications for what happens. The difference is that mental aspects have implications for human action described, explained, and understood in *personalistic* terms, whereas the physical aspects have implications for what occurs described in *physical* terms. The implications for human action that *mental* aspects have derive from their neurological or, ultimately, *physical* aspects, and the way the neurological process in question is related to the rest of the brain (the body and the environment).

I should perhaps add that, even though the mental aspect of a head process is not a physical aspect, nevertheless incredibly intricate neurological (ultimately physical) conditions must be satisfied for the mental aspect to be what it is. A desire for a glass of wine is only a desire at all, let alone the particular desire that it is, if it has very detailed, specific neurological features, and is situated in a specific way in a very specific kind of brain with the right kind of neurological structure and state, so that the neurological process that the desire is will interact with other neurological processes in the brain in the required fashion.

Despite what I have said, it may still be thought that if physics determines everything that occurs, then there can be no room whatsoever for the mental to have any kind of influence on what occurs, whether this is depicted by means of personalistic explanations or in any other way. But a further crucial point needs to be taken into account. It is not *just* physics that determines causally what goes on. It is physics *infected by the mental*, physics *organized, shaped, and structured by the requirements of the mental*. So the picture that it is just physics that really decides what goes on, and the mental is wholly superfluous, is entirely wrong. It is *not* just physics that decides what goes on. It is physics *impregnated* with the requirements of the mental.

I have already, in effect, made this point. If there are true personalistic explanations of a person's actions – especially if there are such explanations that attribute free will to the person in a sense not too far short of "perfect free will" as indicated above – then it follows that the near miracle of treble comprehensibility obtains. Neurological processes that occur in the person's brain must be very precisely structured, and must be very precisely related to the rest of the brain (body and environment), these in turn being very precisely structured, if what the person does is to be trebly comprehensible in the way required for fairly free human action. Desires, perceptions, intentions, decisions, and so on are only these things if the neurological components of these mental states and processes have precisely the required physical structures and features. In short, the truth of personalistic explanations of human action demands that the brain is organized and functions in precisely the way required for brain processes to *be* the mental processes the personalistic explanations attribute to the person. The physical, as I have said, is impregnated with the requirements of the mental. Free action enslaves physics, as it were, to do its bidding. The physical world is imbued with mind.[37] It is not just physics that causes human action, but physics intricately and delicately organized and structured to meet the requirements of mind.

This account of how there can be free will in a physicalist universe throws all the mystery onto the miracle of treble comprehensibility. How can creatures come to exist in a physicalist universe that are trebly comprehensible? That is the key problem that has to be solved. It is tackled in the next chapter.

There are two further questions concerning free will that I shall try to answer in chapter 7. These are: How can free will be enhanced in a physicalistic universe? What grounds are there for holding that the basic problem should be reformulated as a question, not about mere free will, but rather about wisdom? (The assumption here is that wisdom implies free will but not vice versa.)

DO WE HAVE FREE WILL?

This intricate philosophizing is all very well – the cry may go up – but the all-important question is: Do we have free will? It is not enough to argue that it is possible; we need to know that it really does exist!

Here is an argument in support of the idea that we do have free will, or at least that we have no reason to doubt that it exists. We doubt that we have free will because of what physics tells us about the world. But if what modern physics tells us about the world is largely correct (in that physicalism is true), then humanity has made an astonishing discovery of real value, which could not have been made without free will. The argument goes like this. Physicalism is either false or true. If false, it poses no threat to free will. If true, that establishes that science has been extraordinarily successful in acquiring theoretical knowledge and understanding about the nature of the universe – especially granted the argument of chapter 4, which shows that physicalism is a major item of current scientific knowledge. But science, in order to have met with such extraordinary success, requires that the scientists who achieved this success acted freely in their scientific work, in deciding what experiments to perform, what experimental results and theories to accept and reject, what arguments and theoretical derivations to regard as conclusive and inconclusive. We could only have discovered the truth – physicalism – in short, if we had acted freely. The truth of physicalism, discovered by us, establishes the reality of free will, since without free will, we could never have discovered that physicalism is indeed true. In short, if physicalism is true, we have a proof of the reality of free will![38]

The major weakness in this argument is the assumption that free will is required to create modern science. Computers have been programmed to make genuine contributions to science, and computers do not have free will.

When it comes down to it, perhaps we should invoke a revised version of Descartes's "I think, therefore I am" to establish the reality of free will – or at least that we are entitled to accept that free will is a reality. What is at issue, as I said at the beginning of this chapter, is our existence. If we do not have free will, we do not exist. We are rationally entitled to hold that we do have some free will because in making this assumption we have nothing to lose and everything to gain. We should not allow ourselves to be bamboozled into thinking we do not exist. I exist, therefore I have free will.

There is an analogy, here, perhaps, with the problem of knowledge. Traditionally, this has been taken to be the problem of how we can acquire any knowledge at all. Popper, in my view, correctly transformed this fundamental problem of epistemology so that it becomes "How can we acquire *more* knowledge?" or "How can we *improve* our knowledge?" It may seem illegitimate just to presuppose at the outset that we do already have some knowledge, but without that presupposition we are lost. We are rationally entitled to assume that we do have some knowledge, and the fundamental task is to improve what we have, because if we have no knowledge we have no basis for acquiring it. I suggest something similar holds for the problem of free will. The fundamental problem is not "Do we have free will?" or "Can we have free will in a physicalistic universe?" Rather it ought to be "How can we best go about *increasing* or *improving* what free will we do already possess, granted we live in a physicalistic universe?"

We may also wonder whether it is enough to ask how *free will* can be enhanced. Is it not more important to enhance *our capacity to realize what is of value in life* – our *wisdom* in other words? Here I take "wisdom" to be "the capacity, the active endeavour, and the desire to realize (experience and create) what is of value in life, for oneself and others." Free will is included in the idea of wisdom so characterized, it may be argued, but the reverse is not the case. We can hardly be wise if we do not have free will, but we might have bags of free will and at the same time be very unwise. Wisdom, in the sense indicated, is perhaps more fundamental, more desirable, of greater value, than mere free will.

These are questions I will reconsider in chapter 7.

FREE WILL WILDLY IMPROBABLE

So far I have argued that free will is *possible* in a physicalistic universe. The argument has also revealed, however, that free will is wildly, almost inconceivably *improbable*. If I am to have free will, physical processes going on in my brain, my body, and my environment must be such that they accord precisely with what I see, think, feel, decide, and do – so that I am in control of both the sequence of my inner mental processes and my outward actions. My brain and body must be so beautifully and intricately designed that physical processes occurring in my brain *are* my inner conscious thoughts, feelings, desires, and decisions to act, these mental processes following one another in time in just the way for them to be *my* mental processes, all controlled and decided by *me*. Furthermore, my decisions to act must in reality initiate and guide my actions, so that I do what I have decided to do, and it is my decision that controls my actions, physical processes in my brain, body, and environment unfolding in accordance with physical law in just the way required to make all this possible.

Put another way, free will in a physicalistic universe requires that there is something like *dual control* of my inner mental processes and actions. I must be in control; and the physical universe must be in control. And, wildly improbably, almost miraculously, the physical universe and I must persistently agree in almost every detail. What I decide to think and do must agree with what the physical universe determines occurs in my brain, body, and environment.

Put yet another way, if I am to have free will in a physicalistic universe, then I must be trebly comprehensible. I must be comprehensible (in principle) *physically*; I must be comprehensible *purposively*; and I must be comprehensible *personalistically*. Furthermore, the personalistic explanations for my actions must be such that they correctly hold me responsible for what I do – and responsible for what I decide to do – even though, simultaneously, there is, in principle, a purely physical explanation of everything that goes on in connection with my decisions and actions, couched purely in terms of physical states of affairs and physical laws, with no mention of conscious decisions and meaningful human actions at all. Both kinds of explanation must be true simultaneously, from moment to moment, an almost inconceivably improbable state of affairs of pre-established harmony.

For me to have free will, both I and the physical universe must, as it were, be in control. There must be dual control. But that requires a wildly improbable *matching* of what I decide to think and do, and what physics determines occurs.

It is this extraordinary improbability of free will existing in a physicalistic universe which may well be the implicit, underlying reason why so many people find the whole idea of free will in a physicalistic universe to be inconceivable, indeed impossible.

But the wildly improbable may, nevertheless, be possible. And there is, in fact, a partial explanation for the existence of free will in the universe. It comes from Darwin's theory of evolution – the subject of the next chapter. Darwin helps us understand how and why free will, wildly improbable in our physicalistic universe, has nevertheless come to exist.

6

Evolution of Life of Value

∞ Darwinian theory helps explain how and why purposive
life of value has evolved; two versions of the theory, purposive and
purposeless; resistance to recognition of purpose in nature explained
and criticized; principle of noncircularity; sentience,
consciousness, and language ∞

Charles Darwin's theory of evolution constitutes a major stride
towards solving the intellectual part of our fundamental problem
– the problem of how life of value can exist embedded in the physical universe. It is, however, vital that Darwin's theory is interpreted
properly, so that it becomes capable of improving our understanding
of how life of value has evolved in this physicalistic universe.

Darwin's theory holds that all life on earth, in all its multiplicity
and diversity, has evolved gradually during the last three-and-a-half
to four billion years from some primitive source, the source being
some relatively simple capsule of chemicals that began to reproduce
itself. One hypothesis concerning the origin of life, which seems to
me to be highly plausible, pursued especially by Nick Lane, is that
life began under the sea in alkaline hydrothermal vents.[1] Once the
initial blob of chemicals began to reproduce itself in its given environment, two key Darwinian mechanisms, responsible for evolution,
began to operate. First, some of the reproduced entities exhibited
slight variations, these variations being maintained in subsequent
reproductions. And second, those variations best able to survive and
reproduce in the given environment will be the variations that will
tend indeed to survive and reproduce. Darwin's theory of evolution,
boiled down to its essence, asserts that all life on earth has evolved
from some primitive beginning by means of these two mechanisms
of (1) inheritable variations and (2) natural selection – the tendency
of those variations best at surviving and reproducing in the given

environment to survive and reproduce. Gradually, as more and more varieties emerged to survive and reproduce, so diversity of life forms grew and grew. For the first two billion years or so, there were only single-cell organisms. Then life forms emerged that consisted of many cells. Algae, sponges, molluscs emerged; and then fish, plants, fungi, insects, reptiles, mammals, primates, and eventually, in the last 200,000 years or so, human beings.

Darwinian theory can be given two very different interpretations. On the one hand, it can be interpreted as explaining purposiveness away; on the other, it can be interpreted as explaining how purposiveness has gradually emerged and evolved in an ultimately purposeless, physicalistic universe.

The champion of the purposeless view is perhaps Richard Dawkins. In his *The Selfish Gene*, Dawkins argues that Darwinian theory should be interpreted to be about genes. The unit of selection, he argues, is the gene, and genes are not purposive. Of course, in calling genes "selfish," it sounds as if Dawkins does believe genes are purposive. But Dawkins is adamant: "selfish" is a mere metaphor for the tendency of those genes that survive to be the ones that are good at replicating themselves. Dawkins does acknowledge that living things exhibit design, and in doing so, acknowledges a kind of purpose, especially if the distinction between something being well and ill designed is admitted. How well a thing is designed depends crucially on the purpose for which it is used. A table may be well designed if the purpose is to have supper round it, but very ill designed if the purpose is to use it as a boat. Dawkins would reply, no doubt, that design means merely well adapted, well constituted, to survive in the given environment.

Some years ago, I heard Dawkins give a lecture on the subject at the London School of Economics. In order to illustrate the fallacy of attributing purposes to animals, Dawkins played a clip from the BBC TV sitcom *Fawlty Towers* in which John Cleese, in a fury, beat his car with a branch in punishment because it would not start. The intended implication was clear. It is as misguided for us to attribute purposes to living things as it is for Fawlty to attribute a purpose (stubbornly refusing to start) to his car.

This attitude that Darwinism should be interpreted as eliminating purpose from nature seems to be rather widely upheld by biologists. According to this attitude, evolution is all about "chance and necessity" to quote the title of a book by Jacques Monod.[2] One sees the tendency implicit in the complicated answers that evolutionists give to the question: What is life? Once it is acknowledged that all living things are purposive, the answer is very simple and entirely obvious: living things are naturally occurring purposive entities. That this answer is rarely given in biological textbooks is an indication of just how widespread the anti-purpose view is.

It sounds crazy to deny that animals actively pursue purposes in their lives – and of course it is crazy. How, then, can it be that many evolutionary biologists do deny this? They do not deny the facts of animal activity. What they downplay, however, or even deny altogether, is the crucial role that purposive action plays in evolution, and the implications that this has for the whole way in which Darwinian theory is understood. According to the purposive version of the theory, all living things are purposive; their basic goals are survival and reproductive success. A basic task of Darwinian theory is to explain how and why the multitude of diverse purposive beings, alive today and in the past, came to be. Furthermore, according to the purposive version of Darwinian theory, the purposive actions of living things have played a major role in directing evolution itself. The strivings of generations upon generations of animals (our ancestors), during millions of years to live, to survive, to find food, to escape from predators, to mate, to rear offspring has done much to shape the course that evolution has taken. As evolution has progressed, the strivings, the purposive activity, of animals have played an increasingly important role in the way evolution has proceeded. We owe our existence to the purposive strivings of these animal ancestors of ours.

The anti-purpose view fails to stress this all-important aspect of Darwinian evolution, or rejects it outright. The emphasis instead, as I have said, is on "chance and necessity," on purely mechanical, purposeless mechanisms of evolution, and Darwinism is regarded as explaining purpose away rather than helping to explain how it has emerged and evolved. Purpose, in any full-blooded sense, and in any sense that has a substantial influence on the course that evolution takes, tends to be removed, or leached away, from the scene.

This anti-purpose view, however, faces a devastating objection: How can it cope with our human world? There are just two possibilities. Either our human world is held to be full of purposive action; or it is held to be devoid of it. The first option faces the serious objection that this creates a hiatus, a gulf, between the purposeless natural world and the purposeful human world. This is thoroughly anti-Darwinian in character: the whole tendency of Darwinism is to deny the existence of such dramatic, abrupt fissures in the evolutionary process. The second option is even more objectionable: it means we all live devoid of purposes in life, purpose being no more than an illusion. The anti-purpose version of Darwinism cannot help solve our fundamental problem of understanding how our human world, imbued with purpose and value, can have come to exist in the physicalistic universe; for that we require the purposive version of the theory.

There are many further reasons for rejecting the purposeless version of Darwinism for, as I shall argue in a moment, there are very many ways in which the purposive actions of living things do influence subsequent evolution. I shall argue, indeed, that Darwinism scarcely makes sense unless purpose is attributed to living things. And, of course, the purposeless version renders Darwinism incapable of contributing to our fundamental problem of how life of value can exist in a purposeless, physicalistic universe. The anti-purpose view considerably impoverishes Darwinism, even, ultimately, renders it incoherent.

What lies behind the tendency of biology to downplay the significance of purpose in evolution? A number of misunderstandings, some going far back into the history of science.

First, the claim that purpose has an important role to play in evolution may be misinterpreted to be the claim that evolution itself has a purpose. Evolution has no purpose.[3] The twin key Darwinian mechanisms of random variations and natural selection are wholly blind, mechanical, and devoid of purpose in character – initially at least. That feature of Darwinism is vital, if it is to do what is required: explain how purpose has evolved in a purposeless universe. Darwinism must not presuppose just that which it seeks to explain.

Second, the claim that living things are purposive may be interpreted to mean that this purposive character is *incompatible with physics* or *physicalism*. It may be interpreted to be a modern version of a nineteenth-century doctrine of holism or vitalism, which held that processes go on in living things which cannot even in principle be understood in ordinary chemical and physical terms. This again is a misinterpretation. As we saw in chapter 3, purposiveness can be understood in a thoroughly *compatibilist* sense, so that guided missiles and thermostats are purposive in this sense.

A thing that is purposive in a compatibilist sense is such that all processes associated with it can, in principle, be fully predicted and explained by physics.[4]

A third misunderstanding may be that it is thought that to attribute a purpose to something is to attribute awareness of that purpose to that thing. No, not at all. The guided missile, the thermostat, the bacterium, the spider, and the oak tree have no idea at all of what their purposes are: they are, we may assume, all devoid of sentience and consciousness.

There is a broader, more diffuse misunderstanding lurking behind orthodox reluctance to embrace the purposiveness of living things. It goes back to Galileo. Modern science began, it may be argued, when Galileo rejected Aristotle's view that purpose, or teleology, is to be found everywhere in nature, and adopted instead the modern view that the book of nature "is written in the language of mathematics," as Galileo put it. Interpreting Darwin as explaining how purpose has come to exist in the natural world may be held to constitute a serious backsliding to pre-Galilean, Aristotelian times. But again, this is a misunderstanding. Compatibilism affirms, and does not deny, Galileo's vision.

What, then, does the purposive version of Darwinian theory amount to? It can be put like this.

All living things, including human beings, are purposive – in a compatibilist sense. Plants pursue goals mainly by means of growth. The fundamental purposes of all living things, apart, perhaps, from human beings, are the Darwinian ones of survival and reproductive success. Darwinian theory, indeed, hardly makes sense unless we see living things – that to which it is applied – as things that have these basic purposes. We require there to be entities that pursue the goals of survival and reproductive success for the two basic Darwinian mechanisms to have any purchase or application at all. Without purposive entities, in short, Darwinian theory is devoid of application. To interpret the theory in an anti-purpose way is to render the theory incoherent.

Darwinism is to be interpreted as a theory about the evolution of living things living out their lives, pursuing goals, in diverse environments. Furthermore, and most importantly, the activity of living things in pursuing their goals has an impact on the way evolution proceeds. Purposive action becomes a vital part of the Darwinian mechanisms of evolution. And as purposive action becomes increasingly elaborate, involving enhanced mobility, perception, memory, learning, parental care, awareness, and communication, so the role that purposive action has in the mechanisms of evolution becomes increasingly pronounced. A key feature of the purposive version of Darwinism is, in short, that as evolution proceeds, *the mechanisms responsible for evolution themselves evolve.* These mechanisms are not static, as the anti-purpose version of Darwinism would have it. They evolve, as purposive action comes to play an increasingly important role.[5]

In 2014, fifteen evolutionary biologists published an article in two parts in *Nature* entitled "Does Evolutionary Theory Need a Rethink?," seven of the authors in favour, eight against.[6] Those in favour of a rethink criticized the "gene-centred," orthodox view, and defended what they called the "extended evolutionary synthesis (EES)," a view which incorporates crucial elements of what I am calling here the "purposive" view, even though purpose is not mentioned. They summed up their version of Darwinism like this: the "'gene-centric' focus fails to capture the full gamut of processes that direct evolution. Missing pieces include how physical development influences the generation of variation (developmental bias); how the environment directly shapes organisms' traits (plasticity); how organisms modify environments (niche construction); and how organisms transmit more than genes across generations (extra-genetic inheritance). For [the orthodox, gene-centric view] these phenomena are just outcomes of evolution. For the EES, they are also causes."[7] The EES view, here summarized, refers to many of the aspects and consequences of purposive action and, crucially, emphasizes that these have a causal role in evolution, but purposive action itself is not mentioned. Those against the proposed rethink argue that orthodox Darwinism can accommodate the phenomena the critics refer to.

What is striking about this clash of views about how Darwinian theory is to be interpreted is that even those who argue for the EES view, for the rethink, cannot quite bring themselves to mention the key unifying idea of the interpretation they espouse, namely, that purposive action of living things plays a crucial role in the mechanisms of evolution, a role of evolving significance as evolution proceeds. The "gamut of processes that direct evolution" that the EES view refers to are all associated with, or products of, purposive action, and yet purposive action itself, the key idea missing from the orthodox view, is not mentioned. So powerful are the pressures in biology not to acknowledge purpose in nature that even those who oppose the orthodox gene-centred version of Darwinian theory submit to these pressures, and do not mention the key idea that the theory is about how purposiveness evolves in the natural world, purposive action itself playing an increasingly important role in the Darwinian mechanisms that help explain how and why this evolution has come about.

It is important to appreciate that purposive action has two roles in the purposive version of Darwinian theory. First, Darwinism is to be interpreted as being fundamentally about the evolution of *life being lived* as one might say, living things actively pursuing their life goals; it is not primarily about genes or bodily structure. Second, Darwinian theory is to be interpreted in such a way that justice is done to the role that purposive action plays in the Darwinian mechanisms responsible for evolution – the increasingly important role that purposive action plays, as evolution proceeds. Let us now consider illustrations of these crucial points.

The two key mechanisms of Darwinian evolution are, as I have already indicated, (1) random inheritable variations, and (2) preferential selection of those best fitted to survive and reproduce. Purposive action of living things comes to play a role in evolution via mechanism (2). The activity of living things and, in particular, changes in the activity of living things, can have a major impact on selection – on what characteristics have survival value, and what do not – and thus on the way subsequent evolution proceeds.

A striking example of purposive action affecting evolution, very widely distributed among living things, is provided by the predator/prey relationship.

Foxes hunt rabbits; and rabbits flee and hide from foxes. Foxes tend to catch and kill those rabbits less good at escaping from their attention. If, by chance, a mutation occurs that renders the rabbit that has it better at escaping from the fox, the tendency will be for that rabbit to survive and reproduce, offspring who inherit the mutation being better at escaping foxes too. An evolutionary step will have occurred that renders rabbits better at escaping foxes as a result of two factors: (1) a mutation, a random variation; and (2) the purposive actions of foxes hunting rabbits. Both (1) and (2) are vital in bringing about the evolutionary change in rabbits. It would not have occurred without (1); but nor would it have occurred without (2). In the absence of (2), the mutation would provide no extra survival value, and so would not spread throughout the population of rabbits.

Foxes, in hunting rabbits, unconsciously breed rabbits better and better at escaping from them. But equally, rabbits, in escaping from foxes, unconsciously breed foxes to be better and better at catching and killing rabbits. If, by chance, a mutation occurs in a fox that renders it better at catching rabbits, that fox will tend to survive and reproduce, offspring who inherit the mutation being better at catching rabbits. Foxes who lack the mutation will not be so good at catching rabbits, will go hungry, and will not be so good at surviving and reproducing. As a result, an evolutionary change will have occurred in the fox population as a result of two factors: (1) a random mutation; and (2) the purposive activity of rabbits in escaping from foxes. As before, both are vital. If rabbits made no effort to escape foxes, or were hopeless at it, possessing a gene that made the fox good at catching rabbits would incur no survival value.

This way in which purposive action plays a role in evolution, by means of the predator/prey relationship, is very widely distributed throughout the living world. Relatively few animals have no predator. Almost certainly, purposive action played a vital role in evolution by means of the predator/prey relationship in the early stages of life on earth, for the two billion years or so of single-cell organisms, before multi-cell organisms came into existence. Single-cell life forms eat, or engulf and digest, other single-cell life forms. Some will be better at engulfing; others better at escaping.

In his wonderful book *The Living Stream*, an early defence of the purposive version of Darwinism, Alister Hardy gives the example of the evolution of camouflage. Caterpillars that do not have good camouflage are eaten by birds. Caterpillars with mutations that provide better camouflage will tend to survive and reproduce. The perceptiveness of birds breeds caterpillars with better camouflage. But equally, the better camouflage will tend (if appropriate mutations happen to occur) to breed birds more perceptive, able to see and eat the caterpillar despite its better camouflage. It is the purposive, perceptive activity of birds that is, in part, responsible for the evolution of good camouflage.

Those who uphold what I have called the anti-purpose version of Darwinism recognize, of course, the importance of the evolutionary processes I have illustrated by means of the fox and the rabbit, the caterpillar and the bird. What is not emphasized, however, is that these evolutionary processes exemplify *purposive action playing a crucial role in evolution*. It is this orthodox failure of emphasis that so distorts and impoverishes Darwinian theory.

In addition to the misunderstandings concerning "purpose" that I have indicated above, there is another reason why orthodox evolutionists fail to stress the role that purpose plays in Darwinian evolution. It is fear of Lamarckism.[8] Lamarck held that acquired characteristics are inherited. From the standpoint of Darwinism, this is heresy – although in a moment we shall see that a version of Lamarckism is actually a component of orthodox Darwinism, properly understood.

Consider the giraffe with its long neck. Lamarckism holds that it got its long neck as a result of ancestors stretching to eat leaves high up in trees; these ancestors acquired longer necks as a result, which were inherited by offspring. Anti-purposive Darwinism denies this vehemently: the long neck came about as a result of random mutations, which were not caused in any way by the actions of giraffe ancestors.

Both are wrong. Lamarckism is wrong in holding actions of ancestors *caused* the long necks to develop; anti-purpose Darwinism is wrong in holding the actions of ancestors played no role. In order for the giraffe to develop its long neck, it is essential that ancestors did indeed strive to eat leaves high up in trees (and leaves nourishing to eat were available there), since otherwise chance mutations which produced longer necks would have had no survival value, and would not have spread through the population of proto-giraffes. (Long necks have all sorts of disadvantages, so definitely would not have evolved if they did not have considerable survival value given the current way of life.[9]) Acknowledging that proto-giraffes' striving to eat leaves high up in trees played a crucial role in the evolution of the giraffe's long neck does not imply Lamarckism at all, because it does not amount to holding that this activity is the sole *cause* of the long neck.

There is another reason why orthodox biologists have failed to stress the role of purposive action in evolution. Acknowledging that it does play an important role may seem to undermine the explanatory power of Darwinian theory. If Darwinian theory is to explain how ostensibly purposive living things have come to exist in a purposeless universe, the theory cannot itself, it would seem, appeal to purposive action, for that would be to presuppose the very thing that is to be explained. It would render the theory circular and nonexplanatory.

There is a straightforward solution to this problem. The purposive version of Darwinism includes the following basic principle:

Principle of Noncircularity: The theory must not presuppose what it seeks to explain. If, at some stage in evolution, Darwinian theory itself employs purposive explanations, the theory must explain how purposiveness of this type has come into existence at this stage of evolution *without using the very type of purposive action that is being explained.*

As long as this principle is observed, Darwinian explanations that employ purposive explanations can avoid being trivially circular – presupposing the very thing to be explained.[10] Darwinian accounts of evolution may employ purposive explanations, at certain stages of evolution, but if so, Darwinian theory must explain how things that exemplify these notions of the purposive have come into existence *in a way which makes no appeal to these explanatory notions.* Thus, if an appeal is made to empathy in order to explain some evolutionary development, an explanation for the prior evolution of empathy must be given *which does not itself employ empathy as an explanatory notion.* Or, if parental care is employed to explain some evolutionary development, the existence of parental care must itself be explained without this explanation itself invoking parental care.

There is yet another possible misunderstanding that may prompt some biologists to incline toward the anti-purpose view. It may be thought that the claim that purposive activity of animals plays an important role in the path that evolution takes amounts to the claim that evolution itself is purposive in character, or takes a path that corresponds to the purposes of animals. Not at all. When the purposive actions of an animal have an effect on the course of evolution, the purpose of the animal is not at all to produce the evolutionary outcome it does produce. The fox breeds rabbits better at escaping, but the purpose of the fox is quite different: it is to catch and eat the rabbit. Evolution evolves to *incorporate* purposiveness in the mechanisms of evolution, but that does not mean that evolution itself becomes purposive. It does become purposive, however, when people successfully breed animals, birds, and plants with specific purposes in mind. We see here a particular manifestation of the general point that *the mechanisms responsible for evolution themselves evolve as evolution proceeds.*

What other ways are there in which the purposive actions of creatures can influence subsequent evolution? The giraffe case, just indicated, illustrates another general way in which this can occur. Merely to pursue certain sorts of food – and in particular, to change the food one pursues – can have consequences for the way one's own species evolves, quite apart from any impact on any other species. A creature needs a variety of characteristics and skills to detect, capture, kill, and eat food. Mutations that enhance these characteristics will tend to spread through the population. But what these characteristics and skills are may well depend on what kind of food is sought. A change in the kind of food sought may change the skills or bodily characteristics required, and so change what kind of mutations will have survival value (and so spread throughout the population). Decisions creatures make about what to eat may have dramatic consequences for subsequent evolution!

Darwin, famously, discovered that some fifteen different species of finch on the Galápagos Islands have beaks that differ in size and shape, related to the different food sources birds of each species habitually seek.[11] It is not reasonable to suppose that the mutations determining beak size and shape came first, and the bird then looked around for a suitable source of food to use it on. It is much more reasonable to suppose that different flocks of finch already pursued different food sources and, given each specific choice, quite specific changes to beak size and shape would have survival value, so that only those (random) mutations that led to those specific changes in the beak would spread throughout that population of finch (only that specific kind of change having survival value). The purposive actions of finches to seek certain food sources came first; the beak changes (the result of random mutations) came second. Purposive action led the way to subsequent evolutionary change.

It is reasonable to suppose that, throughout the animal world, whenever a species is especially equipped to obtain the food it lives on, the purposive activity of seeking that source of food came first, and mutations that led the species to be well adapted to obtain that food came second. And indeed, more generally, whenever we find a species of animal well adapted to the way of life it leads, in all its diverse range of purposive actions in the given environment, it is reasonable to suppose that the purposive actions came first and the (random) mutations, having survival value relative to that way of life, came second. Change the way of life in any particular way, and what has survival value changes, so that what random mutations will spread throughout the population will change as well.

Consider the following, highly simplified account of how a dog-like creature may evolve into an otter. The dog runs about on land, catching land creatures to eat. One day puppies are born that, because of a mutation, have flippers instead of legs. Disaster! The puppies die. But now suppose at some earlier time, a dog discovered, perhaps by accident, that fish in a river are good to eat. Others imitate, and the local group takes to catching fish. Now, given this new food source and way of life, the puppies with flippers are born.[12] Success! They survive and reproduce because they are especially good at catching fish. The dog evolves into an otter. And the prior change in activity, from pursuing food on land to pursuing fish in a river – a change which might not have any genetic change associated with it – plays a crucial role in the subsequent evolution: dog to otter. Without the prior change in purposive activity, the subsequent evolutionary development, dog to otter, would not have occurred.

It is possible that a particular, ancient, purposive act of "eating" may have had momentous consequences for subsequent evolution. All creatures that have evolved from eukaryotic cells – fish, insects, reptiles, birds, and mammals – are made up of cells that contain mitochondria. Mitochondria are units in the cell, with their own DNA, that produce energy for the cell. Without mitochondria, fish, mammals, etc., would not be possible. But, thanks to the work of Lynn Margulis,[13] we now know that mitochondria exist because two or three billion years ago, a primitive cell engulfed, or ate, another, and the engulfed cell survived and became simplified over time to form the mitochondria of today. All the creatures of land, air, and sea owe their existence to a primitive purposive act of eating.[14]

What other kinds of purposive action are there that have had an impact on evolution? Karl Popper in lectures gave the example of actions that lead to particular environmental conditions in which to live. He suggests that fish acquired lungs and legs, and began to live on land, only because ancestors took to living in shallow sea near the shore. For fish living in that environment, at risk of being stranded on land by the tide, chance mutations that increased the capacity to live out of water would have had survival value – mutations that would have had no survival value whatsoever for fish living in deep sea far from the land. Animals of all kinds are constantly moving into new territory, new environmental conditions with new challenges, dangers, and potential rewards: this way in which purposive action can influence subsequent evolution is clearly very widespread throughout the animal kingdom.

Not only do animals move into new environments; they also, on occasion, themselves change the environment in which they live by creating dams, nests, burrows, webs, and tools. Beavers, birds, badgers, spiders, and chimpanzees, as a result of living with, or in, what they create, change what does, and what does not, have survival value. Specific characteristics and skills are needed to create the artifact in question, maintain it, and survive and reproduce when living in association with it. Mutations that enhance these characteristics and skills will have survival value, and will thus tend to spread through the population, but only if the creature in question is creating and living with the artifact in question – dam, nest, or whatever it may be.[15]

Sexual selection and offspring selection are further examples of ways in which purposive action influences evolution. Peahens prefer to mate with peacocks that have the most elaborate display of tail feathers: thus genes that produce splendid tail feathers are selected for, and tend to spread throughout the population. Peacocks with poor tail display are not chosen, and so leave no offspring. Again, parents decide to favour certain offspring over others, when feeding, in response to certain characteristics or signals; those are selected for, as a result, and go on to produce offspring in turn, the mutations that exaggerate the characteristics or signals in question spreading through the population as a result.

What about plants? Is their evolution influenced by purposive action? Yes! This is perfectly clear in the case of flowers and fruit. If it were not for the purposive actions of mammals, birds, and insects in pollinating proto flowers, eating proto fruit, and thus spreading pollen and seeds, flowers and fruit, as we know them today would not have evolved. Purposive actions are essential for the evolution of flowers and fruit. Furthermore, plants that are eaten by animals evolve means to protect themselves from being eaten. Thistles and other plants develop sharp spikes to discourage foraging. Bracken develops a range of poisonous chemicals to discourage being devoured. Nettles sting. Such evolutionary developments, widespread throughout the plant world, have occurred only because of the purposive actions of insects, caterpillars, mammals, and birds.

Do plants influence evolution as a result of the only kind of purposive action that plants in the main engage in, namely, growth? There is one evolutionary development that can definitely be associated with the capacity for growth of other plants. In a jungle, where sunlight is in short supply, if a break in the canopy develops, as a result of the fall of a tree perhaps, young plants in the patch of sunlight thus created tend to grow quickly, to get ahead of the competition. This capacity for rapid early growth has arisen because of the capacity for rapid growth of other plant species. Here, the purposive actions of plants – growth – have had an impact on the evolution of plants.

This capacity of the activity of living things to affect evolution can perhaps be divided into two categories: those that affect the evolution of descendants (one's own species, in other words); and those that affect the evolution of other species. This distinction becomes somewhat blurred, however, because changes in the way members of another species act with which the first species interacts is likely to lead to evolutionary changes in the first species as well. Foxes may breed rabbits to be better at escaping from them; this is likely, in turn, to have an impact on the subsequent evolution of the fox.

Almost everything a creature does is likely to have an influence on what has survival value, what does not, and thus an influence on the subsequent evolution of descendants – and of other species interacting with descendants. In particular, any *change* in the way of life is likely to have such an influence. A change of environment, whether because of migration, climate change, or change in the presence or behaviour of other species; a change in the kind of food that is sought; a change in measures taken to evade danger; a change in mating, rearing of young, interactions between members of the same species, or interactions with other species: all such changes in the way of life, and indeed any change in the way of life, is likely to influence what subsequently does, and does not, have survival value, and thus influence the evolution of descendants. The proper conclusion to draw, it would seem, is that purposive action of creatures has a ubiquitous influence over subsequent evolution (along with the occurrence of random mutations, of course).

Some changes in the way of life are brought about by mutations in genes that influence behaviour; other changes in the way of life occur without any genetic change at all. But, whatever the cause of the change in the way of life, insofar as it has an impact on subsequent evolution, it is a case of purposive action influencing evolution.

We need a new slogan for Darwinian evolution. Alongside "nature, red in tooth and claw" or "random inheritable variations and natural selection," we should perhaps put the slogan "life breeds itself into existence." Living things, in their interactions with both members of other species and members of their own, unconsciously *breed* their fellow creatures, often breeding other species against the interests of their own, as in the predator/prey relationship.

As I have already remarked, as purposive activity of living things becomes increasingly diverse, complex, and sophisticated in character, so the impact that purposive action can have on evolution becomes increasingly pronounced and sophisticated. Purposive action comes to play an increasingly important role in how evolution proceeds. Sexual selection and offspring selection did not play much of a role for the first two billion years of life on earth when single-cell creatures alone existed. Sex, and care for young, had not been invented. These forms of selection are only possible once sex and care for young have evolved. A key feature of the purposive version of Darwinism, which is absent in the anti-purpose version, is that *the mechanisms of Darwinian evolution themselves evolve as evolution proceeds.*

This becomes especially apparent when evolution by cultural means arrives on the scene. This evolutionary development requires that the capacities to learn, and to imitate, have already evolved. It then becomes possible for an individual creature to learn something new – a new source of food, a new place to sleep, a new way to intimidate fellow creatures, perhaps. Others imitate the discovery, and a new way of life has evolved *without any genetic changes having taken place whatsoever.* This constitutes a new way in which ways of life can evolve – by "cultural means" as we may call it. Such evolution by cultural means may well, of course, usher in subsequent evolutionary developments that do involve genetic changes, as in the simplified case, given above, of the dog-like creature becoming an otter as a result of discovering how to catch and eat fish. But evolution by cultural means as such does not involve genetic evolution. It involves the evolution of new purposive activity, this activity possibly leading to the creation of new artifacts: tools, weapons, items of communication. In one sense, evolution by cultural means is highly Lamarckian in character, in that it involves the inheritance of acquired characteristics; but in another sense, it is non-Lamarckian, in that it does not involve offspring acquiring new bodily characteristics merely as a result of being born to parents who have acquired these characteristics themselves as a result of the activities they engaged in, in their lives (which is what Lamarck had in mind). The reproduction of aspects of a way of life by means of imitation does not compete with, or replace, reproduction by means of sex and birth; it presupposes and supplements these "gene-based" methods of reproduction, as one may call them.

In order to construe evolution by cultural means as the development of a new *method of reproduction,* it is essential that Darwinism is interpreted along purposive lines, as a theory about the evolution of *life,* the evolution of *individuals engaged in living, engaged in purposive activity* (of one kind or another). For evolution by cultural means involves not new genes or new bodily characteristics but merely *new purposive activity, new actions, new ways of life.* If the Dawkins, anti-purpose version of Darwinism is adopted, and if, in particular, the theory is interpreted to be about the evolution of genes, of DNA, then evolution by cultural means does not involve an evolutionary step at all because nothing new genetically is involved. Evolution by cultural means is rendered almost invisible.

Those who adopt anti-purpose versions of Darwinism do, however, recognize evolution by cultural means – except that it is interpreted quite differently from the above, and is referred to differently, as simply "cultural evolution." Cultural evolution is interpreted to involve not a new method for reproducing and modifying ways of living, but rather the evolution of a new kind of entity: the unit of culture. Dawkins has even invented a term for it, which has gained widespread currency: the *meme.* Songs (whether of birds or humans), jokes, sayings, the content of books, plays, slogans, theories are all memes.

For Richard Dawkins, cultural evolution involves the evolution of *a new kind of entity,* the meme.[16] A meme reproduces itself by entering the brains of human beings (or other animals) and inducing them to recreate the meme in question, much as a virus enters the nucleus of cells and induces them to replicate the virus in question. Those memes that happen to be good at this method of reproduction will be the ones that will tend to reproduce and multiply.

The meme account of cultural evolution gains much of its appeal from the analogy with the gene-based version of Darwinian theory. Both involve entities – memes or genes – which replicate themselves by getting their hosts to act so as to promote the reproduction of the entity in question – the meme or gene. We have seen, however, that the gene-based version of Darwinism is a dreadful distortion of the theory, embodying a profound misunderstanding of its nature. Darwinian theory is a theory of the evolution of purposive life, not purposeless DNA. This purposive version of Darwinian theory cannot be applied to memes because memes are not purposive things.[17]

Meme evolution is at best an amusing diversion, not a serious contribution to Darwinian theory. But, whatever one thinks of it, there can be no doubt that the perspective of what I have been calling *evolution by cultural means* is the proper, fundamental one to adopt, with far greater scope and explanatory power than the meme view. A group of animals may come to hunt and eat a specific kind of prey as a result of evolution by cultural means (learning and imitation), but there is, here, no obvious *meme*. Chimpanzees strip twigs of leaves and branches and use what results as a tool to catch and eat termites; this is known to be a product of evolution by cultural means. Again, there is no *meme*. What matters is not the twig as such, but the twig used as a tool – the twig as an integral part of purposive action.

This last point is crucial. Memes only mean anything when integrated into the purposive action of which they form a part. Dissociated from the life that creates and uses them, memes are just meaningless objects or processes. In order to be made sense of, memes need to be put into the context of, and interpreted in terms of, the purposive life that creates and uses them.[18]

Evolution by cultural means has been found to be widespread throughout the animal world. In order to occur, all that needs to have evolved is the capacity to learn, to remember, and to imitate. The first two go far back into evolutionary history, and there is reason to suppose that the capacity to imitate does as well. I have suggested that having this capacity has survival value when there is parental care. The mere fact that your parents exist and have produced you means that they are good at surviving and reproducing, so imitating what they do is quite likely to have survival value. Dinosaurs engaged in parental care, so may have experienced evolution by cultural means over 65 million years ago.

It is, however, when we come to humanity, that evolution by cultural means becomes of profound significance. What marks us out from all other species is the massive extent to which we are the products of evolution by cultural means. Almost certainly, our capacity for language evolved as a consequence of evolution by cultural means. Before we had much of a capacity for language, we began to communicate by means of sounds in a very primitive way, with a very limited vocabulary. Given that way of life, it is not hard to see how and why chance mutations that increase the capacity for language would rapidly spread throughout the population. Those who possess such mutated genes, as a result of having a greater facility for language, would be in a position to have more offspring – either because they are better at attracting mates or because they become powerful in the group and have more mates as a result. What the experts call *co-evolution* takes place.[19] Learning to use language creates the conditions for genes that increase facility with language to spread throughout the population, which in turn makes possible further learning to use language, which in turn increases the conditions for genes for facility with language, when they arise, to become more widespread, and so on.

Sophisticated human language is the foundation of our humanity. It is the bedrock of human history. It makes possible and facilitates the development of everything else about our human world that so strikingly differentiates us from all other species: tools, dwellings, clothes, use of fire and cooking, song and dance, religious belief – and later, cities, ships, democracy, law, books, and all the elaborate technology, science, culture, and traditions of the modern world. What early humans did and made is not so very different from what chimpanzees today do and make, and for thousands of years, human culture and technology evolved only very slowly. The Babylonians, however, differ in their way of life profoundly from chimpanzees, and we, in turn, differ profoundly from the Babylonians. The pace of historical change has accelerated, especially after the scientific revolution in the seventeenth century and the invention of the idea of social progress in the eighteenth century.

The great triumph of the purposive version of Darwinism is that it reveals how human beings and human history emerge seamlessly from earlier mammalian evolution. Much that seems, at first glance, distinctive of early humans turns out to be not so very different from what can be found in the mammalian world, and the evolutionary – or co-evolutionary – processes behind early human development and history are all to be found in the pre-human world.

However, if Darwinian theory is to account for human history, it must provide some kind of account of the evolution of sentience, consciousness, free will, and life of value. Here, I will be brief, and urge the reader to consult my earlier and more detailed discussions of these issues.[20]

The purposive version of Darwinism cannot explain the evolution of sentience and consciousness for reasons spelled out in chapter 3.[21] It can, however, give an account of what it is that needs to evolve if, we may conjecture, sentience and consciousness are to emerge.

My proposal is that sentience emerges as a result of a change in the way brains control purposive action. There is a wasp that flies around looking for a place to bury its egg; when it finds a feasible hole in the ground, it places the egg on the ground and inspects the hole. If it is found to be satisfactory, the wasp returns to the egg, and buries it in the hole. It looks as if the wasp knows what it is doing. However, if, when the wasp is in the hole, the egg is moved a few centimetres away from the hole, the wasp will return to it, put it back to a pre-determined distance from the hole, and reinspect the hole. And it will repeat this many times. The wasp's brain employs what may be called *sequential control*. Each small step in the overall action of burying the egg is controlled separately; each step has to be completed properly before control of the next step is triggered.

This is, I conjecture, very different from the way a lioness is induced to hunt. Brain processes occur in the lioness's brain that prompt the lioness to act in such a way as to put a stop to these processes. This can only be done by finding something to eat. The lioness is prompted to hunt, the brain processes that prompt this activity being experienced by the lioness as hunger. We have here a very different way in which the brain controls or guides purposive action. The final goal – to find and eat prey – is actively represented in the brain by the brain processes experienced as hunger; the lioness must work out what to do in order to realize the goal. I have called this *motivational control* to contrast it with sequential control.

Motivational control can, of course, be described in purely purposive, control terms, without any mention of hunger, or any item of sentience. My conjecture is that it is the evolution of motivational control that constitutes the evolution of sentience.[22] Mental life begins with *feeling* and *desire*. We need to accept Tolstoy's amendment of Descartes: "I desire, therefore I am."

Motivational control has, in some respects at least, enhanced survival value over sequential control because of its far greater flexibility, the room it leaves for learning. Lionesses learn how to hunt, and as a result acquire skills in hunting, and new skills if required, that could never be produced by brains that implement the rigid routines of sequential control.

Once sentience has come into existence, it is not hard to see how and why consciousness emerges subsequently. For sentience to become consciousness, we require an elaboration of the capacity to imagine. The act of imagining can be depicted, in control and purposive terms, as follows: an animal or person, imagining he is climbing a tree, arranges for brain processes to occur in his brain which are similar, in relevant respects, to the processes that would occur were he actually to be climbing a tree.[23]

It is not hard to see how and why the capacity to imagine has survival value. A lioness able to imagine can, while stalking a prey, imagine a number of strategies to employ and, as a result, choose the one that seems, in imagination, to work best. Performing actions in imagination can be much less costly than performing them in reality. Performing a course of action in imagination which leads to one's death is much to be preferred to performing it in reality.

Dreaming involves imagining, and we know animals dream. The question of why we dream has long posed a problem to biologists. It is possible that we dream in order to develop the capacity to imagine, and thus have an inner life.

All our inner conscious activity – our thinking, our pondering and wondering, our deliberating, our talking to ourselves, our daydreaming, our entire universe of inner conscious life – is compounded of imagination. Without the capacity to imagine, we might be sentient but we would not be conscious.

The capacity to imagine may have survival value, not just because it aids problem solving, but also because it is required for personalistic understanding of others.[24] In order for me to acquire personalistic understanding of you, I must be able to imagine that I am you – that I have your character; your hopes and fears; your desires and plans; your relatives, friends, and enemies; your context for your life. And I need to be able to imagine what you imagine – what you think, plan, intend to do. As the imaginative life – the conscious life – of my peers becomes enriched, I need to develop a corresponding capacity for enriched imagination too if I am to continue to have a good personalistic understanding of my peers. One can see, in this way, how social life that incorporates elements of mutual personalistic understanding will tend to provoke the development of the capacity to understand others personalistically, and thus the development of the capacity to imagine. Personalistic understanding may even provoke self-consciousness. A child acquires some personalistic understanding of a parent; this prompts the child to become aware of the parent's awareness of herself, and thus awareness of the distinction of "self as viewed by my parent" and "self as I experience myself." As a result of seeing ourselves as others see us, we become aware of what others do not see: our own inner conscious experiences – our inner feelings, desires, thoughts. Personalistic understanding of others may, in other words, provoke a certain kind of personalistic understanding of ourselves – self-awareness, self-consciousness.

Personalistic understanding, and thus imagination and consciousness, is clearly much enhanced by the development and enrichment of communication and language. It is important to appreciate the multilayered character of human communication, and therefore the step-by-step stages in which human communication can be built up from primitive animal communication. Let us suppose A communicates to B. The following stages can be distinguished.

(i)   A acts in its own interests, for example, goes rapidly into flight to avoid a predator; B takes this behaviour as an indication of something (in this case danger) for him, and acts accordingly.

(ii) In addition, A does something whose sole purpose is to communicate to B, even though A has no such conscious intention. Here A might squawk as it goes into flight in a manner characteristic for that species in such circumstances; B reacts accordingly.

(iii) In addition, A has the purpose of signalling to B since, if A knows that it is on its own, it will not signal (e.g., squawk).

(iv) In addition, A has the purpose of communicating the message of the action to B, so that, in the case of the squawk, the bird squawks in order to warn B. If B is present but in no danger, then the bird does not squawk.

(v)   B understands the message, the meaning of the squawk.

(vi) A has the purpose of B understanding the meaning of the message.

(vi) B understands this too.

(vii) A intends B to understand this.

And so on (the multilayers of mutual understanding, initially profoundly significant becoming, as one goes on further, increasingly insignificant).

As Paul Grice has shown,[25] human communication involves, quite essentially, multilayers of mutually understood intentions. If I am to communicate with you by means of language, I must intend this, you must understand that I intend it, and I must understand that you understand. The progressive development of human communication through these stages from its beginnings in primitive animal communication *is* the progressive development of personalistic understanding and self-consciousness. In this sense, the progressive development of communication, first without and then with language, *is* the progressive development of self-consciousness. This progressive enrichment of communication is, at the same time, the progressive enrichment of meaning and knowledge. There is meaning and knowledge even at stage (i), but it is meaning and knowledge of a very meagre kind; once stage (vii) is reached, and assuming that "A intends B to understand that A has the purpose of B understanding the meaning of the message" is all to be understood personalistically, A and B both being sentient and conscious, then something close to full human meaning and knowledge has been attained.[26]

One dramatic consequence of the capacity to imagine (enhanced by communication and language) is that the arena in which one acts can become massively enlarged in both space and time. The merely sentient animal acts in an arena that is, from its own point of view, confined to the here and now. (Squirrels may bury nuts, but do they contemplate the advent of winter in several months' time as they do so?) The animal or person who is *conscious*, who can *imagine*, can be aware of not just the here and now but also far off places and far off times, both in the past and the future. Consciousness creates awareness of history and the future. One can imagine other places, other times, in a way merely sentient animals cannot.

This enlargement of the arena of action in space and time has two dramatic consequences.

First, it makes possible the discovery of the inevitability of death. The merely sentient animal, tied to the here and now, is not in a position to appreciate that a time will come when it no longer exists – except perhaps when it is about to die. But a conscious being, able to explore distant places and times in imagination, can indeed come to appreciate the inevitability of death. Given that evolution is all about survival, the discovery that personal survival is doomed to failure, sooner or later, is likely to be traumatic indeed. And most cultures and societies have worked hard at attempting to deny the inevitability, or reality, of death. Death is construed to be a journey to another place, and many cultures have elaborate rituals and burial rites designed to help people on their way to that other place. It is not an illusion that the modern world has managed entirely to escape from.

The second dramatic consequence has to do with a disruption in the manner in which the way of life is controlled.

In connection with animals that are merely sentient, we can distinguish two control systems. There is the sentient brain that controls immediate actions. And there is what may be called "the master control system,"[27] which controls the way of life. The master control system, by means of hormones and other methods, prompts the sentient brain to pursue diverse goals in diverse contexts by inducing the sentient brain to have various drives or desires. Thus the animal may hunt for nuts and bury them; it may hunt for food to eat; it may seek a mate; it may engage in the task of building a nest, a dam, or a den; or it may feed and care for offspring. These tasks are initiated by the unconscious master control system; it is this master control system that commands the sentient brain to do its bidding by means of the activation of desires or drives: the desire for food, to care for offspring, etc. The sentient brain is the innocent slave of the master control system, utterly enslaved to it without any glimmerings of awareness that this is the case.

Creatures evolve and acquire the capacity to imagine and be conscious – actively conscious in particular of future times. It now becomes possible for the conscious brain (evolved from the sentient brain) to contemplate reaching decisions about how life will be lived, not just from moment to moment but far into the future. But the master control system is still in place, actively engaged in commanding the conscious brain to do its bidding. The outcome is an inevitable, massive conflict between the two control systems. The conscious brain will find itself often at loggerheads with the master control system.

Just such a dramatic conflict is indeed a widespread feature of human nature. The conflict becomes especially pronounced whenever the conscious brain – the official culture – decides upon a way of life that has features that clash in a marked way with the way of life the master control system would tend to determine. Thus Christians, brought up to do the will of God and deny the promptings of the flesh, find themselves inevitably prone to especially severe conditions of conflict. Temptations of the devil, of the flesh, will be an ever-occurrent feature of life. But the conflict is not confined to

Christians; we all inevitably become victims of some version of this conflict as long as we do not simply allow the master control system to take over and determine the pattern of our activities for us. We are confronted by the promptings of the master control systems whenever we have feelings and desires we do not want to have – whenever we have a desire we do not desire.

This conflict between master and conscious control systems probably first came to the fore when people abandoned the hunting and gathering way of life – the way of life in which human beings emerged – and instead took to an agricultural existence.[28] This requires the conscious brain to plan long-term activity over months before there is a reward: planting of seeds, weeding of crops, harvesting. The conscious brain plans the way of life, not the master control system. And the subsequent great historical transitions, into cities, into industrialization, into the modern interconnected world, have only further exacerbated the conflict.

I began this chapter by distinguishing two versions of Darwinian theory: the purposeless version, which interprets the theory as explaining purposiveness away, and the purposeful version, which seeks to explain how and why purposive life has evolved in a purposeless universe. We now see we need a *third* version of the theory, a *personalistic* version as it may be called, one that invokes and explains the evolution of *sentient* and *conscious* life. This personalistic version is identical to the purposive version as far as nonsentient life is concerned, but differs from the purposive version when it comes to *sentient*[29] and *conscious* life. In this case the personalistic version of the theory, employed correctly, attributes sentience and consciousness to living things, and appeals to explanations of their actions in terms of sentient and conscious experiences, feelings, desires, and decisions. ("Personalistic" must be understood to refer to animals as well as to persons.)

The purposive version of Darwinian theory applies to everything that the personalistic version applies to, but leaves out the sentient and conscious aspect of things. The purposive version can refer to and describe communication, thought, dreaming, decision making, deliberation, friendship, enmity, and love – but all interpreted in a thoroughly purposive way, shorn of all sentience and consciousness. The purely purposive interpretation of these terms is such that the terms can apply truthfully to robots that mimic human actions but are bereft of consciousness and sentience.

The purposive version of Darwinian theory can, then, mimic the personalistic version to the minutest detail, but it leaves out almost everything that matters: the experiences, the pains, joys, and sorrows, the conscious awareness of others and oneself, the meaning and value of life in all its rich diversity. Just as we must not abandon the purposive version of Darwinian theory and adopt the purposeless version in its stead, because the latter can mimic the former, so too we must not abandon the personalistic version, and accept exclusively the purposive version, because this latter can mimic the former. We need both purposive and personalistic versions to do justice to all that is inherent in life, whether human or nonhuman.

I have two final comments to make in this chapter, first about *life of value*, and second about *free will*.

The task of this chapter is to explain how Darwinian theory can explain how and why *life of value* has come to be. But what, it may be asked, is life of value?

One possible answer is that sentience is a minimal requirement for life of value. But that may seem too minimalist to be acceptable. Adolf Hitler was sentient – indeed, conscious – but he may well seem to have been altogether too monstrous a person to embody life of value. Perhaps it would be better to specify what is of supreme value in existence, potentially and actually, and characterize everything else as being of value to the extent that it participates in what is of supreme value.

In the next chapter I put forward the conjecture that life of (supreme) value is life lived lovingly – life lived in such a way that that which is lovable is both enjoyed and cared for. Love between persons is supreme, but loving can be extended to *things* – to crafts, to art, to environments and things in the environment. In all sorts of contexts, love is inappropriate, but ingredients of love are not, such as friendship, concern for the welfare of others, justice, tolerance.

How does Darwinian theory, given its personalistic interpretation, help explain life of value when interpreted along such lines? A basic Darwinian aim of all living things is survival. Actively seeking survival is certainly caring for oneself, actively loving oneself, one might say. Christianity has bludgeoned us into thinking that self-love is bad, but it is not: it is the source of all that is good. Self-hatred, or self-abnegation, is not a good basis for loving others. The Jewish sage had it right when he asked,

If I am not for myself, who will be for me?
If I am for myself alone, what am I?
If not now, when?[30]

It is love of self to the exclusion of love for others that is bad (bad
for oneself as well as for others). The other basic Darwinian aim of
all of life is reproductive success. Living things act[31] so as to produce
offspring – in itself a kind of caring for others. Something closer to
loving others emerges when there is parental care, and parental care
goes far back into evolutionary history. Crocodiles care for their
young. Dinosaurs cared for their young. A considerable amount of
animal activity is devoted to caring for others.

Given that the two basic Darwinian aims of all living things –
survival and reproductive success – concern caring for self and for
others, the task of explaining how life of value has evolved cannot pose a problem of principle for the personalistic version of
Darwinian theory. Indeed, one might almost pose the problem the
other way round. Granted that Darwinian theory is all about living
things caring for self and others, how come that we human beings,
who have emerged from this Darwinian evolutionary process, seem
so bad at caring for ourselves and for others? Why is there so much
self-harm, suicide, brutality, murder, and war in the world?

The answer has to do with the fact that caring for self and offspring involves caring for oneself and one's own offspring, not for
others, not for the offspring of others. Furthermore, in the past (and
even today), the higher a male's rank is in his society, so the more
offspring he may be able to produce – a circumstance designed to
provoke competition between males eager to have many offspring.
And there are many other reasons why conflicts between males may
arise. The discovery of the inevitability of death may provoke some
to seek a kind of immortality in conquest, the creation of dynasties,
business empires, institutions, cults and religions, even works of art
and science. All these aspirations can lead to conflict.

In order to give a Darwinian account of the evolution of human
life of value we need to employ the personalistic version of
Darwinian theory. Such an account needs to appeal to evolution
by cultural means in order to do justice to the evolution of consciousness, language, society, culture, and history. Such a Darwinian
account merges seamlessly into anthropology and history. It enables
us to understand how life of value has come into existence in this

physicalistic universe. It tells of how our chimpanzee-like ancestors in Africa came down from the trees and lived, perhaps, beside the sea and estuaries, spending time in the water to catch fish.[32] It tells of the way our human ancestors spread out of Africa into Europe, Asia, Australia, America, new languages and cultures emerging as this diaspora occurred.

And it would provide an explanation for the apparent miracle of the existence of free will – some free will – in this physicalistic universe. Our brains may not meet the very demanding "Fundamental Requirement for Perfect Free Will" formulated in chapter 5. But insofar as our conscious brains do go quite some considerable way toward satisfying this requirement for perfect free will, it is because our brains have been designed by evolution to control our bodies in our given environment so to act that we are as good as can be at doing what needs to be done to survive and reproduce. It is the three-and-a-half to four billion years of evolution that has made it possible for brains and bodies to exist in this physicalistic universe capable of freely achieving goals to the extent that we human beings do have such a capacity.

Can Humanity Really Create a Good World?

∞ Global problems; the urgent need for a revolution in our institutions of inquiry; the Enlightenment; from knowledge-inquiry to wisdom-inquiry ∞

In this chapter I turn to that aspect of our fundamental problem that concerns the *flourishing* of life of value in the physical universe. I argue that in order to give ourselves the best chances of making social progress toward a good world, we need to learn from the astonishing success that science has achieved in making intellectual progress towards greater knowledge.

For thousands of years we lived in small, scattered hunting and gathering tribes, more or less as evolution had designed us to live. Then we discovered agriculture. We built cities. More recently, in the seventeenth century, we discovered how to do science. And modern science and technology made it possible for us to transform the human condition. Science and technology made possible the industrial revolution, modern industry and agriculture, the modern world. For most of us, there have been immense benefits. The whole quality of human life has been enhanced for almost all of us in countless ways.[1] Nevertheless, the dramatic changes in the conditions of human life that have taken place in the last 5,000 years or so, or more strikingly, during the last 200 years, have created two fundamental new problems.

First, our psyches, our instincts – that within us that sets the way we live – were designed by evolution for life in a small, hunting and gathering tribe, not for the modern world. Our instinctive human nature, designed by evolution for life in a hunting and gathering tribe of 150 people or so, is likely to encounter difficulties when confronted by the very different conditions of the modern world, composed of billions of strangers. Our instinctive capacities to solve problems of living we encountered in tribal life may become far less efficacious, even deranged, when it comes to the very different problems of living we encounter in the modern world. Unorganized cooperative action, entirely feasible for a tribe of 150 members,[2] becomes all but impossible for a modern nation, or for the whole world of 7.7 billion – and yet greater cooperative action is what we need if we are to solve many of the problems we face.

Second, the immense new powers to act that we have acquired as a result of modern science and technology have led, not just to great new benefits but also to serious new problems. We are confronted by grave global problems, byproducts of our successes. Here are some of the problems that we face.

There is the explosive rise in the world's population. Some estimate that there will be as many as 11 billion people by the end of the century. There is the destruction of natural habitats, the rapid loss of animals in the wild, and the devastating extinction of species. There is massive and, in some respects, growing inequality in wealth and power around the globe. The richest 1 percent own over 48 percent of the world's wealth, while the poorest half own less than 1 percent. There is the lethal character of modern war, and our abiding proclivity for war. Whereas around 12 million people died in wars in the nineteenth century, over 100 million died as a result of war in the twentieth century, and we are not doing too well in the twenty-first century so far. There is the grave danger of world disaster posed by nuclear weapons poised for use. There is the problem of pollution of earth, sea, and air. There is the problem of growing resistance of bacteria to drugs as a result of the misuse of antibiotics. We face the dreadful possibility that we may return to the state of affairs in the nineteenth century, when trivial infections would lead to death, and diseases such as tuberculosis had no effective treatment. There is the Internet, and the threat it poses to reliable journalism and democracy. And most serious of all, there are the looming disasters of global warming. By the end of the century, large areas of the earth's surface, at present supporting life and agriculture, may become uninhabitable as a result of climate change: drought and rising sea levels.

These threats to our future are all the more serious because they interact with and intensify one another. At a time when the world's population goes up, and more food is required to keep hunger at bay, the capacity of the world to produce food may well go down because of loss of land fit for agriculture due to climate change. Again, as the population increases, the area of the earth's surface capable of supporting human life goes down, due to adverse weather conditions and rising sea levels. Millions of people, in north Africa, parts of Asia, and elsewhere, living in areas that increasingly fail to support any kind of human life, will seek to move into neighbouring areas, also degraded and under threat, and so incapable of accommodating refugees. These are circumstances all too likely to provoke war. As global problems intensify, it becomes all the more important that the nations of the earth find ways to cooperate with one another to discover how best to resolve the crises. But as the crises intensify, conditions likely to provoke violent conflict proliferate, and cooperation becomes all the more difficult to achieve. It is possible that we now have only a very few decades to put in place measures capable of coming to grips with these grave problems. If we do not do what needs to be done, the world may descend into even greater anarchy and chaos than what we have at present.

If we are to resolve these immense global problems that confront us, we need to *learn* how to do it. And that in turn means that our institutions of learning – our universities and schools – need to be well designed and devoted to the task. What we require, in order to tackle in increasingly effective ways the global problems we face, is community learning, social, economic, institutional, and political learning. It is not enough that individuals learn what needs to be done. Communities need to learn. We need to learn how to tackle our problems in increasingly cooperatively rational ways. In a sense, the world's population needs to learn, although, because of massive inequalities in wealth and power, some of us carry a far heavier responsibility for the world's problems than others, and some of us are in a far better position to do something about these problems than others are. Only our institutions of learning – our universities and schools – can help promote the kind of community, social, institutional, cooperative learning that we require. Of course the media, NGOs, charities, pressure groups, can all help. But we need our universities and schools to galvanize the world's population into discovering how to come to grips, effectively, intelligently, and humanely, with the world's problems.

Are universities at present organized for and devoted to the task in hand? The answer to this question is deeply shocking. Far from being devoted to helping humanity learn how to tackle our grave global problems, universities are, if anything, in part *responsible* for the creation of these problems. They are not helping to make things better; on the contrary, they are, in part, responsible for making things worse.

What, we need to ask, is responsible for the genesis of our global problems? Ultimately it is the astonishing intellectual success of modern science and technology. This has, as I have already emphasized, led to much that is of immense benefit. Science and technology have made the modern world possible. But there is a downside. Modern medicine and hygiene have led to population growth. Modern technology has led to modern industry and agriculture, which, in turn, have led to destruction of natural habitats, extinction of species, pollution, and global warming. Scientific and technological advance has led to modern armaments, conventional, chemical, biological, and nuclear, and so to the lethal character of modern war.

If by the "cause" of an event we mean that prior change that led to the occurrence of the event, and without which the event would not have occurred then, without any doubt, it is the astonishing success of modern science and technology that is the cause of all the global problems indicated above. It is not that we have become more wicked, more stupid, or more selfish. Nor can capitalism be said to be the cause, as some would have it. The old Soviet Union, after all, was, if anything, even better at creating appalling environmental and other problems than capitalist countries. And capitalism without modern science and technology would have been relatively impotent. In the context of the history of humanity of the last one or two thousand years, what is new, what has dramatically changed, is the advent, and immense intellectual and technical success, of modern science and technology. This success has made possible modern industry, agriculture, transport, armaments, and medicine, which in turn have led to our current, menacing global problems.

And it is universities that have, by and large, created, nurtured, and promoted the science and technology that have, in turn, led to the crises we now face. Universities, instead of helping us learn how to resolve our global problems, are actually a major part of the *cause* of these problems.

What on earth has gone wrong? After all, a major part of the raison d'être of the university is to help enhance the quality of human life by intellectual, cultural, educational, technological, and practical means. But we have just discovered that the university has been behind the *genesis* of our most serious current global problems – so serious that the future of civilization may even be in doubt.

The problem is this. Universities as at present organized are, when judged from the vital standpoint of helping to promote human welfare, disastrously and damagingly irrational, in a wholesale, structural way, and it is this gross institutional/intellectual irrationality that is responsible for the havoc that universities have helped cause.

Even if our future looked entirely rosy, it would still be important to have institutions of learning rationally designed and devoted to helping us resolve our conflicts and problems of living – rationally devoted to helping us make progress toward as good a world as possible. It would still be important to keep alive critical scrutiny of our institutions of learning to try to ensure that they are performing this task as well as possible. As things are, confronted by a future that looks grim, it becomes all the more important that our institutions of learning are up for the task in hand. The scandal is that they are not. The even greater scandal is that there is hardly any serious discussion at all about this all-important question about how good our schools and universities are when judged from the standpoint of helping us make progress toward a better, wiser, more civilized world. And perhaps the greatest scandal of all is that a full diagnosis of what is wrong, and what needs to be done to put matters right, has been very prominently available in the literature for over forty years.[3] It has been ignored.

KNOWLEDGE-INQUIRY

From the past we have inherited the idea that the proper way for academic inquiry to help promote human welfare is, in the first instance, to acquire knowledge. First, knowledge is to be acquired; then, secondarily, it can be applied to help solve social problems. The *intellectual* aim of inquiry, of acquiring knowledge, is to be sharply distinguished from the *social* or *humanitarian* aim of promoting human welfare. In the first instance, academic inquiry seeks to solve problems of knowledge, not social problems of living. Values, politics, expressions of feelings and desires, political philosophies, and philosophies of life must all be excluded from the intellectual domain of inquiry to ensure that the pursuit of objective, factual knowledge does not degenerate into mere ideology or propaganda. In order to produce what is of real human value – genuine, objective, factual knowledge – inquiry must, paradoxically, exclude from the intellectual domain of inquiry all expressions of human problems, suffering, and values (although of course factual *knowledge* about these things can be developed).

At the centre of knowledge-inquiry there is an even more restrictive conception of *science*, namely *standard empiricism*, the doctrine expounded and refuted in chapter 4. According to standard empiricism, claims to scientific knowledge must be assessed impartially with respect to evidence, with respect to empirical success and failure. Metaphysical theses – theses that are neither empirically verifiable nor falsifiable – are to be excluded from science. (One form of this idea is Popper's famous demarcation criterion: a theory, in order to be scientific, must be *falsifiable*.)

I shall call this traditional conception (and kind) of inquiry *knowledge-inquiry*. By no means everything that goes on in the university today conforms to these edicts of knowledge-inquiry, and by no means all academics support knowledge-inquiry. Nevertheless, it exercises a massive influence over a multitude of aspects of academia: publications, research, funding, education, careers, promotions, interactions with the public. It is the only conception of rational academic inquiry at present generally understood.

Knowledge-inquiry is, however, profoundly and damagingly irrational. What is so damaging is that knowledge-inquiry is both massively influential and profoundly irrational in a wholesale, structural fashion.

What should we mean by rationality? The relevant notion is this: there is some, probably rather ill-defined, set of rules, strategies, or methods which, if put into practice in solving problems or pursuing aims, gives us our best chances of success, other things being equal. These rules of reason don't guarantee success. They don't tell you precisely what to do; rather, they indicate what to attempt. They are meta-rules in the sense that they assume that you can already solve many problems, successfully pursue many aims, in the real world (implementing a wide range of methods); the rules of reason tell you how to marshal these past successes so as to give yourself the best chances of solving new problems, of achieving new aims.

Here are four elementary, utterly uncontroversial rules of reason.

1 Articulate and seek to improve the articulation of the basic
  problem(s) to be solved.
2 Propose and critically assess alternative possible solutions.
3 When necessary, break up the basic problem to be solved into a
  number of *specialized* problems – preliminary, simpler, analogous, subordinate problems – to be tackled in accordance
  with rules 1 and 2, in an attempt to work gradually toward a
  solution to the basic problem to be solved.
4 Interconnect attempts to solve the basic problem and specialized problems, so that basic problem solving may guide, and be
  guided by, specialized problem solving.

Any problem-solving enterprise which persistently violates any
one of 1 to 4 will thereby undermine its capacity successfully to
solve its problems and achieve its aims; it will forego its claim to be
intellectually rigorous, or rational. If academia is to contribute to the
aim of promoting human welfare, the quality of human life, by intellectual means, in a rational way, in a way that gives the best chances
of success, then 1 to 4 must be built into the whole institutional/
intellectual structure of academic inquiry.

But knowledge-inquiry violates *three* of these four most basic
rules of reason. It is as bad as that.

The first point to note is that, granted that academic inquiry has, as
its fundamental aim, to help promote human welfare by intellectual
and educational means,[4] then the *problems* that inquiry fundamentally ought to try to help solve are problems of living, problems of
action. From the standpoint of achieving what is of value in life, it
is what we *do*, or refrain from doing, that ultimately matters. Even
where new knowledge and technological know-how are relevant
to the achievement of what is of value – as they are in medicine
or agriculture, for example – it is always what this new knowledge
or technological know-how enables us to *do* that matters. All the
global problems discussed above require, for their resolution, not
merely new knowledge, but rather new policies, new institutions,
new ways of living. Scientific knowledge, and associated technological know-how have, if anything, as we have seen, contributed to the
creation of these problems in the first place. Thus problems of living
– problems of poverty, ill-health, injustice, deprivation – are solved

by what we do, or refrain from doing; they are not solved by the mere provision of some item of knowledge (except when a problem of living *is* a problem of knowledge).

Second, in order to achieve what is of value in life more successfully than we do at present, we need to discover how to resolve conflicts and problems of living in more cooperatively rational ways than we do at present. There is a spectrum of ways in which conflicts can be resolved, from murder or all out war at the violent end of the spectrum, via enslavement, threat of murder or war, threats of a less extreme kind, manipulation, bargaining, voting, to cooperative rationality at the other end of the spectrum, those involved seeking, by rational means, to arrive at that course of action that does the best justice to the interests of all those involved. A basic task for a kind of academic inquiry that seeks to help promote human welfare must be to discover how conflict resolution can be moved away from the violent end of the spectrum toward the cooperatively rational end.

Granted all this, and granted that the above four rules of reason are put into practice, then, at the most fundamental level, academic inquiry needs to:

1 Articulate, and seek to improve the articulation of, personal, social, and global problems of living that need to be solved if the quality of human life is to be enhanced (including those problems indicated above);
2 Propose and critically assess alternative possible solutions – alternative possible *actions, policies, political programs, legislative proposals, ideologies, philosophies of life.*

In addition, of course, academic inquiry must

3 Break up the basic problems of living into subordinate, specialized problems – in particular, specialized problems of knowledge and technology.
4 Interconnect basic and specialized problem solving.

Academic inquiry as it mostly exists at present can be regarded as putting rule 3 into practice to splendid effect. The intricate maze of specialized disciplines devoted to improving knowledge and technological know-how that goes to make up current academic inquiry is the result. But, disastrously, what we have at present, academic inquiry devoted in the first instance to improving knowledge, fails to put rules 1, 2, and 4 into practice. In pursuing knowledge, academic inquiry may articulate problems of knowledge, and propose and critically assess possible solutions, possible claims to knowledge – factual theses, observational and experimental results, theories. But, as we have seen, problems of *knowledge* are not (in general) problems of *living*; and solutions to problems of *knowledge* are not (in general) solutions to problems of *living*. Insofar as academia does at present put rules 1 and 2 into practice, in departments of social science, development and policy studies, it does so only at the periphery, and not as its central, fundamental intellectual task.

In short, academic inquiry devoted primarily to the pursuit of knowledge, when construed as having the basic humanitarian aim of helping to enhance the quality of human life by intellectual means, fails to put the two most elementary rules of reason into practice: rules 1 and 2. Academic inquiry fails to do (at a fundamental level) what it most needs to do, namely 1 articulate problems of living, and 2 propose and critically assess possible solutions. And furthermore, as a result of failing to explore the basic problems that need to be solved, academic inquiry cannot put the fourth rule of rational problem solving into practice either, namely 4 interconnect basic and specialized problem solving. As I have remarked, *three* of the four most elementary rules of rational problem solving are violated.[5]

This gross structural irrationality of contemporary academic inquiry, of knowledge-inquiry, is no mere formal matter. It has profoundly damaging consequences for humanity. As I have pointed out above, granted that our aim is to contribute to human welfare by intellectual means, the basic problems we need to discover how to solve are problems of living, problems of action, not problems of knowledge. In failing to give intellectual priority to problems of living, knowledge-inquiry fails to tackle what most needs to be done in order to contribute to human welfare. Academia fails to give priority to the tasks of getting clearer about what our problems are, and what we need to do about them. It fails, as a matter of fundamental intellectual priority, to develop imaginatively possible actions, policies, political programs, institutions, ways of living, to be critically scrutinized from the standpoint of their practicality, their capacity, if implemented, to help us realize what is of value to us in life. There is a dreadful failure to take up the task of intelligent public education about what our problems are, and what we need to do about them. These tasks, vital if we are to learn how to solve our grave global problems and make some progress toward a better world, do not get done because they do not fit into the framework of knowledge-inquiry.

Furthermore, in devoting itself to acquiring knowledge in a way that is unrelated to sustained concern about what humanity's most urgent problems are, as a result of failing to put rules 1 and 2 into practice, and thus failing to put rule 4 into practice as well, the danger is that scientific and technological research will respond to the interests of the powerful and the wealthy, rather than to the interests of the poor, of those most in need. Scientists, officially seeking knowledge of truth *per se*, have no official grounds for objecting if those who fund research – governments and industry – decide that the truth to be sought will reflect their interests, rather than the interests of the world's poor. And priorities of scientific research, globally, do indeed reflect the interests of the first world, rather than those of the developing world.[6]

Knowledge and technology successfully pursued in a way that is not rationally subordinated to the tackling of more fundamental problems of living, through the failure to put rules 1, 2, and 4 into practice, are bound to lead to the kind of global problems discussed above, problems that arise as a result of newly acquired powers to act being divorced from the ability to act wisely. The creation of our current global problems, and our inability to respond adequately to these problems, has much to do, in other words, with the long-standing, rarely noticed, structural *irrationality* of our institutions and traditions of learning, devoted as they are to acquiring knowledge dissociated from learning how to tackle our problems of living in more cooperatively rational ways. Knowledge-inquiry, because of its irrationality, is designed to *intensify*, not help *solve*, our current global problems.[7]

WISDOM-INQUIRY

Inquiry devoted primarily to the pursuit of knowledge is, then, grossly and damagingly irrational when judged from the standpoint of contributing to human welfare by intellectual means. At once the question arises: What would a kind of inquiry be like that is devoted, in a genuinely rational way, to promoting human welfare by intellectual means? I shall call such a hypothetical kind of inquiry *wisdom-inquiry*, to stand in contrast to knowledge-inquiry.[8]

As a first step at characterizing wisdom-inquiry, we may take knowledge-inquiry (at its best) and modify it just sufficiently to ensure that all four elementary rules of rational problem-solving, indicated above, are built into its intellectual and institutional structure: see figure 7.1.

The primary change required is to ensure that academic inquiry implements rules 1 and 2. It becomes the fundamental task of social inquiry and the humanities 1 to articulate, and seek to improve the articulation of, our problems of living, and 2 to propose and critically assess possible solutions, from the standpoint of their practicality and desirability. In particular, social inquiry has the task of discovering how conflicts may be resolved in less violent, more cooperatively rational ways. It also has the task of promoting such tackling of problems of living in the social world beyond academia. Social inquiry is, thus, not primarily social *science*, nor primarily concerned to acquire knowledge of the social world; its primary task is to promote more cooperatively rational tackling of problems of living in the social world. Pursued in this way, social inquiry is intellectually more fundamental than the natural and technological sciences, which tackle subordinate problems of knowledge, understanding, and technology, in accordance with rule 3. Social inquiry does, of course, seek to improve knowledge and understanding of aspects of the social world, but it does this as an adjunct to the primary task of promoting increasingly cooperative rational problem solving in the social world. Knowledge is acquired to increase understanding of what our problems are, and in order to assess proposals for solving them.

In figure 7.1, implementation of rule 3 is represented by the specialized problem solving of the natural, technological, and formal sciences, and more specialized aspects of social inquiry and the humanities. Rule 4 is represented by the two-way arrows linking fundamental and specialized problem solving, each influencing the other.

One can go further. According to this view, the thinking that we engage in as we live, in seeking to realize what is of value to us, is intellectually more fundamental than the whole of academic inquiry (which has, as its basic purpose, to help cooperatively rational thinking and problem solving in life to flourish). Academic thought emerges as a kind of specialization of personal and social thinking in

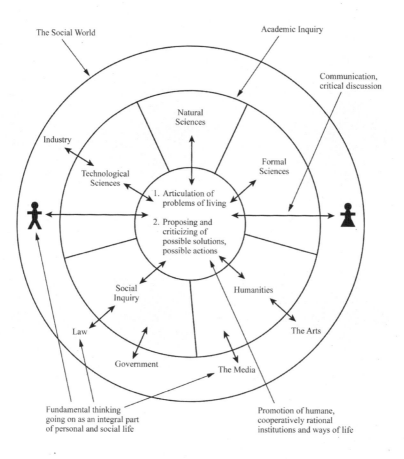

The Social World

Academic Inquiry

Communication,
critical discussion

Natural
Sciences

Industry

Formal
Sciences

Technological
Sciences

1. Articulation of
   problems of living

2. Proposing and
   criticizing of
   possible solutions,
   possible actions

Social
Inquiry

Humanities

Law

The Arts

Government

The Media

Fundamental thinking
going on as an integral part
of personal and social life

Promotion of humane,
cooperatively rational
institutions and ways of life

Figure 7.1 Wisdom-inquiry implementing problem-solving rationality

life, the result of implementing rule 3; this means there needs to be a two-way interplay of ideas, arguments, and experiences between the social world and academia, in accordance with rule 4. This is represented, in figure 7.1, by the two-way arrows linking academic inquiry and the social world.

The natural and technological sciences need to recognize three domains of discussion: evidence, theory, and aims. Discussion of aims seeks to identify that highly problematic region of overlap between what is discoverable, and what it is of value to discover. Discussion of what it is of value to discover interacts with social inquiry, in accordance with rule 4. Wisdom-inquiry might be regarded as a sort of people's civil service, doing openly for the public what actual civil services are supposed to do for governments. Wisdom-inquiry needs just enough power to protect its independence from the pressures of government, industry, the media, and the public, but no more. Its task is to propose, argue for, and suggest, not to dictate.

It may be asked: but if academic inquiry today really does suffer from the wholesale structural irrationality just indicated, when and how did this come about? I turn now to a consideration of that question. The answer leads to an improved version of wisdom-inquiry, and to a new argument in support of my claim that wisdom-inquiry, potentially, is more rigorous and of greater human value than knowledge-inquiry.

THE TRADITIONAL ENLIGHTENMENT

The irrationality of contemporary academic inquiry has its roots in blunders made by the philosophes of the eighteenth-century Enlightenment.

A basic idea of the Enlightenment, perhaps *the* basic idea, was to try to learn from scientific progress how to go about making social progress toward an enlightened world.[9] The philosophes of the French Enlightenment in particular, Voltaire, Diderot, Condorcet, and others, did what they could to put this immensely important idea into practice in their lives. They fought dictatorial power, superstition, and injustice with weapons no more lethal than those of argument and wit. They supported the virtues of tolerance, openness to doubt, readiness to learn from criticism and from experience. Courageously and energetically they laboured to promote rationality in personal and social life.[10]

Unfortunately, in developing the Enlightenment idea intellectually, the philosophes blundered. They thought the task was to develop the social sciences alongside the natural sciences. I shall call this the *traditional Enlightenment program*. It was developed throughout the nineteenth century by Auguste Comte, Karl Marx, J.S. Mill, Max Weber, and others, and built into the institutional structure of universities during the twentieth century, with the creation of departments of social science.[11] Knowledge-inquiry, as we have it today, by and large is the result, both natural science and social inquiry being devoted, in the first instance, to the pursuit of knowledge.

But, from the standpoint of creating a kind of inquiry designed to help humanity learn how to become civilized, all this amounts to a series of monumental blunders. These blunders are at the root of the damaging irrationality of current academic inquiry.

THE NEW ENLIGHTENMENT

In order to implement properly the basic Enlightenment idea of learning from scientific progress how to achieve social progress toward a civilized world, it is essential to get the following three steps right.

1 The progress-achieving methods of science need to be correctly identified.
2 These methods need to be correctly generalized so that they become fruitfully applicable to any human endeavour, whatever the aims may be, and not applicable only to the endeavour of improving knowledge.
3 The correctly generalized progress-achieving methods then need to be exploited correctly in the great human endeavour of trying to make social progress toward an enlightened, wise, civilized world.

Unfortunately, the philosophes of the Enlightenment got all three points wrong. And as a result, these blunders, undetected and uncorrected, are built into the intellectual-institutional structure of academia as it exists today.[12]

First, the philosophes failed to capture correctly the progress-achieving methods of natural science. From d'Alembert in the eighteenth century to Popper in the twentieth (Popper 1963), the widely held view, among both scientists and philosophers, has been (and continues to be) standard empiricism: science proceeds by assessing theories impartially in the light of evidence, *no permanent assumption being accepted by science about the universe independently of evidence.*

But, as we saw in chapter 4, this standard empiricist view is untenable. Science cannot proceed without accepting, as a part of scientific knowledge, the metaphysical thesis that the universe is (more or less) physically comprehensible – whether this thesis is explicitly

acknowledged or not. In order to ensure that we accept as scientifically fruitful a thesis as possible, we need to represent it in the form of
a hierarchy of theses, these theses becoming less and less substantial
as we ascend the hierarchy. (See figure 4.2.) The top two we accept
permanently on pragmatic grounds; their acceptance can only help,
and cannot harm, the pursuit of knowledge, whatever the universe
may be like. Metaphysical theses lower down in the hierarchy are
accepted on the basis of (a) compatibility with theses above in the
hierarchy, and (b) association with empirically progressive scientific
research programs. The outcome – aim-oriented empiricism (AOE) – is
a view of scientific method very different from all versions of standard empiricism. AOE is a meta-methodological view: it specifies how
methods are to be improved in the light of improving knowledge, so
that as we improve our knowledge about the nature of the universe,
we improve our knowledge about how to improve knowledge. Even
though almost all scientists and philosophers since Newton have taken
versions of standard empiricism for granted nevertheless, of necessity,
something like AOE has been put into scientific practice. (Scientists
have professed one thing, done another.) Something of the positive
feedback character of AOE has been put into scientific practice, and it is
that which helps to explain the astonishing progressive success of modern science since the scientific revolution in the seventeenth century.[13]

So much for the first blunder of the traditional Enlightenment, and
how to put it right.[14]

Second, having failed to identify the methods of science correctly,
the philosophes naturally failed to generalize these methods properly.
They failed to appreciate that the idea of representing the problematic
aims (and associated methods) of science in the form of a hierarchy can be generalized and applied fruitfully to other worthwhile
enterprises besides science. Many other enterprises have problematic aims – problematic because aims conflict, and because what we
seek may be unrealizable, undesirable, or *both*. Such enterprises,
with problematic aims, would benefit from employing a hierarchical
methodology, generalized from that of science, thus making it possible to improve aims and methods as the enterprise proceeds. There
is the hope that, as a result of exploiting in life methods generalized
from those employed with such success in science, some of the astonishing success of science might be exported into other worthwhile
human endeavours, with problematic aims quite different from
those of science. I call this hierarchical, aims-improving conception

of rationality *aim-oriented rationality*. It is arrived at by generalizing aim-oriented empiricism, the progress-achieving methods of science implicit in scientific practice despite the fact that scientists pay lip service to standard empiricism.

Third, and most disastrously of all, the philosophes failed completely to try to apply such generalized, hierarchical, progress-achieving methods to the immense, and profoundly problematic, enterprise of making social progress toward an enlightened, wise world. The aim of such an enterprise is notoriously problematic. For all sorts of reasons, what constitutes a good world, an enlightened, wise, or civilized world, attainable and genuinely desirable, must be inherently and permanently problematic.[15] Here, above all, it is essential to employ the generalized version of the hierarchical, progress-achieving methods of science, designed specifically to facilitate progress when basic aims are problematic: see figure 7.2. It is just this that the philosophes failed to do. Instead of applying the hierarchical methodology to *social life*, the philosophes sought to apply a seriously defective conception of scientific method to *social science*, to the task of making progress toward, not a *better world*, but to better *knowledge* of social phenomena. And this ancient blunder is still built into the institutional and intellectual structure of academia today, inherent in the current character of social science.[16]

Properly implemented, in short, the Enlightenment idea of learning from scientific progress how to achieve social progress toward an enlightened world would involve developing social inquiry, not as social *science*, but as social *methodology*, or social *philosophy*. A basic task would be to get into personal and social life, and into other institutions besides that of science – government, industry, agriculture, commerce, the media, law, education, international relations – hierarchical, progress-achieving methods (designed to improve problematic aims) arrived at by generalizing the methods of science. A basic task for academic inquiry as a whole would be to help humanity learn how to resolve its conflicts and problems of living in more just, cooperatively rational ways than at present. This task would be intellectually more fundamental than the scientific task of acquiring knowledge. Social inquiry would be intellectually more fundamental than physics. Academia would seek to learn from, educate, and argue with the great social world beyond, but would not dictate. Academic thought would be pursued as a specialized, subordinate part of what is really important and fundamental: the thinking that goes on, individually, socially, and institutionally, in the social world, guiding individual, social, and institutional actions and life. The fundamental intellectual and humanitarian aim of inquiry would be to help humanity acquire wisdom – wisdom being the capacity to realize (apprehend and create) what is of value in life, for oneself and others, wisdom thus including knowledge and technological know-how but much else besides.

It is our failure to develop social inquiry as social methodology, devoted to getting aim-oriented rationality into the fabric of institutional and social life, that is in part responsible for the genesis of our current global problems and our incapacity to resolve them effectively, intelligently, and humanely. For most of our current global problems are the almost inevitable outcome of our long-term failure to put aim-oriented rationality into practice in institutional and social life, so that we actively seek to discover problems associated with our long-term aims, actively explore ways in which problematic aims can be modified in less problematic directions, and at the same time develop the social, the political, economic, and industrial *muscle* able to change what we do, how we live, the technology we develop, so that our aims become less problematic, less destructive in both the short and long term.[17] We have failed even to appreciate the fundamental need to improve aims and methods as the decades go by. Because of the dominance of knowledge-inquiry, academia cannot even entertain the idea that it has, as a basic task, to help humanity learn how to put aim-oriented rationality into practice in all the diverse contexts of social life. Even worse, academia does not put aim-oriented empiricism and aim-oriented rationalism into practice itself. As a result, the mere *idea* that it is of fundamental importance to put aim-oriented rationality into practice in personal and social life is, as yet, all-but unknown.[18] Conventional ideas about rationality are all about *means*, not about *ends*, and are not designed to help us *improve* our ends as we proceed.[19] Environmental degradation, species extinctions, the threat posed by nuclear weapons, pollution of earth, sea, and air, global warming, and the rest are the outcome.

One outcome of getting into social and institutional life the kind of aim-evolving, hierarchical methodology indicated above, generalized from science, is that it becomes possible for us to develop and assess rival philosophies of life as a part of social life, somewhat as theories are developed and assessed within science. Such a hierarchical methodology provides a framework within which

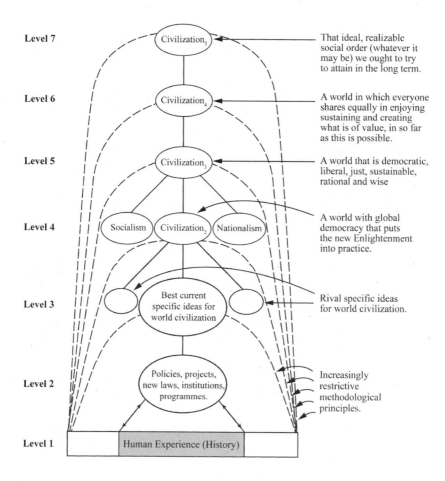

Figure 7.2 Hierarchical social methodology generalized from science

competing views about what our aims and methods in life should be – competing religious, political, and moral views – may be cooperatively assessed and tested against broadly agreed, unspecific aims (high up in the hierarchy of aims) and the experience of personal and social life. There is the possibility of cooperatively and progressively improving *such philosophies of life* (views about what is of value in life and how it is to be achieved) much as *theories* are cooperatively and

progressively improved in science. In science, ideally, theories are critically assessed with respect to each other, with respect to metaphysical
ideas concerning the comprehensibility of the universe, and with respect
to *experience* (observational and experimental results). In a somewhat
analogous way, diverse philosophies of life may be critically assessed
with respect to each other, with respect to relatively uncontroversial,
agreed ideas about aims and what is of value, and with respect to *experience* – what we do, achieve, fail to achieve, enjoy, and suffer – the
aim being to improve philosophies of life (and more specific philosophies
of more specific enterprises within life such as government, education,
or art) so that they offer greater help with the realization of what is of
value in life. This hierarchical methodology is especially relevant to the
task of resolving conflicts about aims and ideals, as it helps disentangle
agreement (high up in the hierarchy) and disagreement (more likely to
be low down in the hierarchy).

Wisdom-inquiry, because of its greater rigour, has intellectual
standards that are, in important respects, different from those of
knowledge-inquiry. Whereas knowledge-inquiry demands that
emotions and desires, values, human ideals and aspirations, philosophies of life be excluded from the intellectual domain of inquiry,
wisdom-inquiry requires that they be included. In order to discover
what is of value in life, it is essential that we attend to our feelings
and desires. But not everything we desire is desirable, and not everything that feels good is good. Feelings, desires, and values need to
be subjected to critical scrutiny. And of course feelings, desires, and
values must not be permitted to influence judgments of factual truth
and falsity. Wisdom-inquiry embodies a synthesis of traditional
rationalism and romanticism. It includes elements from both, and it
improves on both. It incorporates romantic ideals of integrity, having to do with motivational and emotional honesty, honesty about
desires and aims; and at the same time it incorporates traditional
rationalist ideals of integrity, having to do with respect for objective
fact, evidence, knowledge, valid argument, and criticism. Traditional
rationalism takes its inspiration from science and method, romanticism from art, from imagination, and from passion. Wisdom-inquiry
holds art to have a fundamental rational role in inquiry, in revealing
what is of value and unmasking false values; but science, too, is of
fundamental importance. What we need, for wisdom, is an interplay
of skeptical rationality and emotion, an interplay of mind and heart,
so that we may develop "mindful hearts and heartfelt minds."[20] It is

time we healed the great rift in our culture, so graphically depicted by C.P. Snow (1986).

All in all, if the Enlightenment revolution had been carried through properly, the three steps indicated above being correctly implemented, the outcome would have been a kind of academic inquiry very different from what we have at present, inquiry devoted primarily to the intellectual aim of acquiring knowledge.

CULTURAL IMPLICATIONS OF WISDOM-INQUIRY

Wisdom-inquiry does not just do better justice to the social or practical dimension of inquiry than does knowledge-inquiry; it does better justice to the "intellectual" or "cultural" aspects as well. Here, what really matters is the desire that people have to see, to know, to understand, their passionate curiosity about aspects of the world, and the knowledge and understanding they acquire and share as a result of actively following up their curiosity. An important task for academic thought in universities is to encourage nonprofessional thought to flourish outside universities. As Einstein once remarked, "Knowledge exists in two forms – lifeless, stored in books, and alive in the consciousness of men. The second form of existence is after all the essential one; the first, indispensable as it may be, occupies only an inferior position."[21]

Wisdom-inquiry is designed to promote all this in a number of ways. It does so as a result of holding thought, at its most fundamental, to be the personal thinking we engage in as we live. It does so by recognizing that acquiring knowledge and understanding involves articulating and solving personal problems that one encounters in seeking to know and understand. It does so by recognizing that passion, emotion, and desire have a rational role to play in inquiry, disinterested research being a myth. Again, as Einstein has put it, "The most beautiful experience we can have is the mysterious. It is the fundamental emotion which stands at the cradle of true art and true science. Whoever does not know it and can no longer wonder, no longer marvel, is as good as dead, and his eyes are dimmed."[22]

Knowledge-inquiry, by contrast, all too often fails to nourish "the holy curiosity of inquiry,"[23] and may even crush it out altogether. Knowledge-inquiry gives no rational role to emotion and desire; passionate curiosity, a sense of mystery, of wonder, has no place, officially, within the rational pursuit of knowledge. The intellectual domain becomes impersonal and split off from personal feelings and desires; it is difficult for "holy curiosity" to flourish in such circumstances. Knowledge-inquiry hardly encourages the view that inquiry at its most fundamental is the thinking that goes on as a part of life; on the contrary, it upholds the idea that fundamental research is highly esoteric, conducted by physicists in contexts remote from ordinary life. Even though the aim of inquiry may, officially, be *human* knowledge, the personal and social dimension is all too easily lost sight of, and progress in knowledge is conceived of in impersonal terms, stored lifelessly in books and journals. Rare is it for popular books on science to take seriously the task of exploring the fundamental problems of a science in as accessible, nontechnical, and intellectually responsible a way as possible.[24] Such work is not highly regarded by knowledge-inquiry, as it does not contribute to "expert knowledge." The failure of knowledge-inquiry to take seriously the highly problematic nature of the aims of inquiry leads to insensitivity as to what aims are being pursued, to a kind of institutional hypocrisy. Officially, knowledge is being sought "for its own sake," but actually the goal may be immortality, fame, or the flourishing of one's career or research group, as the existence of bitter priority disputes in science indicates. Education suffers. Science students are taught a mass of established scientific knowledge but may not be informed about the *problems* that gave rise to this knowledge in the first place, the problems that scientists grappled with in creating the knowledge. Even more rarely are students encouraged themselves to grapple with such problems. And rare, too, is it for students to be encouraged to articulate their own problems of understanding that inevitably arise in absorbing all this information, or to articulate their instinctive criticisms of the received body of knowledge. All this tends to reduce education to a kind of intellectual indoctrination, and serves to kill "holy curiosity."[25] Officially, courses in universities divide up into those that are vocational, like engineering, medicine, and law, and those that are purely educational, like physics, philosophy, or history. What is not noticed, again through insensitivity to problematic aims, is that the supposedly purely educational are actually vocational as well: the student is being trained to be an academic physicist, philosopher, or historian, even though only a minute percentage of the students will go on to become academics. Real education, which must be open-ended and without any predetermined goal, rarely exists in universities, and yet few notice.[26]

In order to enhance our understanding of persons as beings of value, potentially and actually, we need to understand them empathetically, by putting ourselves imaginatively into their shoes and experiencing, in imagination, what they feel, think, desire, fear, plan, see, love, and hate. For wisdom-inquiry, this kind of empathic understanding is rational and intellectually fundamental. Articulating problems of living, and proposing and assessing possible solutions, is, we have seen, the fundamental intellectual activity of wisdom-inquiry. But it is just this that we need to do to acquire empathic understanding. Social inquiry, in tackling problems of living, is also promoting empathic understanding of people. Empathic understanding is essential to wisdom. Elsewhere I have argued, indeed, that empathic understanding plays an essential role in the evolution of consciousness. It is required for cooperative action, and even for science.[27]

Granted knowledge-inquiry, on the other hand, empathic understanding hardly satisfies basic requirements for being an intellectually legitimate kind of explanation and understanding.[28] It has the status merely of "folk psychology," on a par with "folk physics."

This fulfills a promise I made in chapter 5 to respond to the criticism of personalistic explanation: it fails to meet intellectual standards required of a good explanation. Granted knowledge-inquiry, this may be true, but granted the more rigorous wisdom-inquiry, it is not. Articulating problems of living, and proposing and critically assessing possible solutions – integral to personalistic explanation – have an intellectually fundamental role within wisdom-inquiry.

Aim-oriented rationality and wisdom-inquiry are designed to enhance our capacity to realize what is of value to us in life. They are, in other words, designed to enhance free will – especially, of course, if this is construed as the capacity to realize what is of most value to us in life. Here, then, is the answer to another question left unanswered in chapter 5. In order to enhance free will we need to put aim-oriented rationality and wisdom-inquiry into practice. We need a culture, a social world, that does this.[29]

It may be objected, however, that wisdom-inquiry, unlike knowledge-inquiry, is committed to accepting *human values* in its basic aims, whereas knowledge-inquiry is not. That means wisdom-inquiry lacks a basic *objectivity* and *rigour* possessed by knowledge-inquiry. My reply to this objection is that it is actually the other way round.

First, there are, inevitably, and as a matter of desirability, values inherent in the aims of knowledge-inquiry, too. Inevitably, the pursuit of knowledge must select out some matters to seek knowledge about while ignoring endlessly many other matters. This selection will be done in part on the basis of what is deemed to be significant, of interest, important, or of value. Furthermore, it is not just inevitable that such a selection should be made: it is desirable. We want to develop knowledge about what is useful, significant, important, or of value. The difference between the two views is that wisdom-inquiry is much more explicit about its value-commitments – a gain in objectivity and rationality.

Second, wisdom-inquiry, in implementing the hierarchy of aims of aim-oriented empiricism and aim-oriented rationality, subjects aims, ideals, and values to sustained critical scrutiny in an attempt to improve them. Value commitments are open to *rational* appraisal and improvement. This is not the case as far as knowledge-inquiry is concerned.

CONCLUSION

Humanity is in deep trouble. We urgently need to learn how to make progress toward a wiser, more civilized world. This in turn requires that we possess traditions and institutions of learning rationally designed – *well designed* – to help us achieve this end. It is just this that we do not have at present. What we have instead is natural science and, more broadly, academic inquiry devoted to acquiring knowledge. Judged from the standpoint of helping us create a better world, knowledge-inquiry of this type is dangerously and damagingly irrational. We need to bring about a major intellectual and institutional revolution in the aims and methods of inquiry, from knowledge-inquiry to wisdom-inquiry. Almost every branch and aspect of academic inquiry needs to change.

A basic intellectual task of academic inquiry would be to articulate our problems of living (personal, social, and global) and propose and critically assess possible solutions, possible actions. This would be the task of social inquiry and the humanities. Tackling problems of knowledge would be secondary. Social inquiry would be at the heart of the academic enterprise, intellectually more fundamental than natural science. On a rather more long-term basis, social inquiry would be concerned to help humanity build hierarchical methods of problem-solving into the fabric of social and political life so that we may gradually acquire the capacity to resolve our conflicts and problems of living in more cooperatively rational ways than at present. Natural science would change to include three domains of discussion: evidence, theory, and aims – the latter including discussion of metaphysics, values, and politics. Academia would actively seek to *educate* the public by means of discussion and debate, and would not just *study* the public.

This revolution – intellectual, institutional, and cultural – if it ever comes about, would be comparable in its long-term impact to that of the Renaissance, the scientific revolution, or the Enlightenment. The outcome would be traditions and institutions of learning rationally designed to help us acquire wisdom. There are a few scattered signs that this intellectual revolution, from knowledge to wisdom, is already under way.[30] It will need, however, much wider cooperative support – from scientists, scholars, students, research councils, university administrators, vice chancellors, teachers, the media, and the general public – if it is to become anything more than what it is at present, a fragmentary and often impotent movement of protest and opposition, often at odds with itself, exercising little influence on the main body of academic work. I can hardly imagine a more important work for anyone associated with academia than, in teaching, learning and research, to help promote this revolution.

8

What Is of Real Value in Life?

∽ Reasons for doubts about value; value and evolution;
intrinsic value; value relativism; value objectivism;
aim-oriented rationalism ∾

IMPLICATIONS OF WHAT HAS BEEN DONE SO FAR

How can there be life of value – how can it exist and flourish – if the universe really is more or less as modern science tells us it is? This is perhaps the nub of our fundamental problem.

We need to take note of just how fundamental this question of life of value is. If in reality nothing is of value, in itself as it were, that means everything we experience and do, our whole life, our whole human world, is devoid of value. If human life, and sentient life more generally, is devoid of value, morality and law cease to have much meaning. For morality depends, surely, on persons, and sentient animals, being of value. And law in turn depends on morality: not everything immoral can be illegal, but everything illegal ought to be immoral.

Previous chapters have chipped away at this core problem. In chapter 3 we saw how the experiential world can exist even if the universe really is more or less as modern physics tells us it is. Physics (and that part of science reducible in principle to physics) is about only an aspect of the world: that aspect that exists at one instant that determines (perhaps probabilistically) what occurs next. Physics cannot predict (or explain) the experiential, and if physical theory is extended to include the experiential, it ceases to be explanatory. Excluding the experiential from physics is the price we pay to have the marvellously explanatory theories that we do have in physics. The silence of physics about the experiential is thus no reason whatsoever to hold that the experiential does not exist. Grass really is green and the sky really is blue, and our inner experiences and states of consciousness exist as well. All this is profoundly relevant to the value of our lives. Annihilate the experiential world, and life would become meagre indeed – mere physical processes unfolding in accordance with physical law. The familiarity of the experiential world can dim our eyes and dull our ears falsely to its utterly miraculous character.

Chapter 4 underlines how serious the fundamental problem is. Physicalism is not just metaphysical speculation, a toy idea discussed by philosophers. Once science is properly understood, in terms of aim-oriented empiricism, it becomes clear that physicalism is a central component of current scientific knowledge, more securely established, indeed, than our best physical theories – relativity, quantum theory, the standard model. The implications of physicalism for human life, its nature and value, need to be taken very seriously indeed.

In chapter 5 we saw how it is possible for us to have free will in a worthwhile sense even if physicalism is true. Free will is essential if we are to exist as persons, as beings of value. Devoid of free will, we are bereft of the power to perform actions in the world; we become automata, mere puppets of the physical universe. But free will in a physicalistic universe is also wildly improbable. It requires the miracle of double comprehensibility. We need to be comprehensible simultaneously in two very different ways: comprehensible physically and comprehensible purposively, or rather personalistically, and in such a way that free will can be ascribed to us, to our actions.

Chapter 6 reveals that Darwinian theory helps explain how double comprehensibility has got into the world, and thus how living things have evolved so as to have gradually acquired enhanced powers to act and free will. But, in order to fulfill this role, Darwinian theory must be interpreted as a theory about the evolution of purposive life and not as a theory that explains purposiveness away. Darwinian theory makes a profound contribution to enabling us to understand how life of value has come to exist.

Chapter 7 tackles the problem of how human life – and other forms of life too – can best flourish, granted we exist embedded in the physical universe. Around 12,000 years ago we stepped out of small, scattered hunting and gathering tribes, took up agriculture, and began the journey toward the modern world, transforming the conditions of life as we did so. During the last 200 years or so, modern science and technology have brought great benefits, but have also led to grave global problems, byproducts of our successes.

Granted that we were designed by evolution to cope with the conditions of life of hunting and gathering tribes of some 150 members, are we capable of coming to grips effectively with our current global problems, in a world of over 7.7 billion people, rapidly changing, charged with inequality and conflict?

Our global problems are in part the outcome of our failure to develop and implement properly the great Enlightenment idea of learning from scientific progress how to achieve social progress towards an enlightened world. We have failed to anticipate the undesirable consequences of our science-and-technology facilitated actions, or have failed to heed anticipations when they have been made, and take appropriate action. In order to do these things, it is essential to build aim-oriented rationality (arrived at by generalizing aim-oriented empiricism) into our institutions, social endeavours, and culture. In particular, aim-oriented rationality needs to be applied to academia to transform knowledge-inquiry into wisdom-inquiry, so that we may come to have what we so urgently need, institutions of learning rationally designed and devoted to helping us improve our personal and social lives as we live.

If we put the problem of coming to grips with our global problems into the context of our fundamental problem, the profound importance of aim-oriented rationality becomes all the more apparent. There are three crucial points we need to appreciate. First, we are a part of the physical universe: free will is problematic. Second, evolution designed us to cope with hunting-and-gathering life, not the very different conditions of life in the modern world. Third, evolution designs creatures to be good at pursuing the *fixed* aim of survival and reproductive success, but not good at actively *modifying* or *improving* this aim – or even able to do it.[1] But it is precisely this, active modification and improvement of personal, social, and institutional aims *actually being pursued*, that we need to perform to solve our global problems. Evolution has not equipped us for such a task; and the task is monumental, given that over 7.7 billion people are involved. We urgently need to discover how to exploit aim-oriented rationality so that our science-and-technology-facilitated actions may move into more desirable directions.

Modern science and technology have brought us great benefits. But at the same time they have led to new actions (via modern industry, agriculture, and armaments) that have created horrendous new global problems. Modern science provides us with an inspiring vision of the cosmos that, at the same time, contains grim implications for the meaning and value of human life in that it embeds us in the physical universe. But on top of all this, there is another, potentially very hopeful, message that comes from modern science: we can learn from scientific progress how to achieve social progress toward a wise, enlightened world. We can take seriously the task of tackling our problems in an aim-oriented rationalistic fashion.

That, in summary, is what I have done so far to try to show that life of value is possible and can flourish further even though our entire human world is an integral part of the physical universe. Endless questions remain unanswered of course. That is inevitable, granted that our concern is with the most fundamental problem we can consider, in thought and life. In particular, problems remain about what is of value in life. That is what I now consider in this penultimate chapter of the book.

QUESTIONS CONCERNING WHAT IS OF VALUE

What is genuinely of value in life? How do we decide? Is the answer obvious, or is it deeply mysterious? What kind of question is it in any case? In asking what is genuinely of value, are we asking a factual question? Or is the whole issue of what is of value purely subjective, any one person's answer being as good, or as bad, as any other's? But if that is the case, it is all subjective, and nothing is of value objectively, does that not mean that, ultimately, nothing really is of value? Is this the reason why the view that nothing is of value has a certain currency in our times when, quite possibly, life has never been so good for so many? Can we learn about what is of value in life? If so, how? How can anything be ultimately of value when we are a part of the physical universe, and all our actions, thoughts, and feelings are subject to physical law? How can anything be of ultimate value as far as I am concerned when, sooner or later, I will die and everything I have done, thought, enjoyed, and suffered will be as if it has never been? How can anything be of value to any of us if, in the end, the human race will die out and disappear, and it will be as if we have never existed? Is it not all rather grim?

On the other hand, it may seem that there are so endlessly many utterly obvious answers to the question "What is of value?" that it hardly counts as a serious question at all. Life is of value. So are happiness, friendship, laughter, joy, love, enjoyment, pleasure, sex, good company, fun, intimacy, beauty, the natural world, great art and great science, education, democracy, justice, freedom, kindness – even food, drink, drugs, and rock and roll – the list of good things in the world goes on and on. How could anyone think that the question "What is of value?" poses a serious *problem*? And for those in desperate straits – hungry, homeless, poor, imprisoned, enslaved, threatened with injury or death – the question "what is of value?" has all-too obvious an answer: sustenance, shelter, money, freedom, safety.

But then, for some of us at least, a mood can come down upon us in which the world no longer seems to be so charged with value. All those things and circumstances which, on other occasions, seemed supercharged with value, now seem to have had their intrinsic value leached from them, so that they now seem devoid of value, or no longer attainable in a form that has any value. All colour, all value has drained away from the world, and we are left with mere simulacrums of happiness, friendship, love, and all those other things supposedly so supremely desirable.

This capacity of the value-aspect of things to leach out of existence is interpreted, officially, as a feature, not of the world, but of the individual. It indicates depression, even clinical depression. The proper response to it is not philosophical discussion but psychiatric treatment: lithium perhaps or Prozac, and therapy possibly. Those who ask, despairingly, "What is there that is of ultimate value?" need, not an answer, but appropriate psychiatric treatment.

But this attitude toward doubts about the reality of the value of things has a slightly sinister aspect. It seems all too reminiscent of Aldous Huxley's *Brave New World*, in which people are led to imbibe Soma to keep them happy. There would indeed be something seriously wrong with a society that treats those who have profound doubts about orthodox views of the world with drugs. Philosophical problems could be suppressed in that way, but hardly solved.

Why is the value aspect of things, for some of us at least, on some occasions, so frail, so vulnerable to disappearing? The answer, I think, is that we become aware of the value aspect of things via our *desires* and *feelings*, our motivational and emotional responses to things, and our desires and capacity to feel may become locked in despair, or frozen in numbness. Not everything that we desire is desirable, and not everything that feels good is good, of course, but bereft of the capacity to desire and feel, we cannot make value discoveries for ourselves, we can only parrot the value discoveries of others, or know in a cold, purely intellectual way that something is of value – or is deemed to be of value. It is because we discover and experience what is good or of value via our desires and feelings, and these can become locked and obsessive, and so unresponsive to the particularities of what we experience, that the value features of things can seem to be so vulnerable to disappearance.

But clinical depression is not the only reason for becoming haunted by the possibility that there is nothing in existence that is genuinely, ultimately, of value. We may be led to adopt such a view because, almost unconsciously, we fall victim to arguments or considerations, floating around in our culture, which seem to carry such implications. The conditions of the modern world may prompt such an attitude.

First, there are the considerations that have been the concern of this book so far: the grim implications of modern science – or its apparent grim implications. We are nothing but indescribably minute specks of physical systems caught up in the remorseless flow of physical phenomena in a vast and impersonal cosmos. I have done what I can to combat that reason for philosophical despair.

Second, we may despair of anything in life having any real value because, whatever we do, it all ends in death and comes to nothing. Undoubtedly, the discovery of the inevitability of death, when first made in the depths of prehistory, must have been traumatic. Animals, for the most part, do not know that death is inescapable. The discovery is made when the capacity to imagine develops, distant places and times can be imagined, the arena in which one acts is vastly extended in space and time, an arena which contains one's death, sooner or later, implacably, sometime in the future. The urge to survive is deeply implanted within us by evolution: the discovery that, sooner or later, our efforts to survive will inevitably be defeated is bound to be unspeakably traumatic. An enormous amount of human ingenuity has gone into attempts to deny, or circumnavigate death. Is there a solution to the problem of death? Not one, perhaps, that brings much comfort. For something to be authentically of value it is not necessary that it be deathless, or eternal. Most of what is of most value, the stuff of our lives, is fleeting, perishable, here one minute and gone the next. The more we value the eternal, the more of what is really of value in life will slip through our fingers. Perhaps what is of most value can blaze into existence when we stare death calmly in the face, and enjoy and celebrate our lives despite its looming presence. Besides, the real fear may be, not death, but rather not living, or only partly living, and then dying. It is perhaps the dreadful possibility that we have not yet come into the full realization of what it is to be alive, so that we participate in what there is of most value in existence, and then we die, that is the real paralyzing death-fear. But that could be diagnosed as a fear of life rather than of death. Much better to exist and then cease to exist than never quite to exist and then die, so that one's one opportunity for existence is lost forever. The real terror is not ceasing to exist, but rather, much worse, never quite existing in the first place.

A third spectrum of reasons for doubting that life has value comes from the difficulty of a journey we all have to make these days, in one way or another, from the "closed" to the "open" society, as Karl Popper would put it.[2] We begin life, if we are fortunate, in the more or less closed society of the family – or perhaps the local community, our local tribe: one view of the world, one set of values more or less taken for granted. Then the impersonality and diversity, the fragmentary character, of the modern world crashes into our lives. We become aware of a multiplicity of ways of life, beliefs, and values. Viewed from this perspective, the secure world of our parents, or local community leaders, their easy convictions, may seem faintly ridiculous. At some point in our lives, we are confronted by the problem of choice: how do we decide what to believe, what to value, how to live? And we are not just confronted by the multiplicity of lives in the social world around us; many of us become aware of people – billions of people – living lives very different from ours in distant places. And we may become aware of the very different lives that people lived in the past – and thus aware of the very different lives that will, no doubt, be lived in the future. Our whole word and way of life may seem to be no more than a somewhat arbitrary juncture in a history of rapid change. Inevitably, the meaning and value of our lives, the very substance of our being, is thrown into doubt. But it is an unhelpful, corrosive, silent doubt, eating away invisibly at the authenticity and integrity of life. It is doubt that corrodes, not doubt from which one can learn. Our "open" societies may contain many different faiths, values, ways of living, customs, and traditions; they do not contain much by way of hints as to how one can learn and grow, exploiting this diversity.[3] Doubt is not generally regarded as a universal condition, even a blessing facilitating learning, growth, and progress. Too many creeds denounce doubt as a sin. In these ways, the multiplicity and impersonality of modern "open" societies can erode belief in the value of life.

THE SOURCE OF VALUE

Where do values come from? They come from evolution. As soon as a living thing has come into existence pursuing aims, whether bacterium, plant, or animal, it becomes possible to refer to what is of value to that living thing, and what is of disvalue; what is good or beneficial (food, protection from a predator), and what is bad or harmful (a predator, a threat of extinction, a high wall blocking the route to a goal). Anything that helps a creature attain its goals, or is the realization of a goal, is of value to that creature; anything that obstructs or prevents the attainment of its goals is a disvalue to it. What is of value, or disvalue, is a purely *factual* matter. And we may regard the notion of value as becoming progressively enriched as insentient life becomes, first, sentient, and then conscious and self-conscious, as we human beings mostly are.[4]

This evolutionary account of value interprets what is of value to a creature to be merely what is of use to that creature in the pursuit of its aims. But we do not just value what we can make *use of* in our efforts to achieve our aims. We may also hold something to be of value even though it does not, in any way, aid – or constitute – the realization of one of our aims. I may, for example, value the snow leopard of the mountains of Asia – value that snow leopards continue to exist in the wild. But their continued existence does not aid me in my realization of my aims in life in the slightest – not unless I take on God-like responsibilities, and decide to adopt as my aims the welfare of everything I value.

But the evolutionary account of value can easily be extended to take this distinction into account. The problem with the above account is that it is a view of value restricted to animals. We human beings differ from other sentient animals in that we have enhanced powers of imagination. We are, as a result, conscious. And we can collaborate with other human beings to engage in joint actions. All this enormously extends aims that we can be regarded as having. I can imagine aims I might have if my circumstances were different, or if I had powers to act that I do not in fact have. This allows me to invent a whole universe of what is desirable which vastly overshoots what I can realistically desire (and hope to achieve). Human desire notoriously overshoots practicality in a way that animal desire does not. Furthermore, I can join with others to engage in the pursuit of aims that I could not pursue on my own with a remotely realistic hope of success. I can sign a petition to save the snow leopard from extinction, and perhaps, thereby, help save the snow leopard in reality. I can have an aim that demands collaboration from others – such as the aim to create peace on earth. This vast extension of the aims I can be held to have vastly extends what I may hold to be of value. It enables us to make sense of the idea that a person can value something, such as the snow leopard, for its own sake entirely, apparently unrelated to any aims in life that that person may have – although actually imaginatively extended aims of the person are involved. The basic features of the above aims-related view of value remain in place. It enables us to make sense of the idea that a person holds something to be of *intrinsic* value, of value in its own right as it were, and not just of value because it is of use to someone. And that immediately raises the question: what is it for something to be of intrinsic value, of value in its own right? Is this a factual issue? Or is it merely a matter of opinion? And what is of intrinsic value – or what should we hold to be of intrinsic value? How do we decide? These are the questions I try to answer in what follows.

RELATIVISM

Relativism is the view that the many different traditions, ways of living, and values that exist are all equally viable; all views about what is of value deserve respect equally, unless actively causing harm in a way that violates the law.

It is surprising how widely relativism is taken for granted in liberal, democratic societies, for relativism has very disturbing implications.[5] If any system of values is as good, or as bad, as any other, this means the values of, say, Adolf Hitler are as good, or as bad, as those of Albert Einstein or Martin Luther King. Relativism cancels the very possibility of there being valid grounds for rejecting an utterly obnoxious set of values.[6] Furthermore, relativism implies that, ultimately, nothing is objectively, in reality, of value. For if some things are of value objectively, in reality, then only those systems of value that hold these things to be of value would be correct; all the other systems of value that disagree would be false – and that contradicts relativism.

Given that relativism has these grim, nihilistic implications, why, one may ask, would any sane person want to hold such a view? Those who uphold relativism do so, I suggest, out of a misguided desire to defend liberalism against what are seen as dogmatic, authoritarian, illiberal alternative doctrines.[7]

I have in mind versions of what may be called *dogmatic objectivism*. A dogmatic objectivist claims to know for certain that his values are correct, all other, clashing systems of value being inferior and false. Many Victorian travellers and anthropologists instinctively assumed that their own values and culture represented superior civilization in contrast to the primitive, false values of the tribal people they encountered. Today, religious and political dogmatists and fundamentalists of various hues claim to know for certain what is of value, all other clashing views about what is of value being unquestionably false.

Relativism arises as a reaction against such doctrinaire, authoritarian views. In seeking to defend the right of each group of people, or of each individual, to uphold their own values, the relativist argues that all views about values need to be treated equally. In the interests of liberalism – the rights of groups or individuals to hold their own views, whatever they may be – relativism rejects the *objectivism* of dogmatic objectivism. But this is a disaster, for the reasons given above. It ends up destroying the very thing relativism seeks to defend, namely liberalism, respect for the views and values of groups and individuals. Relativism implies that liberal values are on a par with all others, no better or worse than those of criminals and fanatics.[8]

The objectionable ingredient in dogmatic objectivism is not the objectivism, as relativism holds, but rather the *dogmatism*, the claim to know for certain what is of value. Relativists overlook a third position: *conjectural objectivism*. This holds that what is of value is indeed an objective matter, and precisely for that reason our views about what is of value can only be *conjectural*. When we encounter people who hold values that differ from our own, we ought not to take it for granted that we are correct and they are wrong. Rather, we should seek to discover what we can learn from each other. Victorian anthropologists might indeed have had much to learn from the primitive people they encountered. The Pygmies of the tropical rain forests of central Africa, as described by Colin Turnbull in *The Forest People*, are free of dogmas and superstitions. They have hardly any crime, and manage their affairs in an instinctively cooperative way.[9] Victorians would have had quite a lot to learn from the Pygmies about civilization.

In rejecting the *objectivism* of dogmatic objectivism, relativism manages to intensify what is really wrong with the doctrine, namely its *dogmatism*. Dogmatic objectivist Victorians may have known their values were correct, but it was at least possible that they were wrong. Granted relativism, the very possibility of being wrong disappears. It does not even make sense to say that one's values are inadequate, or false in some way. It becomes impossible to learn about what is of value. At most, one's values may improve relative to one's own values; but relative to some other, equally viable set, this change will represent the very opposite: decline, degeneration.

Relativism gains false credence from overlooking the most viable alternative: conjectural objectivism. I now consider the merits and problems of this doctrine.

CONJECTURAL OBJECTIVISM

Assertions about what is of value and what of disvalue are, in some sense, correct and incorrect, true and false. But in what sense? One possibility is that such assertions are just straightforwardly *factually* true and false. As long as we are clear as to what it means to say of something that it is of value, the assertion that it is of value is a straightforwardly factual assertion, true or false depending on whether or not it really is of value, in the relevant sense. And this is the case whether we are talking about people, human actions, institutions, works of art and other artifacts, other living things, or aspects of the natural world. Let us call this view *conjectural value realism* (or just value *realism* for short).[10]

Value realism may seem, at first sight, a somewhat dubious doctrine. It is widely taken for granted that questions of *fact* and questions of *value* belong to two wholly distinct realms. Questions about fact concern simply *what is the case*, what exists in the world, what is factually true or false. Questions about value concern what is, for us, good or bad, desirable or undesirable. No body of purely factual statements, however comprehensive, can imply anything about what is good, what bad, what is, or is not, of value, a point emphatically stressed by David Hume.[11]

Of course, if we stipulate at the outset that *facts* are, by definition as it were, value-neutral, then Hume's point follows immediately. If we exclude value from fact by definition of "fact," then of course no body of facts, so defined, can imply anything about value. But suppose we do not do this. Suppose we leave it as an open question as to whether the domain of *fact* includes *value* – so that this possibility is not just excluded at the outset by mere definition. What *reasons* are there for holding that the realm of fact does not include the realm of value?

As we have seen, if in declaring something to be of value we mean that it is of value to this person or group of people, then the declaration is factual. But the issue before us is rather different. It is, rather, Can we make sense of the idea that this object – this sentient creature perhaps, or this person, this deed, or this work of art – is of value *intrinsically, in its own right*, independently of whether it is of value to this or that person or purposive agent? Can it be straightforwardly true, factually, that this person is of value? This sentient creature? This work of art? This human act? These buildings, this city, this woodland, this beautiful countryside? Can it ever be factually true of anything that it possesses some value feature? Or is the very idea a nonsense? Let us consider objections to the idea that what is of value can be a *factual* matter.

It may be objected that people notoriously disagree about what is of value, and there seems to be no procedure for resolving differences and reaching agreement. All this is very different from the realm of fact.

But people differ over undeniably factual issues, too, and such differences of views can be interminable, and apparently irreconcilable. Such differences of views arise even in science – in cosmology, for example. The mere fact that people hold different views about what is of intrinsic value does not mean that the domain of intrinsic value does not exist. I shall have more to say about how clashing views about what is of value can be resolved below.

It may be thought that value features, if they exist, must be inherently mysterious. One might, with the common sense Oxford philosopher G.E. Moore, think of the Good as an unanalyzable property which cannot be defined.[12] Or one might suppose, even more radically, with the novelist Robert Pirsig, that there is something called Quality that is the basic stuff of existence, undefinable, neither objective nor subjective, from which everything else emerges.[13] Value might be thought of as some sort of mysterious invisible fluid, valuable things being soaked in it, valueless things being bereft of it.

Might chemists one day distil drops of this precious fluid in a flask? The whole idea is surely preposterous.

But we don't have to resort to such ideas in order to defend the existence of value features in the world. There are endlessly many value features that we are all entirely familiar with, and often attribute to people: kindness, courage, generosity, friendliness, sincerity; and their opposite, cruelty, cowardice, meanness, coldness, insincerity. And there are, of course, all sorts of other value features: graceful, entrancing, beautiful, life-enhancing; and brutal, ugly, obnoxious. It may well be a *fact* that a person is kind, or generous, or mean, or cruel: such facts carry value implications.

It may be objected: the meanings of these words may combine factual and evaluative aspects, but that does not mean that *reality* is composed of both aspects. We must split up these supposed features into two aspects, the purely *factual* aspect – the aspect that exists in the world – and the evaluative aspect – our evaluation of what exists.

But does not this objection presuppose the very thing that is at issue? What compels us to hold that the value aspects of these features cannot exist, as a part of reality, real factual features of persons?

It might be argued that *science* tells us that facts are, in themselves, value-neutral. But does science tell us this? In chapter 3 we saw that physics, and that part of natural science in principle reducible to physics, can say nothing about the experiential – colours, sounds, and smells as we experience them, and our inner experiences. A major part of natural science simply ignores a basic aspect of reality: the experiential aspect. Is it not reasonable to suppose that science also ignores the value aspect of reality? And just as the fact that physics is silent about the experiential aspect provides no grounds for holding that the experiential does not exist, so likewise, the fact that science is silent about the value aspect of reality provides no grounds for holding that this aspect does not really exist.

But, it may be objected, the only way we can tell whether something is of value or not is by means of our emotional responses to that thing. That shows that values are subjective, not factual features of the objective world.

Is that correct? Why should we not hold that value features of things are like perceptual features of things? In order to detect the redness of a rose, the yellowness of sand, I need to have a certain sort of inner visual experience, but that does not mean that the perceptual properties, red and yellow, are purely subjective. Or rather, as we saw in chapter 3, there are two ways of drawing the distinction between objective and subjective. The first has to do with existence: if something exists, it is objective; if it appears to exist but in reality does not, then it is subjective. The second distinction has to do with something being impersonal or personal. If it is not in any way related to human physiology or experience, it is objective; if it is related, in an essential way, to our physiology, psychology, or experiences, then it is subjective. The all-important point is that something may be objective in the first sense, subjective in the second sense. Colours (and other perceptual qualities) as we experience them are a perfect example: they exist out there in the world and are thus objective in the first sense, but they are subjective in the second sense.

Why not hold that value features are the same? The value aspect of a generous person or generous action exists objectively (in the first sense) out there in the world, as a part of reality; it is, nevertheless, subjective in the second sense because of its relationship with human aspirations, desires, and emotions. The subjectivity, in the second sense, of value features is entirely compatible with these value features existing objectively, in the first sense, as objectively as colours and sounds. It is the failure to distinguish these two very different ways of drawing the distinction between objective and subjective that condemns so many to conclude that values must be subjective – because of the relationship between what is of value and our all-too human emotional responses to things.

But just as the "value as fact" view seems to be coming out on top, a dreadful snag emerges. If we hold that colours, as we see them, exist objectively (in the first sense) in the world, we must also agree that very different colours perceived by people suffering from various forms of colour blindness also exist – and very different colours perceived by other sentient creatures, and other possible conscious persons. A person suffering from red-green colour blindness finds it difficult, if not impossible, to distinguish red from green. Such a person must see a colour I do not see, for to me red and green are easy to distinguish. All these other colours that we "normal sighted" people do not see exist just as objectively (in the first sense) as the colours I do see.

Linking the perception of value features to the perception of colour – the perception of perceptual qualities – has the consequence that value features perceived by people with emotional responses to things that I may judge to be "morally deranged" exist just as objectively as value features I perceive – I having, I hope, emotional responses that are not deranged. I see a person who is generous and kind-hearted; a follower of Hitler sees a person who is weak and pathetic. We may deplore the value judgments of the follower of Hitler, but are we justified in holding that, whereas value features we perceive really do exist, those the follower of Hitler perceive do not? Is the universe of value features so constructed that our good values exist, but others' bad values do not? The follower of Hitler finds glory and magnificence in parades celebrating a future Nazi state; to us such parades are menacing and horrible. But can we declare that value features of glory and magnificence just do not exist – because we deplore them – whereas being menacing and horrible do exist – because that is what we experience them to be? There seems to be something inherently suspect about trying to justify values on the grounds that good values exist and are true, bad values don't exist and are false.

The "value as fact" view does not, it seems, solve the key problem of distinguishing what is really of value from what merely seems to be of value to some people. Despite that failure, it may nevertheless be the case that there are authentic value features of people or things that we can discover. It may well be a fact that some person is kind, generous, honest, or life-enhancing: these factual features that a person can possess have an inherent value dimension to them, which we can discover.

Furthermore, is it not a fact – if indeed it is a fact – that our life is meaningful and of value whatever anyone may think about the matter? Surely, we do not want the significance of our life to depend on mere *choice* – even if it is rational choice?

Perhaps we can declare that a thing is of value if a hypothetical person who may be called "a reliable value perceiver" perceives it to be of value. There would seem to be two possibilities here.

First, we might hold that if a thing has a certain intrinsic value, then the "reliable value perceiver" will indeed judge its intrinsic value accordingly, granted the hypothetical "value perceiver" has perceived correctly. A view explicated along these lines would be a version of value realism. Value features of things really do exist in the world; they can be perceived or experienced by us, and more reliably perceived by the "reliable value perceiver."

Second, we may hold that what is of intrinsic value just is what the "reliable value perceiver" decides is of value. Value features do not exist out there in the world, real features of things, persons, and events. They are, rather, what the "reliable value perceiver" decides to be of value. The snow leopard is not really, intrinsically, of value, in itself; it is just that the "reliable value perceiver" deems it to be of value.

As long as an acceptable characterization of the "reliable value perceiver" can be given, this second option does not degenerate into something that is equivalent to value relativism. For, according to this second option, even though there are no value facts, there are, nevertheless, correct value judgments, in a certain sense of "correct." These are the value judgments that agree with those of the "reliable value perceiver."

But how can an acceptable account of the "reliable value perceiver" be given? All actual people are limited, in one way or another, in their interests and sympathies; we require a person free of all such limitations. We require a person who is free of the prejudices and self-delusions that all actual people suffer from, to a greater or lesser extent. We need an emotionally responsive person whose emotional responses to things accurately reflect objective realities rather than the moods or misconceptions of the person in question. But these apparently impossible requirements do not even begin to address the greatest difficulty: whether we judge a candidate "value perceiver" to be "reliable" or not is bound to depend on what systems of values we uphold. A person who holds that the greatest good in life is service to others will come to a quite different judgment as to what constitutes "reliability" from that of a person who holds personal success, or power, to be the greatest good. We build our system of values into our characterization of the "reliable value perceiver," and then, surprise, surprise, the value perceiver, so characterized, detects just that to be of value which agrees with our presupposed system of values. The whole procedure is viciously circular. It presupposes just that which it delivers.

There is another problem that confronts the attempt to characterize an ideal "perceiver" or "judge" of what is of intrinsic value. It is tempting to appeal to reason. What is of real value is what "reason" decides is of value – what it is rational to hold to be of value. False values are irrational or nonrational values. But can reason be in a position to determine what is of value? Certainly traditional conceptions of reason, which hold emotion and desire to be irrational or nonrational, seem dreadfully ill equipped to decide such an issue. We surely do need to consult our emotions and desires when it comes to deciding what is of value. Considerations such as these have led some philosophers to conclude that only intuition can determine what is, and what is not, of value – but that does not seem to be much of an improvement, first because intuitions are, all too blatantly, fallible, and second because they differ from person to person, so that the appeal to intuition could not conceivably deliver agreed, "correct" judgments of value. Not everything we desire is desirable, and not everything that feels good is good.

These difficulties can be overcome, I suggest, if we invoke aim-oriented rationalism. The hierarchical character of aim-oriented rationalism (AOR) is designed specifically to overcome the viciously circular problem. Given two clashing views about what is of value, we go up the hierarchy of aims, ideals, or values of AOR until we discover that lowest level that is in agreement with the two views. The merits of the two views are then assessed in terms of (1) agreed values and (2) experience. AOR makes it possible to explore questions of value without initial views about what is of value prejudging the outcome.

AOR resolves the problem of the inevitable limitations of any one individual person. AOR is designed to be put into practice by many individuals acting cooperatively.

Finally, AOR solves the problem posed by the point that neither reason nor emotion nor intuition can suffice to disclose what is genuinely of value. AOR is a synthesis of traditional rationalistic considerations – evidence, logic, criticism, knowledge, science – and traditional romantic considerations – emotional and motivational integrity, imagination, art. Both kinds of consideration are essential. The moment it is recognized that reason, the authentic article, must include strategies for the improvement of aims when they are problematic (as they often are), it becomes clear that authentic reason must call upon both intellectual and motivational considerations, so that each interacts appropriately with the other (motivation reminding intellect what drives it, intellect critically assessing motivation for inadequacies). As I have already remarked, AOR puts our minds and hearts in touch with one another, so that we may develop "mindful hearts and heartfelt minds."

Put in a nutshell, we may say that what is of authentic, intrinsic value is disclosed by the successful application of AOR in the search for what is of value.

There is another point that should, perhaps, be taken into account. In tackling the problem of value skepticism – which is, in effect what we have been discussing – we should compare it with the traditional philosophical problem of skepticism about factual knowledge: How can we know anything? Descartes tried to solve this problem by identifying, among what we took to be knowledge, that nugget that proved impossible to doubt. He hit upon "I doubt, I think, therefore I am." But this whole traditional search for certainty, upon which knowledge can be built up, is the wrong approach.[14] We should rather take what we hold to be our knowledge, the whole body of it, some parts no doubt more secure than others, some no doubt false, and ask: How can we *improve* this body of knowledge? How can we weed out falsehood, enhance content, reliability, and explanatory power?

Should we not take a similar approach granted we face the problem of value skepticism? Instead of trying to establish what is of value from scratch, as it were, without any initial input of value conjectures (for that would prejudge the whole issue), we should rather take the body of our current value conjectures as our starting point and ask: How can this body of value conjectures be *improved*? In seeking to improve our value conjectures, we should consult others, compare our value conjectures with theirs, listen to and learn from others. As I have already remarked, we should put aim-oriented rationality into practice cooperatively with others, in seeking to discover how we can, together, improve the value conjectures we hold – and, of course, of far more significance, the value of our lives. That basic commitment to engage with others in the attempt to improve value conjectures has, perhaps, within it something like a basic moral edict: when possible, resolve conflicts and problems by means of discussion rather than manipulation or violence. (But, of course, those who do violence to others need to be restrained by means of violence – whether the restraining is done by police or an army.)

Finally, I would like to indicate the kind of consideration that persuades me that what is of intrinsic value really does exist in the world.

Think of a friend or relative that you have known personally, neither a saint nor a fiend, who has lived her life and has died. A number of people have known this person, in different contexts and to differing degrees. The deceased person will have revealed different aspects of her personality to these friends, lovers, and acquaintances. No one, it is all too likely, knows all that there is to be known about this person. No one knows all the good qualities of this person. Even the dead person, when alive, may not have been aware of her good qualities; she may have undervalued herself, been too aware of failings and insufficiently aware of countless acts that have brought pleasure, delight, and happiness to others. No one sees all that is of value in this person. But we should not conclude that it therefore does not exist. To do so would have the dreadful consequence that it is only those who are widely believed to be of value that really are of value, and those who have quietly contributed much to the quality of people's lives, unnoticed and unsung, are nothing, and have done nothing.

9

Implications

⚬ Revolution for philosophy proposed in this book; basic tasks of philosophy: keep alive thinking about our fundamental problem; put the problem at the heart of philosophy, education, and academia; spell out implications for thought and life; help turn knowledge-inquiry into wisdom-inquiry ⚬

The chief implication of this book is that our fundamental problem – how our human world can exist and best flourish embedded in the physical universe – ought to be at the heart of our society, our culture, our human world. Everyone ought to have some awareness of the problem, its open character, the diverse attempts that have been made to solve aspects of it. It should be possible for anyone to ponder the problem, from time to time, and put much more specific problems that arise in life into the context of our shared, fundamental problem. It would be good, too, if there was some awareness of some of the other ways in which the fundamental problem can be formulated – formulations that take the existence of God for granted, for example – together with an awareness of the relative merits and demerits of these diverse formulations.

A basic task for philosophers is to keep alive imaginative and critical – that is, rational – thinking about the problem, and to encourage nonphilosophers everywhere to ponder the problem seriously, now and again. The problem does not, of course, belong to philosophers: it is not their property; it does not constitute their special disciplinary territory. On the contrary, it is the job of philosophers to encourage everyone to take personal possession of the problem, as it were, and to think about it, from time to time. Philosophers may try to solve philosophical aspects of the problem, as I have tried to do in this book, but they need to recognize that the most fruitful contributions may come from outside academic philosophy altogether. Charles

Darwin has contributed more to the problem than any philosopher, but Darwin, in his scientific work, would not even have considered himself as making a contribution to the problem, and may not have recognized the problem, as I have formulated it, in the first place.[1]

IMPLICATIONS FOR PHILOSOPHY

Philosophers need to put their own house in order. The diverse branches of philosophy – metaphysics, epistemology, theory of mind, history of philosophy, philosophy of science, political philosophy, moral philosophy, aesthetics, and so on need to be organized and pursued in such a way that these are all aspects of the fundamental problem: how can our world exist and best flourish embedded as it is in the physical universe? This fundamental problem must not disappear beneath a morass of intricate specialization. And philosophy must not become so esoteric, so riddled with specialized vocabulary, that it is wholly unintelligible to the nonphilosopher. Introductory courses in philosophy need to concentrate on discussion of the fundamental problem, there being as much discussion of relevant background knowledge – theoretical physics, cosmology, evolutionary biology, neuroscience, anthropology, history, psychology, literature – as of the philosophical issues themselves. Philosophy should not be introduced via a history of philosophy: it requires a rather sophisticated understanding of the fundamental problem as it confronts us today in order to get into perspective the work and efforts of earlier philosophers. We need to appreciate the impact that current scientific knowledge and understanding has on the way we formulate the problem today in order to be able to assess the extent to which seriously inadequate scientific knowledge of earlier times distorted the work of earlier philosophers: Plato, Aristotle, Descartes, Locke, Leibniz, Berkeley, Hume, Kant.

One way of highlighting the difference between orthodox philosophy as it is mostly practised in universities today, and philosophy as done in this book, critical fundamentalism devoted to tackling aspects of our fundamental problem, is to have a look at introductions to philosophy, and compare them with this book. I have looked at fourteen such books.[2] Not one of these fourteen introductions takes philosophy to be the enterprise of tackling, and keeping alive thinking about, our fundamental problem! Even worse, not one even gets round to formulating, let alone trying to solve, the human world/physical universe problem. The nearest that any of these books gets to tackling this problem is to tackle the mind-body problem, a subordinate bit of our fundamental problem. But the mind-body problem, if discussed at all, tends to emerge only around chapter 6. These introductions to orthodox philosophy conceive of the discipline in terms of its recognized sub-branches: metaphysics, epistemology, perception, philosophy of science, moral philosophy, mind-body problem (or the philosophy of mind), political philosophy, history of philosophy. Insofar as these sub-branches have *problems* associated with them, these introductions do discuss components of our fundamental problem, for the simple reason that all problems are, of course, subordinate aspects of our fundamental problem. But what they do not do is put these subordinate problems into the context of our fundamental problem. And that, as often as not, distorts the way the subordinate problem is formulated and tackled.[3] To take just one example, orthodox philosophy all too often introduces and discusses problems of perception as arising in connection with illusions and hallucinations. But that, as we saw in effect in chapter 3, entirely misses the point. The problem arises because of the view of the universe that came to the fore with the birth of modern science: the corpuscular hypothesis or, more generally, physicalism. One cannot even begin to discuss the problems of perception properly without putting them into the context of the human world/physical universe problem.

One of the fourteen introductory books I consulted begins rather promisingly with the words "Philosophy is the love of wisdom ... It is the contemplation or study of the most important questions in existence, with the end of promoting illumination and understanding, a vision of the whole."[4] But the rest of the book follows orthodox lines; the mind-body problem is fifth in a list of philosophical questions.

Ragland and Heidt's book *What Is Philosophy?* consists of answers given to this question by six philosophers: Barry Stroud, Karsten Harries, Robert Brandom, Allen Wood, Martha Nussbaum, and Karl-Otto Apel. Not one gives an answer similar to the answer of the present book.

One striking feature of orthodox academic philosophy is that it rarely has fruitful implications for disciplines and human endeavours outside philosophy, and rarely claims to have such implications.[5] As Wittgenstein said, "Philosophy ... leaves everything as it is."[6] That is in striking contrast to the approach to philosophy pursued in this book. As I hope I have made clear, there emerge from the discussion of previous chapters implications for a range of disciplines and human endeavours far beyond the confines of philosophy itself. In chapter 4 I argued for aim-oriented empiricism. This has important implications for theoretical physics and, indeed, for the whole of natural science.[7] The solution to the problem of theory unity has implications for quantum theory.[8] The discussion of chapter 6 has important implications for Darwin's theory of evolution, and for the way the biological world is understood more generally.[9] The argument of chapter 7 has dramatic implications for social science and the humanities, and for academic inquiry as a whole. Chapter 7, far more strikingly, has profound implications for personal, social, political, and institutional life: we should endeavour to put aim-oriented rationality into practice as we live.

The crucial question of course is: If implemented, would these implications be fruitful or disastrous? As I indicated in chapter 2, one way to assess the merit of a philosophical idea is to determine whether its implications are fruitful or harmful. The *arguments* of chapters 4 and 7 claim to show that implementing aim-oriented empiricism and aim-oriented rationality in science, in social science and the humanities, in academic inquiry as a whole, and in social and institutional life, would be beneficial. In order to assess the merit of what is proposed in these chapters, it is vital to determine whether the relevant arguments are valid. But even if the arguments are valid, it might turn out that these ideas are such that, when attempts are made to put them into practice in intellectual and social life, the results are not so good. These ideas may be excellent in theory, but not so good in practice. All sorts of unforeseen difficulties might emerge to frustrate their fruitful implementation. Two kinds of consideration need to be taken into account: the validity of philosophical arguments, and how good or bad the results are when attempts are made to put the philosophical ideas into practice in life. We may, of course, learn how to improve philosophical ideas as a result of what we experience when we attempt to implement them. As I remarked in chapter 7, aim-oriented rationality is a framework designed to facilitate just such learning – learning about philosophies as a result of what ensues when we try to put them into practice.

I have said enough, I hope, to make clear that the approach to philosophy taken in this book differs substantially from current orthodox academic philosophy – from the spectrum of views and approaches to be found in philosophy departments in universities today.

So far I have discussed what might be called the internal nature of philosophy – how and why philosophy needs to change to take up its basic, proper task: to keep alive imaginative and critical (i.e., rational) thinking about our fundamental problem. But these matters of good housekeeping internal to philosophy are hardly the most urgent issues for professional philosophers to attend to.

An urgent, primary task for philosophers is to move heaven and earth in order to ensure that the human world/physical universe problem comes to have the central role it needs to have in education, science, and scholarship. Every university ought to have a symposium, open to everyone at the university from undergraduate to vice-chancellor, that meets regularly and devotes itself to exploring the fundamental problem. An important task for the symposium would be to explore interactions between the fundamental problem and the more specialized problems of diverse disciplines: theoretical physics, neuroscience, history, anthropology, evolutionary theory, and so on. Interactions need to go in both directions: the results of specialized research may influence the way the fundamental problem is formulated, and may influence attempts to solve aspects of it; and ideas thrown up in discussion of the fundamental problem may suggest new avenues for specialized research. All the disciplines of academic inquiry, from the formal and natural sciences to the technological sciences, the social sciences, and the humanities need to conduct both research and education in such a way that there is some awareness of the significance of the fundamental problem for the discipline in question. A basic disciplinary task for critical fundamentalist philosophy is to get these points across to academic colleagues – or at least engage them in discussion of the issues.

Philosophers should also argue for a revision of the primary and secondary school curriculum. In schools, too, there needs to be some exploration of the fundamental problem. When I was at school, admittedly decades ago in the 1940s and 1950s, we pupils were presented with a series of subjects – English, chemistry, history, mathematics, biology, physics – but no discussion whatsoever as to how these distinct domains coexisted in one universe. We had no inkling as to how Shakespeare could be accommodated within a world of chemistry, or how history could be subsumed within the physical universe. The absolute educational silence about these questions of integration could only mean, it seemed, that there was no problem here at all! None of this constituted much of an encouragement to engage in critical thinking. As I have argued elsewhere, education in schools, from five-year-olds onward, needs to include a philosophy discussion seminar devoted to the questions, problems, and issues that interest and excite the children involved, the task being to learn how to engage in cooperative discussion, so that speakers are listened to, and responded to, and everyone does not speak at once.[10]

But awareness of the character of our fundamental problem, our efforts to solve aspects of it, and their merits and demerits, must not be confined to universities and schools. Some awareness of these things needs to be found in all walks of life: politics, law, the media, theatre, personal and social life. We ought all to be aware of the fact that when it comes to fundamental issues, we are all confronted by uncertainties and baffling dilemmas.

FROM KNOWLEDGE-INQUIRY TO WISDOM-INQUIRY

There is a further, even more substantial professional task awaiting critical fundamentalist philosophers. It is to make out the case, to all and sundry, for the urgent need to transform academia so that knowledge-inquiry becomes wisdom-inquiry. What would this transformation involve?

To begin with, it would require physicists to renounce allegiance to standard empiricism and instead adopt and implement in scientific practice aim-oriented empiricism (AOE). The metaphysical theses of AOE, and their hierarchical organization, need to be acknowledged as key items of theoretical knowledge in physics. Every effort needs to be made to improve those most likely to need improvement – theses low down in the hierarchy. Elsewhere I have spelled out detailed implications of AOE for physics and its history.[11] And more broadly, natural scientists need to renounce standard empiricism and accept and implement instead that version of AOE which recognizes that there are problematic assumptions concerning values and the social use of science inherent in the aims of science, in addition to metaphysical assumptions; these need sustained imaginative and critical attention, as an integral part of science itself, in an attempt to move the aims and priorities of scientific research in the direction of the best interests of humanity.

AOE, more or less implicit in scientific practice, is a good part of the reason for the astonishing success of modern science over the centuries.[12] It needs and deserves to be taken as a model for all problem-solving endeavours. AOE needs to be generalized to form aim-oriented rationality (AOR), designed to help us solve problems, and improve aims implicit in problems, whatever we may be doing. It is our failure to take AOE and AOR seriously, in our scientific, political, industrial, agricultural, and international life that is, in part, responsible for the genesis our current global problems, and our current incapacity to deal with them humanely and decisively. Almost all these problems have arisen because we have failed to recognize the problematic character of aims we have pursued – one or other dimension of "progress" facilitated by modern science and technology. When problems have been recognized, we have failed to take appropriate action, even when we know what we need to do, and know how to do it – as in such cases as habitat destruction, pollution, and global warming.

A proper basic task for academic inquiry is to help humanity put AOR into practice in diverse social and institutional endeavours so that what we strive to achieve may cease to be so plagued with harm, and may come to be increasingly in our very best interests. But before academia can make out a convincing case for the urgent need for the rest of the social world to put AOR into practice, it needs to put its own house in order, and put AOR into practice itself. What does this involve?

It involves taking seriously that a proper, basic aim of academia is to help promote human welfare by intellectual, technological, and educational means. That means that problems of living need to be put at the heart of the academic enterprise. The basic task of academia is to help humanity resolve conflicts and problems of living in increasingly cooperative and rational ways. Problems of knowledge and technological know-how are important but secondary. Social inquiry and the humanities have, as their proper, central task, to help promote cooperatively rational tackling of problems of living in the social world. The pursuit of knowledge about the human world is to be carried on as a secondary activity, to improve understanding of what our problems of living are, and to assess the viability of proposed solutions. A long-term task of social inquiry is to help humanity get into the fabric of social and institutional life the aims-and-methods improving meta-methodology of AOR. Social inquiry is, as I have remarked in chapter 7, social *methodology* or social *philosophy*, not primarily social *science*. The whole domain of social science has been fundamentally misconceived. This new kind of social inquiry – social methodology devoted to helping humanity tackle problems of living – is intellectually more fundamental than natural science, the latter being concerned with subsidiary problems of knowledge.

Public education, intelligently conducted, about what our problems are, and what we need to do about them, ought to be a central task of social inquiry and the humanities. But education needs to go in both directions. Nonacademics, grappling with problems of living in the real world, may have as much, or more, to teach academics, as the other way round. What really matters, of course, is the quality of thinking that goes on in the social world, guiding personal and social life.

Whereas knowledge-inquiry has two distinct aims, the intellectual aim of knowledge, and the social aim of helping to promote human welfare (primarily by the provision of knowledge and technology), wisdom-inquiry has just one basic aim, a synthesis of the intellectual and the social: to seek and promote wisdom, understood to be the capacity, the active endeavour, and possibly the desire, to realize what is of value in life, for oneself and others – wisdom thus including knowledge, technological know-how and understanding, but much more.

Wisdom-inquiry is what emerges when the damaging intellectual defects of knowledge-inquiry are put right. We need urgently to bring about a revolution in the academic enterprise – a series of revolutions! First, we need a revolution in the philosophy of science, acceptance of one or other version of standard empiricism being replaced by advocacy of aim-oriented empiricism.[13] We need a revolution in philosophy as a whole, so that it comes to devote itself to keeping alive imaginative and critical thinking about our fundamental problem. We need a revolution in natural science so that scientists, instead of attempting to do science in conformity with standard empiricism, come to adopt and implement aim-oriented empiricism instead. We need a revolution in the social sciences and humanities so that the basic task becomes to help humanity resolve conflicts and problems of living in increasingly cooperative and rational ways, an associated task being to help humanity feed aim-oriented rationality into personal, social, and institutional life. We need a revolution in academic inquiry as a whole, from knowledge-inquiry to wisdom-inquiry.[14] And finally, we need the revolution that really matters, a social revolution that enhances our capacity in life to solve problems of living in cooperatively rational ways, and proceed in accordance with the edicts of aim-oriented rationality.

Is there not an element of absurdity in expecting academic philosophers to bring about this series of revolutions, intellectual, institutional, social, and political? There is. The plea to help bring about these revolutions goes out to everyone who has any say whatsoever in our educational and academic institutions, our social and political life. Nevertheless, academic philosophy bears an especially heavy burden of responsibility for the close-to disastrous state of affairs that confronts us today.

First, academic philosophy is responsible in failing to develop philosophy as the enterprise that keeps alive imaginative and critical thinking about our fundamental problem *at the heart of the academic enterprise*, influencing and being influenced by all the other disciplines, from theoretical physics to the study of literature. A university system that kept alive the symposium, indicated above, devoted to explorations of the fundamental problem, would possess the capacity to think actively and effectively about academic inquiry as a whole, what its tasks ought to be, how well it pursues them, what changes need to be made to ensure that academia serves the best interests of humanity as well as possible. The conglomeration of specialized disciplines that is academia as it exists at present provides no arena for the exploration of such vital questions.

Second, academic philosophy bears a heavy burden of responsibility for the state of affairs we find ourselves in today because of its lamentable failure to pursue what may be called *the philosophy of inquiry*. Knowledge-inquiry and wisdom-inquiry are two rival philosophies of inquiry. They constitute two rivals views as to what ought to be the overall aims and methods of academic inquiry. We have inherited the former from the past. It is still massively influential today. The edicts of knowledge-inquiry are, to a considerable extent, built into the institutional structure of academia, influencing such things as research and education, funding, character of disciplines and how they are related to one another, criteria for publication, what constitutes a contribution to thought, what determines academic promotion, and how academia is related to the rest of the social world. Nevertheless, knowledge-inquiry is damagingly irrational. It needs to be replaced by wisdom-inquiry, more rigorous, and of greater potential human value. If academic philosophy recognized that *the philosophy of inquiry* is an important branch of philosophy, these issues would have come to attention long ago – especially as they have been spelled out in the literature repeatedly since 1976.[15] As it is, even though *philosophy of science* flourishes, *philosophy of inquiry* does not. And *the study of higher education* hardly does justice to the issues at stake.

Academics today concern themselves with their own careers, the fate of their research group, their Department possibly, at a stretch their particular discipline perhaps, but they all ignore serious questions about what the overall aims and methods of the academic enterprise ought to be. The outcome is that it is left to politicians and bureaucrats to reach decisions about such matters. We should not be surprised that the results do not correspond to the best interests of humanity.

CONCLUSION

Two great problems of learning confront us. There is, first, the problem of learning about the nature of the universe, and learning about ourselves and other living things as a part of the universe. And second, there is the problem of learning to become civilized. We have solved the first great problem of learning. We did that when we created modern science. We discovered how to learn about the universe. But we have not yet solved the second great problem of learning.

It is this combination of solving the first problem and failing to solve the second, that puts us into a situation of unprecedented peril. For, as a result of solving the first problem, we have vastly increased our power to act. The astonishing intellectual success of modern science and technology, since their creation in the seventeenth century, have made it possible for us to develop modern industry, modern agriculture, armaments, medicine, hygiene – the modern world. These immense new powers to act we have acquired as a result of the immense success of science have led to great benefits for people around the globe. But they have also led to our current spate of global problems: population growth; habitat destruction; species extinctions; lethal modern war; nuclear weapons; pollution of earth, sea and air; climate change; and the rest. We are in a situation of unprecedented crisis.

But there is a solution! We can learn from the solution to our first great problem of learning how to solve the second one. We can learn from scientific progress how to achieve social progress toward a better, wiser world.

This is an old idea. It goes back to the Enlightenment of the eighteenth century, especially the French Enlightenment. But, as we saw in chapter 7, the philosophes botched the job of developing this simple and profound Enlightenment idea properly. The outcome is what we are burdened with today: knowledge-inquiry.

In order to create institutions of learning of the kind we really need, rationally designed, *well designed*, to help us solve *both* great problems of learning, we do not need to thrash about in the dark, trying out this idea, that suggestion. We have before us clear guidelines as to what we need to do. Academic inquiry as it exists today is, substantially, the result of the Enlightenment effort to learn from scientific progress how to achieve social progress toward an enlightened world, but it is a *botched* effort. We have clear instructions as to what we need to do before us. We need to correct the intellectual/institutional defects in the kind of inquiry that comes down from us from the Enlightenment. Knowledge-inquiry needs to become wisdom-inquiry.

What we need, then, is a much more emphatic realization of the seriousness of our situation. And academics today need just a small portion of the energy and courage of the Enlightenment philosophes to push through the changes that we so desperately require.

APPENDIX

Why Philosophy Lost Its Way

*೧ Some time after Descartes, philosophy lost the plot because of
intellectual failures in connection with two of its most basic problems:
the mind-body problem and Hume's problem of induction. We need a
revolution in philosophy – integral to the revolution
we need in academia as a whole and, of far greater moment, the
revolution we need in our human world ೧*

In the last chapter we saw that philosophy has lost its way. It has profoundly misunderstood what its proper task is and, as a result of this
failure, our intellectual, cultural, and social life has suffered, and continues to suffer. We have failed to learn how to solve the grave global
problems that threaten our future – and we continue to fail. Instead
of acquiring the capacity to make social progress toward as good a
world as possible, we seem to stumble toward looming disaster.

At once the question arises: why? Why has philosophy failed so
disastrously? Why has it failed to put critical fundamentalism into
practice, to the extent of failing even to imagine that this is the
proper thing for philosophy to do? Why has it betrayed the best
interests of humanity in this way? In this appendix I try to answer
this question.

As it happens, suggestions as to why philosophy has failed so badly
are scattered throughout this book. Here, I gather up these scattered
suggestions, reinforce them, and add to them. As we proceed, it may
seem increasingly baffling that philosophers should have overlooked
such a vital task for philosophy as to get critical fundamentalism
up and running. If so, I shall count that failure as a success. For it
would mean that I have made out such a convincing case for critical
fundamentalism that it is all but impossible to see how philosophers
over the centuries could have failed to get the point.

One very obvious point to make is that philosophers have perhaps simply failed to appreciate just how damaging rampant specialization is, or have failed to appreciate that it is the proper task of philosophy to counteract mere specialization by keeping alive thinking about our fundamental problem. Instead of seeking to counteract the evils of mere specialization, academic philosophy has tended, in the twentieth and twenty-first centuries, to seek out eagerly, even desperately, its own specialized niche.

Once specialized intellectual standards become established, they determine what gets published, what gets noticed, and so such important matters for academics as funding, recognition, and careers. Too many academic philosophers seem to have been unable to resist such pressures. They have engaged in a highly specialized, esoteric kind of philosophy, and, as a result, have condemned their work to sterility.[1] Observance of specialist intellectual standards makes critical fundamentalism unthinkable.[2]

There are, however, even more important reasons for the failure of philosophy to take up critical fundamentalism. These have to do with intellectual blunders made in response to two of philosophy's most basic problems: the mind-body problem and the problem of induction. I take these in turn.

THE MIND-BODY PROBLEM

In chapter 2, pages 28–33, I gave a preliminary account of the intellectual failings in connection with the mind-body problem that led philosophy after Descartes to fail to put the human world/physical universe problem centre stage. We saw there that modern philosophy began well with Descartes's brilliant attempt at the solution to the human world/physical universe problem with his doctrine of Cartesian dualism (as it subsequently came to be called). It quickly became apparent, however, that Cartesian dualism creates more problems than it solves. Above all, it creates the horrendous problem of how, if we are confined to our Cartesian Minds, we can know anything about the physical universe, of which we can have no experience. Because of these difficulties, philosophers who came after Descartes in the main rejected Cartesian dualism.

At once there ought to have been a return to the problem that Cartesian dualism tries but fails to solve: the human world/physical universe problem. If that had happened, and philosophy had put centre stage, in thought and life, the problem of how human life of value can exist and best flourish embedded as it is in the physical universe, philosophy might have had a career after Descartes every bit as intellectually fruitful and successful as natural science (of which it would have formed a part). Especially would this have been the case if the fundamental problem had been tackled in such a way that it had interacted, in both directions, with all the more specialized and particular problems of science, thought, and life. Standard empiricism and knowledge-inquiry would almost certainly have evolved into aim-oriented empiricism and wisdom-inquiry long ago, perhaps in the early nineteenth century, and we would now live in a world very different from the one we endure today.

But this did not happen. Even though philosophers after Descartes in the main rejected Cartesian dualism,[3] they continued to be obsessed by the problems that Cartesian dualism generates. Instead of returning to the original problem that, implicitly, gave rise to Descartes's attempted solution in the first place, paradoxically, they struggled with the implications of Descartes's untenable solution. They agonized about how we can know anything about the physical universe if we are confined to the universe of Mind. They struggled to understand how physical events in the brain could cause, and be caused by, mental events in the Mind. They grappled with the problem of how there could be free will if determinism held sway in the physical universe. Singularly, they failed to return to the more fundamental human world/physical universe problem that Descartes may be construed to have tried, and failed, to solve.[4] Having rejected Descartes's attempted solution, the rational thing to do would have been to return to the problem it sought to solve. Philosophy did not begin to do that. Instead it struggled to solve problems *generated* by Cartesian dualism, even though Cartesian dualism itself had been rejected!

This obsession of philosophers after Descartes with problems generated by Cartesian dualism, even though the doctrine itself had been rejected, had further disastrous consequences for philosophy. It led to the acceptance of doctrines that made it impossible even to *formulate* the human world/physical universe problem. The apparent impossibility, given Cartesian dualism, of the Mind knowing anything about the physical universe led Bishop Berkeley to deny that there is any such entity. There are, according to Berkeley, only our perceptions;

nothing exists independent of perception.[5] David Hume was led to adopt a similar position: for him, we can only have knowledge of *sense impressions*. Only those ideas that can be traced back to prior sense impressions are meaningful; everything else is meaningless.[6] Immanuel Kant was led to hold that all we can know about the real world – the *noumenal* world as he called it – is that it exists; we cannot know anything more about it.[7] These doctrines make it impossible even to formulate our fundamental problem, the human world/physical universe problem.[8] Critical fundamentalism is dead.

Kant was passionately interested in natural science; the whole project of his *Critique of Pure Reason* might be said to be a (thoroughly misguided) attempt to save Newtonian science from Hume's devastating attack. Nevertheless, those who came after Kant, and were especially influenced by his emphasis on the *phenomenal* world, the world of human experience, lost interest in science and became increasingly immersed in the direct study of human experience by means of personal introspection. Science, and even reason, dropped out of the picture as Continental philosophy flourished. As I remarked in chapter 2, Kant led on, unwittingly, to Fichte, Schelling, Schleiermacher, Hegel, Schopenhauer, Husserl, Heidegger, Sartre, and Derrida; and to doctrines such as idealism, phenomenology, existentialism, structuralism, post-structuralism, and deconstructionism. The physical universe and natural science have all but disappeared: the human world/physical universe problem cannot even be stated, let alone tackled rationally.

Even philosophers who took science and reason seriously did not do much better. J.S. Mill defined matter as the permanent possibility of sensation.[9] The Logical Positivists – Moritz Schlick (1882–1936), Rudolf Carnap (1891–1970), Carl Hempel (1905–1997), Otto Neurath (1882–1945), Hans Reichenbach (1891–1953), Friedrich Waismann (1896–1959), Herbert Feigl (1902–1988), and Philipp Frank (1884–1966) – sought to establish that all metaphysics is meaningless because it cannot be verified empirically, which, once again, has the consequence that our fundamental problem, the human world/physical universe problem, cannot even be stated because its statement would be meaningless.[10]

Thus, for much of the history of philosophy since Descartes, philosophers of almost all schools have conspired to render our fundamental problem impossible to state, and even meaningless. Critical fundamentalism becomes, as a result, impossible. There could hardly be a greater betrayal of philosophy as it ought to be pursued. No wonder philosophy has dwindled in significance over the centuries.

Even today, almost all those philosophers who tackle aspects of the mind-body problem still fail to put it into its proper context of the broader, more fundamental human world/physical universe problem, as we saw in chapter 3 in connection with the discussion of the minimalist version of the two-aspect view on pages 66–9. As I pointed out there, the mind-body problem needs to be put into the more fundamental context of the human world/physical universe problem in order to facilitate the solution to the problem – the philosophical part of the problem, at least.[11] Modern philosophy began well with Descartes's brilliant attempt at the solution to an important part of the human world/physical universe problem, but then disaster set in. The subsequent philosophical tradition rejected Descartes's attempted solution but failed to return to the problem it sought to solve, namely the human world/physical universe problem. Instead, philosophers became obsessed with problems that Cartesian dualism generates *even though Cartesian dualism itself had been rejected*. As a result of this blunder, philosophical doctrines were developed that made it impossible even to formulate the human world/physical universe problem. Critical fundamentalism became impossible, and philosophy condemned itself to intellectual poverty.

But in recent decades, all this has changed dramatically, it may be objected. Many philosophers of science these days defend scientific realism, take the metaphysics of science seriously, and even formulate and discuss the human world/physical universe problem explicitly.[12] Thus Wilfrid Sellars discussed the problem of reconciling "the manifest image" and "the scientific image" (corresponding roughly to "the human world" and the "physical universe") decades ago.[13] Smart, Nagel, Dennett, and Chalmers[14] all discuss crucial elements of the human world/physical universe problem, to refer to just a few of the flood of books published on diverse aspects of the problem. Does not all this mean that critical fundamentalism is now alive and well? It does not, as we saw in the last chapter.

THE IMPOVERISHMENT OF PHILOSOPHY

Philosophers themselves recognize that their discipline faces a serious problem of intellectual legitimacy.[15] Other academic disciplines – most notably mathematics, the natural and technological sciences

– make important discoveries and achieve undeniable and remarkable progress. Philosophy, by contrast, does not. It is hard to pick out any discovery philosophy has made in recent times which would be generally recognized as undeniable and really important.[16] As I indicated in chapter 2, philosophers themselves tend to tell the following historical story to account for the progressive impoverishment of their discipline.[17]

Once upon a time, philosophy was extraordinarily fruitful and successful. In the seventeenth century it created modern science. Science began as natural philosophy – that branch of philosophy devoted to the study of nature. One can hardly think of a more significant step in history than the creation of modern science. It has made the modern world possible. But then science broke away from philosophy and established itself as an independent discipline. Thus philosophy gave birth to one of humanity's most successful endeavours ever, empirical science, and in the process lost a great chunk of its body – an astonishingly successful chunk to boot.

And this process of profound creation, dissociation, and severe depletion happened again and again down the centuries, leaving philosophy ever more impoverished and diminished as a result. The moment a part of philosophy became successful, it broke away from its parent discipline, became independent, and left philosophy further reduced in significance. After philosophy had given birth to natural science, it gave birth in the eighteenth and nineteenth centuries to the social sciences. Economics, psychology, anthropology, sociology, political science all emerged from philosophy, tore themselves away from their parent discipline, established themselves as independent empirical social sciences, and thus left philosophy more and more depleted. Then logic and linguistics became distinct from philosophy and established themselves as successful independent disciplines. Finally, in the twentieth century, cosmology, hitherto a branch of philosophy, became a successful empirical science dissociated from philosophy.

Academic philosophers, in the English-speaking world at least, became anguished as to what there was left for philosophy to do. It was decided that two tasks remained: attack bad philosophy – especially metaphysics; and engage in analysis – analysis of propositions or concepts. Philosophy ceased to tackle problems of the real world – that was the job of science – and instead engaged in the spurious intellectual activity of conceptual analysis.[18]

William Lycan, in a recently published paper, tells the story as a universally accepted platitude. He asks whether there have been any "permanent contributions" to philosophy since ancient Greece, and answers, "In one way, uncontroversially so: every science originated from philosophy, acquired some methodological underpinning, split off, and acquired a new name. Physics, biology, chemistry. Later, economics; psychology at the turn of the twentieth century; and in 1957, theoretical linguistics."[19]

But all this is nonsense. Even if the key points of the previous chapters of this book are ignored, especially points of chapters 2, 4, 7 and 9, nevertheless there is still an overwhelming case for the need to keep alive thinking about our fundamental problem, to be conducted in such a way that it interacts with the more specialized problem solving of the natural and social sciences and the humanities. Not only do results of the specialized sciences need to influence thought about our fundamental problem; the influence needs to go in the other direction as well, in that our best ideas about how to solve our fundamental problem may well have fruitful implications for research in the specialized sciences. The five views as to how the fundamental problem is to be solved, spelled out in chapter 2, have diverse implications for neuroscience, psychology, biology, physics. Furthermore, sustained thinking about our fundamental problem, carried on in such a way that it interacts with more specialized research is needed to counteract the rampant specialization that is such a feature of academia today. It is needed to ensure that academia puts into practice the four elementary rules of rational problem solving formulated in chapter 7, page 158. In failing to do all this, philosophy ensures that academia violates, in a structural way, *three* of the four most elementary rules of reason conceivable – rules 1, 2, and 4.

All this assumes we ignore key points made in this book. But if these points are *not* ignored but are, on the contrary, taken fully into account, the case for critical fundamentalism becomes overwhelming. In chapter 4, I made clear that it is a grave mistake to think that science needs to be, even can be, pursued independently of philosophy.[20] The orthodox, standard empiricist conception of science is untenable.[21] Physics, in persistently accepting unified theories only, makes a persistent, profoundly problematic *metaphysical*, or *philosophical*, assumption about the universe: it is such that physicalism is true. Even if some version of physicalism happens to be true (and it may not be), the specific version of physicalism accepted at any stage as physics proceeds is almost bound to be false, and will need to be replaced and improved. Physics needs actively to explore ideas for improved versions of physicalism as it proceeds, at the same time developing improved methods, such as symmetry principles, as it does so – all within the framework of aim-oriented empiricism. In other words, the task of improving the metaphysics of physics, and its associated methods, becomes a vital task of physics itself. That is, the philosophy of physics (insofar as it is devoted to the assumptions and methods of physics) becomes a vital part of physics itself. Physics cannot be dissociated from metaphysics, from philosophy of science, from philosophy, and the attempt to dissociate physics from philosophy damages physics and undermines its rationality, its intellectual integrity (in that it results in influential and problematic assumptions escaping critical appraisal).[22] In brief, physics ought to be pursued as natural philosophy within the methodological framework of aim-oriented empiricism, and not as science dissociated from philosophy. The traditional history of philosophy, told above, which concedes that science justifiably splits off from philosophy, gets things horribly wrong.

The blunders of this traditional history of philosophy are, if anything, even worse when it comes to the social sciences. Psychology, sociology, anthropology, economics, and the rest ought *not* to be pursued as empirical sciences dissociated from philosophy. Indeed, as we saw in chapter 7, they ought not to be pursued as empirical sciences at all – not, at least, when viewed from a fundamental standpoint. Rather, viewed from this standpoint, the social sciences are social *philosophy* or social *methodology*. Their primary concern is to promote increasingly cooperatively rational tackling of problems of living in the social world. On a more long-term basis, an additional concern is to get into the fabric of social life the aim-improving, progress-achieving methods of aim-oriented rationality arrived at by generalizing aim-oriented empiricism – the methods of science actually responsible for scientific progress, implicit in scientific practice to a considerable extent, despite misguided efforts of the scientific community to do science in accordance with the edicts of standard empiricism.

Insofar as social inquiry, as it ought to be pursued, does engage in empirical research to improve knowledge and understanding of social phenomena, it does so within the more fundamental framework of social philosophy and methodology. It does so to improve our understanding of what our problems of living are – including, of course, our grave global problems – and to assess critically proposals as to what we need to do to solve our problems of living, and thus make progress toward as good a world as possible. Empirical research into social phenomena is conducted as an integral part of, and to facilitate, increasingly cooperatively rational tackling of problems of living.[23]

Here, the orthodox philosophical view that it is entirely proper for social inquiry to dissociate itself from philosophy, and set itself up as empirical science, could not be more wrong. On the contrary, social inquiry needs to be pursued, not fundamentally as social science, but rather as *social philosophy* or *social methodology*. It is not just that social inquiry ought not to dissociate itself from philosophy. Rather, it ought *to continue to be philosophy itself* – social philosophy!

The implications of all this are, I hope, clear. It may in fact be the case that, over the centuries, philosophy has lost great chunks of its body as components have become successful, and have split off from their parent discipline, leaving philosophy severely depleted, an impotent shadow of its former self. But if so, it is all a disastrous mistake. It is not just philosophy that has been severely damaged and diminished by this process. Natural science and social inquiry have been damaged too. Our whole human world has suffered in that, as a result, we have failed to develop institutions of learning rationally and effectively devoted to helping us make progress toward a wiser, more civilized world. Nothing of the kind ought to have happened. Philosophy ought all along to have been pursued as critical fundamentalism, keeping alive thinking about our fundamental problem, engaged everywhere fruitfully with problem-solving going on in more particular circumstances: natural science, social inquiry, the humanities, technology, politics, industry, economics, law, the media, environmental problems, education. Critical fundamentalism potentially contributes to, and receives contributions from, all areas of problem solving in both thought and life.

Why, then, it may be asked, in even greater bafflement, has this not happened? If it is so obvious that it is vital to keep critical fundamentalism alive and kicking for almost all departments of thought and life, why have philosophers been blind to this need?

A part of the answer is that philosophy – that part of philosophy that values natural and social science – has taken for granted, almost without question, the orthodox, standard empiricist conception of science. This holds, as we have seen, that in science contributions are to be assessed impartially with respect to evidence, *there being no role whatsoever in science for metaphysics or philosophy*. Take this orthodox, standard empiricist conception of science for granted, and the story that philosophers tell about the reason for the decline of philosophy since the seventeenth century does gain a certain superficial plausibility. It becomes understandable, just about, that philosophers should see the history of their discipline as a process of immensely successful chunks breaking away and establishing themselves as independent empirical sciences, leaving academic philosophy today as a terminally unsuccessful, non-empirical residue.

But, as we have just seen, and as we saw in greater detail in chapter 4, standard empiricism is untenable. We need to reject standard empiricism and accept aim-oriented empiricism (AOE) in its stead. If we do, the story philosophers tell about the slow decline of philosophy becomes even more nonsensical. The idea that empirical science needs to break away from, and dissociate itself from, philosophy is just wrong. Natural science ought to be pursued as *natural philosophy*, a synthesis of science, metaphysics, and philosophy of science conducted within the methodological framework of AOE.

The argument for AOE has been in the literature since 1974, and has been developed in many publications since.[24] One would have thought that philosophers would have pounced on this argument, since it reveals that the story about the inevitable decline of philosophy is wrong – philosophy having a vital role to play as a part of science. Nothing of the kind has happened. The argument has been ignored, right down to the present.

FROM NATURAL PHILOSOPHY TO THE NEWTONIAN CONCEPTION OF SCIENCE

This dogged determination of philosophers to ignore the argument for AOE becomes all the more extraordinary when one takes into account that modern science *began as natural philosophy* – and only became *science* for rather disreputable reasons.

Kepler, Galileo, Descartes, Newton, Boyle, Hobbes, Huygens, Hooke, Locke, Spinoza, and Leibniz were all natural philosophers.

All were prepared to think about fundamental problems of metaphysics and philosophy in addition to tackling more specialized
problems of physics, astronomy, chemistry, physiology, psychology,
mathematics, mechanics, and technology. Philosophy as imaginative
and critical thinking about fundamental problems was alive and
well – and highly creative and productive. Both Kepler and Galileo
made careful observations and performed experiments, as good scientists should; but they also adopted a metaphysical view of nature
that held that "the book of nature is written in the language of mathematics," as Galileo famously put it. They both adopted the view, in
sharp contrast to the orthodox Aristotelian metaphysics of the time,
that simple mathematical laws govern the way natural phenomena
occur, and this metaphysical view played a crucial role in the discovery and acceptance of their great scientific discoveries concerning the
motions of the planets (Kepler), and the motion of terrestrial objects
(Galileo). Descartes, Huygens, Boyle, Newton, and others adopted
diverse versions of the then metaphysical view that the universe is
made up of atoms.

But then science did indeed break away from metaphysics, from
philosophy. A key event in this process was the publication of
Newton's *Principia*. Newton claimed, in the third edition at least,
to have derived his laws of motion and law of gravitation from the
phenomena by induction, thus apparently rendering philosophy and
metaphysics irrelevant.

Paradoxically, the first edition of Newton's *Principia*, published
in 1687, was quite explicitly a great work of natural philosophy.
There are, in the first edition, nine propositions all clearly labelled as
"hypotheses," some quite clearly of a metaphysical character. By the
third edition, the first two of these hypotheses had become the first
two "Rules of Reasoning," and the last five hypotheses, which concern the solar system, had become the "Phenomena" of later editions.
One hypothesis disappears altogether, and one other, not required
for the main argument, is tucked away among theorems. In the third
edition, there are two further "rules of reasoning," both inductive
in character. In connection with the second of these, Newton comments, "This rule we must follow, that the argument for induction
may not be evaded by hypotheses."[25] And Newton adds the following remarks concerning induction and hypotheses: "whatever is not
deduced from the phenomena is to be called an hypothesis; and
hypotheses, whether metaphysical or physical ... have no place in

experimental philosophy. In this philosophy, particular propositions are inferred from the phenomena, and afterwards rendered general by induction. Thus it was that ... the laws of motion and of gravitation were discovered."[26] In these and other ways, Newton sought to transform his great work in natural philosophy into a work of inductive science.

Newton hated controversy. He knew his law of gravitation was profoundly controversial, so he doctored subsequent editions of his *Principia* to hide the hypothetical, metaphysical, and natural philosophy elements of the work, and make it seem that the law of gravitation had been derived, entirely uncontroversially, from the phenomena by induction. Because of Newton's immense prestige, especially after his work was taken up by the French Enlightenment, subsequent natural philosophers took it for granted that success required that they proceed in accordance with Newton's methodology. Laws and theories had to be arrived at, or at least established, by means of induction from phenomena. Metaphysics and philosophy had become irrelevant, and could be ignored. Thus was modern science born, and natural philosophy, which had given rise to modern science in the first place, was quietly forgotten.[27]

Newton's inductivist methodology is still with us. It is known today as "inference to the best explanation."[28] (Newton did not ignore explanation. His Rules of Reasoning stressed that induction required one to accept that theory which is simplest and, in effect, gives the best explanation of phenomena.)[29] Scientists today may not hold that theories can be "deduced" from phenomena by induction, but they do hold that evidence alone (plus explanatory considerations) decides what theories are accepted and rejected in science. In other words, they take for granted one or other version of *standard empiricism*, the doctrine that evidence decides in science what theories are to be accepted and rejected, with the simplicity, unity or explanatory power of theories playing a role as well, but not in such a way that the world, or the phenomena, are assumed to be simple, unified, or comprehensible. The crucial point, as I have said, inherited from Newton is that *no thesis about the world can be accepted as a part of scientific knowledge independently of evidence, let alone in violation of evidence.* In essence, Newton's methodology of evidence and theory still dominates the scene. The decisive split between science and philosophy and the trivialization of the latter, which is one outcome, persists down to today.

HUME REFUTES THE NEWTONIAN
CONCEPTION OF SCIENCE

It is perhaps just about understandable that scientists and philosophers should, even today, doggedly uphold this Newtonian conception of science even though it was refuted decades ago.[30] It takes
time, perhaps, for philosophical arguments to sink in. What makes
the situation absolutely extraordinary, however, is that what I am
calling the Newtonian conception of science was refuted, not just
decades ago, but nearly three centuries ago, in 1738! It was decisively refuted by David Hume in his *Treatise of Human Nature*.[31]

Hume's argument, decisively demolishing the idea that theories
can be verified by evidence by means of induction, can be put like
this. However much evidence we gather in support of a law or
theory, it cannot verify it, or even render its probability greater than
zero. This is because any physical law or theory makes infinitely
many predictions, not just about the past and present, but the future
too, and possible states of affairs that have not, as yet, occurred (and
may never occur). We must always be infinitely far away from verifying all these infinitely many predictions of the theory. Put another
way, however well-established a theory is by evidence, there will
always be infinitely many different theories that agree about the evidence we have gathered so far, but disagree, in different ways, about
predictions for phenomena we have not yet observed, because they
are in the future, or because they concern possible states of affairs
or experiments not yet created. For example, if the accepted theory
is Newton's law of gravitation, one rival, until now just as empirically successful as Newton's theory, might assert: everything occurs
as Newton's theory predicts until 2050, when gravitation abruptly
becomes a repulsive force. Another such rival might assert: everything occurs as Newton's theory predicts except for gold spheres
in outer space over one thousand tons in mass, which attract each
other in accordance with an inverse cube law (instead of the inverse
square law of Newton's theory). These rivals are horribly disunified
and somewhat implausible: they are, however, for the moment, just
as empirically successful as Newton's theory. We can even concoct
endlessly many disunified rivals to Newton's theory that are even
more empirically successful by adding on to Newton's theory additional, independently testable hypotheses whose predictions have
been "verified."

Evidence cannot verify a theory. It cannot even select a theory, since infinitely many disunified rivals will always fit the available evidence equally well, or even better. (As I explained briefly in chapter 4, pages 73–4, a theory is disunified – to degree N – if it makes N different assertions about the actual and possible phenomena to which it applies; it is unified if N = 1.)

This argument, derived from Hume, demonstrates decisively that scientific laws and theories can never be verified by evidence to any degree of probability greater than zero however much supporting evidence we accumulate. It was a slightly more elaborate version of this argument that I employed in chapter 4 to refute standard empiricism, and make the way clear for the acceptance of the more rigorous conception of science of aim-oriented empiricism (AOE).

One would have thought that philosophers would have pounced triumphantly upon this result long ago, and argued for the rejection of the Newtonian conception of science and the revival of the more rigorous conjectural and metaphysical conception of natural philosophy to replace it.[32] That would have healed the split between science and philosophy, reintegrated the two, and massively restored the significance and good fortunes of philosophy. Bafflingly, philosophers have done nothing of the kind.[33] They have done just the opposite. They have insisted on trying to defend the Newtonian conception of science against Hume's attack right down to today,[34] and they have failed.[35] And it is no mystery why they have failed. Hume's argument is valid. The Newtonian conception of science must be rejected.

Thus, in striving to do the impossible and save Newton from Hume, philosophers help sustain the split between science and philosophy, and thus condemn their discipline to continuing triviality. The more one looks into the matter, the more baffling the whole thing becomes.

Philosophers may have persisted in believing that Hume's refutation of the Newtonian conception of science must, somehow, be invalid because they have thought that there is no alternative conception available. If that were the case, to accept that Hume is right would be to accept that there is no such thing as science.[36] But we have seen that such a view is a sheer mistake. There does indeed exist a viable alternative to what I am calling "the Newtonian conception of science." It is the view that science is really natural philosophy, conjectural in character, and such that metaphysical

conjectures are an integral part of scientific knowledge. As we have
seen, modern science began, in the hands of Kepler, Galileo, and
others, with the adoption of this hypothetical, natural philosophy
view. Furthermore, it was Newton's view, initially at least. It is the
view to be found in the first edition of Newton's *Principia*. The great
achievements of the *Principia* – Newton's laws of motion, his law of
gravitation, and their successful application to the solar system and
other phenomena – were all done within the framework of conjectural, metaphysical natural philosophy. Only later, in the second and
third editions of the *Principia*, did Newton transform the whole conception of science that was presupposed, so that conjectural natural
philosophy became inductivist, verificationist Newtonian science.
And Newton made this dramatic change for the very bad reason
that he hated criticism, and wanted to give his work the appear-
ance of being beyond criticism because it had all been derived by
induction from the evidence. What Hume's argument shows is that
Newton's dishonest, neurotic attempt to deflect criticism away from
his results just does not work.[37] Newton's law of gravitation cannot
be derived from the phenomena by induction – and nor can any
other physical law. Furthermore, as we saw in chapter 4, whereas
Hume's argument decisively demolishes the Newtonian conception
of science, and all standard empiricism conceptions accepted by
scientists and non-scientists alike today, it does not demolish conjectural and metaphysical natural philosophy and, in particular, the
version of it that I expounded in chapter 4: aim-oriented empiricism
(AOE). I there sketched how it is that AOE is able to do what standard empiricism cannot do – solve Hume's problem of induction.
As I have shown in much greater detail elsewhere, reasons can be
given for accepting metaphysical, physical, and empirical statements
of scientific knowledge at all the levels of AOE. Hume's problem of
induction is solved.[38]

Given all these points, it would seem to be bizarre in the extreme
that philosophers should persist in trying to save the Newtonian
conception of science from Hume's attack. Especially as, in doing
this, philosophers help to preserve the division between science and
philosophy, and the insignificance of the latter.[39]

Most philosophers, however, believe there are decisive arguments
against the idea that Hume's problem can be solved by appealing
to metaphysical principles – and thus to natural philosophy. As Bas
van Fraassen has put it so strikingly (in a remark I have quoted

on other occasions), "From Gravesande's axiom of the uniformity of nature in 1717 to Russell's postulates of human knowledge in 1948, this has been a mug's game."[40] First, any such approach has seemed hopeless because there can be no reason to accept the *truth* of any such metaphysical principle independent of evidence. And second, if evidence is appealed to, and some metaphysical principle – such as the uniformity of nature – is justified on the basis that it has supported empirical progress in science, and then that empirical progress in science is in turn justified by an appeal to the uniformity of nature, the whole procedure becomes viciously circular. One presupposes the very thing one seeks to justify.

Both objections fall by the wayside, however, given AOE.

First, AOE makes no attempt whatsoever to justify the truth of any metaphysical principle, by reason or in any other way. On the contrary, the basic argument is that physics inevitably makes a profoundly problematic metaphysical *conjecture*, which may well be false. Precisely because such a presupposition is no more than a *conjecture*, the specific version of it that is presupposed at any stage in the development of physics is all too likely to be false, it is essential that it is made explicit within physics so that it can be critically assessed and, we may hope, improved. It is the irrevocably *conjectural* character of the implicit metaphysical presuppositions of physics, together with their influential role in physics, that makes it so important to make them explicit, so that they can be critically assessed and improved. In the circumstances, it is pretending that science is pursued within the framework of standard empiricism, so that no such metaphysical assumption is made, that is the real mug's game. That pretence undermines the intellectual rigour of physics in suppressing influential, problematic metaphysical presuppositions which need *criticism* and *improvement*.

Second, the circularity problem is solved within the framework of AOE, as we saw briefly in chapter 4, note 20, and as I have shown elsewhere in some detail.[41] The positive feedback procedure of allowing metaphysical conjectures to influence choice of physical theory and, at the same time, of allowing physical theory to influence choice of metaphysical principles will, if done properly, go wrong only in certain sorts of "malicious" universes. Crucially, our universe is not such a malicious universe. That at least is asserted by one of the metaphysical theses in the hierarchy of theses of AOE: the thesis of "meta-knowability" at level 6. (It asserts that the universe is such that we can learn how to learn). And, absolutely crucially, the argument justifying acceptance of meta-knowability as an item of scientific knowledge makes no appeal whatsoever to the success of science. Meta-knowability thus provides a rational justification for the positive feedback procedure of permitting acceptance of meta-physical conjecture and physical theory to influence each other.[42]

There is perhaps one final crucial point that needs to be made to make plausible my claim that aim-oriented empiricism solves Hume's problem. It surely just does happen that scientific laws and theories are verified by evidence. If a hypothesis makes a variety of new predictions and, when they are checked, they all turn out to be correct, and no refutations are discovered, then surely our whole attitude to the hypothesis is transformed. Even if it is not the final truth, nevertheless we take its standard predictions to be reliable – even to the extent of trusting our lives with them (when we cross bridges, fly in airplanes, and take modern medicines). The Newtonian conception of science – putting Hume's argument entirely on one side for the moment – can do justice to all this. Conjectural natural philosophy and AOE cannot.

What AOE does provide, however, is a perfect *simulacrum* of verification of theory by evidence.[43] Why cannot a physical law or theory, such as Newton's law of gravitation, Einstein's theory of general relativity, or quantum theory, be verified by evidence? Primarily, because endlessly many grossly disunified versions of these theories can be concocted that make different predictions for as-yet unobserved phenomena, but are even more empirically successful than the theory we accept. However, granted physicalism, all these empirically more successful, disunified rivals are excluded from consideration because they clash with physicalism. Just that is what happens in scientific practice. Given a physical theory that accords reasonably well with both *physicalism* and *the evidence*, it is astonishingly difficult to think up a rival theory that satisfies both requirements even better, or even just as well. It is this that leads us to hold that a unified physical theory that has met with empirical success, and has not been refuted, has been verified by the evidence.[44]

Thus AOE provides a perfect simulacrum of verification of theory by evidence without it actually being verification. It is not verification because it requires acceptance of physicalism, which is a conjecture – even though one we are justified in accepting. There is a justification for the *acceptance* of physicalism as a part of scientific knowledge, but no justification of its truth. Standard empiricism dishonestly pretends to verify theories by means of evidence but does not in reality because of implicit, unacknowledged metaphysical conjectures; by contrast, AOE is openly and honestly conjectural in character, and furthermore subjects acknowledged metaphysical conjectures to sustained critical scrutiny.

The Newtonian and standard empiricist conceptions of science, by contrast, are quite unable to justify the manner in which theories are accepted in science. They may hold that an acceptable theory must be both *unified* and *empirically successful*, but no justification is forthcoming for persistent preference for unified over disunified theories even when the latter are more successful empirically. (And there is a failure to say what it is for a theory to be unified, as well.) The Newtonian and standard empiricist conceptions of science dishonestly pretend to verify theories by means of evidence but do not in reality because of implicit, unacknowledged metaphysical conjectures; AOE, by contrast, is openly and honestly conjectural in character, and furthermore subjects acknowledged metaphysical conjectures to sustained critical scrutiny.

One final point. Aim-oriented empiricism does not solve Hume's problem of induction, it may be argued, because it provides only a *simulacrum* of verification, not *real* verification. *Real verification* is what is required for a real solution to the problem.

What this final objection reveals, however, is a failure to appreciate just how all-pervasively cosmological conjectures lurk in our claims to knowledge – even in our humblest items of common sense knowledge, let alone in the far grander, more extensive claims to knowledge of science. I "know" (1) that this room in which I sit, as I type out these words, will continue to exist for the next ten seconds. But even this incredibly humble, particular item of common-sense knowledge has a cosmological assumption implicit in it. For in making this claim to knowledge I am implicitly claiming to "know" (2) that the entire cosmos is such that nowhere in it does there now occur a cosmic explosion that will travel at near infinite speed to engulf and destroy the earth, and this room and me, in the next five seconds. (1) is only true if (2) is true. If (2) is false, and a cosmic explosion is occurring now somewhere in the universe that will engulf me in the next five seconds, then (1) is false as well. Thus, I only "know" (1) if I "know" (2) as well.

If even our humblest items of common-sense knowledge have such cosmological conjectures implicit in them, we should not be surprised at all to learn that scientific knowledge, of far, far greater empirical content, has such cosmological or metaphysical conjectures implicit in it as well. It is just *that* that the argument for aim-oriented empiricism, spelled out in chapter 4 – a development of Hume's argument – shows to be the case. Newton's disreputable attempt to put his *Principia* beyond criticism has fooled all of us into thinking that our common sense and scientific knowledge is free of implicit assumptions about the nature of the universe. It is not. With every step we take we implicitly make an assumption about what kind of universe we are in. We are, in a sense, never free of implicit answers to our fundamental problem, implicit in what we do and how we think.

It is worth noting that the problem of induction arises because the attempt is made to *dissociate* science from its fundamental problem – what kind of universe is this? – the attempt being made to *specialize* in other words, and violate the basic idea of critical fundamentalism (which is of course to keep alive thinking about fundamental problems in such a way that it both influences, and is influenced by, more specialized problem solving, in accordance with basic rules of rational problem solving formulated on page 158). In seeking to remove *metaphysical hypotheses* from natural philosophy (theories being arrived at by induction from phenomena), Newton sought, in effect, to do just that: construe science in such a way that intellectual rigour required it to exclude all metaphysical hypotheses about the ultimate nature of the universe, and attend only to empirically testable laws and theories, and evidence.

But this attempt to construe science in such a way that it is dissociated from metaphysical speculation about the ultimate nature of the universe, far from delivering a *rigorous* conception of science, does exactly the opposite: it generates Hume's insoluble problem of induction. It is profoundly *irrational* to try to specialize in this way, to dissociate science from sustained thinking about the fundamental problem that science seeks to solve.

It ought to have been obvious that science cannot be dissociated in this way from its fundamental problem – from metaphysical views about what sort of universe this is.[45] A universe of the kind envisaged by the ancient Greeks, the outcome of the wilful deeds and conflicts of rather adolescent gods, would require a very different kind of science from the one that we have today. It would be a science that seeks to improve our knowledge and understanding of the gods: who they are, what they want, what pleases and displeases them, what we can do to induce them to behave in ways beneficial to us. In such a universe, attempting to do science as we do it today might be profoundly counterproductive. It might anger the gods and prompt them to harm us in ways that ancient Greek myths portray so vividly!

The problem of induction is, in short, a product of *specialization*. I pointed this out decades ago, in Maxwell 1980, 46–7, and 74n34.[46] The point has been, of course, ignored.

CONCLUSION

Modern philosophy since Descartes has been a bit of an intellectual and humanitarian disaster. It began well with Descartes's attempted solution to our fundamental problem, but then lost the plot, as we have seen, as a result of becoming obsessed with problems generated by Cartesian dualism *even though, paradoxically, Descartes's view itself was widely rejected*! The basic task of critical fundamentalism of keeping alive imaginative and critical (i.e., rational) thinking about our fundamental problem was lost sight of. This happened in part because of long-standing intellectual failures in connection with two basic philosophical problems.

First there was the failure just mentioned, the failure just to *formulate* adequately the mind-body problem – or rather the human world/physical universe problem. As a result of becoming locked into problems generated by Cartesian dualism – even though Cartesian dualism had been rejected – philosophers down the centuries expounded a series of doctrines that made it *impossible* to formulate the human world/physical universe problem. Philosophy as it should be pursued – as critical fundamentalism – was lost sight of and betrayed. And even if, today, things have improved a bit so that it is now possible at least to *formulate* our fundamental problem, this is still not the way academic philosophy is pursued. Traditional conceptions of philosophy linger on.

Second, there has been the failure to solve the problem of induction ever since it was first formulated by Hume in 1738. This failure is the result of the dogged conviction of philosophers that it must be possible to verify scientific theories by evidence to some degree of probability at least, and thus defend the Newtonian conception of science against Hume's skepticism. Formulate the problem in that way, and it is insoluble. But it should have been obvious, all along, that this is the wrong way to formulate the problem. Hume's argument is valid. It shows decisively that the Newtonian conception of science (still, essentially, taken for granted by scientists and non-scientists today) is untenable. But this should have been obvious in any case, on other grounds. Modern science began as natural philosophy, metaphysical conjectures about the nature of the universe an inherent element of the enterprise. The first edition of Newton's *Principia* is quite explicitly a very great contribution to natural philosophy in just this sense. But then, in subsequent editions, Newton did what he could to deceive the reader into thinking that he had derived his laws of motion and law of gravitation from evidence by induction. Hating controversy, he did what he could to pull the wool over people's eyes – and succeeded all too well! The outcome was the dissociation of science from philosophy, the impoverishment of the latter as a result, and the insoluble problem of induction as a bonus.

Refuse to abandon natural philosophy, develop it within the framework of AOE, and philosophy continues to be a vital, integral part of natural science. It retains its vitality and significance, and Hume's problem of induction is resolved. If natural philosophy had indeed developed in this way, in line with the first edition of Newton's *Principia*, our intellectual, cultural, and social worlds would now be very different from the way they are.

We need urgently to reform philosophy so that it takes up its proper basic task of keeping alive thinking about our fundamental problem. At the heart of the university, interacting in both directions with all more specialized disciplines from physics to the humanities, we need to have a seminar devoted to exploring, imaginatively and critically, the problem: *How can our human world exist and best flourish embedded as it is in the physical universe?* Take this problem seriously, along the lines I have indicated in this book, and it is at once obvious that there is a horrendous enigma as to how people, an integral part of the physical universe, can succeed in improving the aims they pursue in life so that they come to realize what is genuinely of value. We have come to be aim-pursuing beings in the physical universe as a result of Darwinian evolution. But Darwinian evolution presupposes a fixed basic aim for all life: survival and reproductive success. The mechanism of evolution may be very good at enhancing our capacity to achieve pre-set aims; but these mechanisms do nothing to create the capacity to *improve* basic aims so that it is not just survival and reproductive success that we pursue (or some rein-terpretation of this aim such as imagined survival and reproductive success via religion, political power, wealth, creative endeavour, or fame), but survival of *what is of value*, and reproductive success that is *of value*. Somehow we have to learn how so to evolve aims and methods, at personal, institutional, and social levels, so that basic aims implicit in our actions, all too likely to be problematic, evolve toward what is of value. And for that, our institutions of learning, our schools and universities, need to be so designed that they help us with the task. We need urgently to transform our universities around the world – or at least where this can be done – so that they come to have, as a basic task, to help us resolve conflicts and problems of living in more cooperatively rational ways. And, as an integral part of that task, we need social inquiry and the humanities in particular to help us get aim-oriented rationality built into our institutions, into our cul-ture and social world, so that the milieu in which we live facilitates the discovery of what is of value, and how it is to be realized.

If philosophes of the eighteenth century Enlightenment had done their job properly, and had put all their wit, argument, and pas-sion into creating wisdom-inquiry, we might have been able to avoid some of the tragedies and horrors of the nineteenth, twentieth, and twenty-first centuries, and we might now live in a world very differ-ent from the one that confronts us, menaced by grim inequalities, war, nuclear weapons, devastation of the natural world, the insane politics of Trump, Putin, and Xi Jinping, and the impending disasters of climate change. If we delay much longer in creating institutions of learning rationally devoted to helping us realize what is of value in life, our social-economic-political world may become so grim that academic reform becomes impossible, or irrelevant.

The reader of this book may come to the conclusion that what I argue for amounts to such a vast intellectual, institutional, cultural, and social change that it is hopelessly utopian to think it could all come about. But revolutions in the way people think and live have come about in the past. It can be done. There is hope for the future.

Notes

CHAPTER ONE

1 Quarks are electrically charged particles, either one-third or two-thirds of
the charge of the electron. Three quarks go to make up a proton, and three
different quarks to make up a neutron. They interact with one another via
the exchange of particles called gluons. Gluons stick quarks together to
form protons and neutrons, and they do this so firmly that it is impossible
to isolate individual quarks.

2 Philosophers tend to discuss components of this fundamental problem
such as: What does science tell us about the world? Does it provide
knowledge of unobservable, fundamental physical entities? Or does it
provide knowledge about observable phenomena only? How is the mind,
or consciousness, related to the brain? What knowledge do we acquire as
a result of perception? Can we have free will if the universe is deterministic? How are moral statements to be analyzed? What is it for something to
possess intrinsic value? Three books by philosophers that do discuss many
aspects of the fundamental problem are Smart 1963; Nagel 1986; and
Chalmers 1996. For my own earlier efforts at tackling the fundamental
problem, see Maxwell 2001a; 2010a; 2019a. For even earlier efforts, see
my first three published papers: Maxwell 1966; 1968a; 1968b, extracted
from my master's thesis, "Physics and Common Sense: A Critique of
Physicalism," 1965, Manchester University. I differ from many of my philosophy colleagues in that, unlike them, from the outset I have put the fundamental problem at the heart of all my work: see Maxwell 2019a,
chapters 1 and 2.

3 Paleontology is the study of fossils; ecology is the study of interactions between different living things, and between them and the environment; neuroscience is the study of the brain.

4 Galileo reinvented the telescope, pointed it at the night sky, and made many discoveries, including the one about the Milky Way, which he reported in his book *The Starry Messenger*, published in 1610: see Galileo 1957, 21–58.

5 1 billion = 1 thousand million = 1,000,000,000 = 10^9.

6 A light year is the distance light travels in one year. In one second light travels 186,000 miles. A light year is roughly 6 million million miles (10^{12} miles).

7 There are 118 elements, but elements at the top end of the scale – elements that have the greatest number of protons in their nuclei – tend to decay rapidly, being short-lived. Ninety-eight elements are found naturally on earth, some in minute quantities.

8 For nontechnical introductions to the mysteries of wave/particle duality and quantum theory, see Al-Khalili 2003; Kumar 2008; Rae 1992; Squires 1986. For my own views about how to solve the quantum wave/particle mystery, see Maxwell 1976b; 1988; 1994b; 2017b, 135–51; 2018a.

9 See Lane 2009, chapter 1.

10 For a fascinating account of the evolution of photosynthesis on earth, together with an account of the history of the scientific work struggling to understand how it works, see Morton 2009. See also Lane 2009, chapter 3.

CHAPTER TWO

1 I suggested this pyramid structure of problems and their attempted resolution in Maxwell 1980.

2 For Plato's actual arguments for the idea that philosophers should rule, see Plato 1970. For a devastating criticism, see Popper 1962, vol. 1.

3 These introductory remarks (amplifying what I said in the preface) are intended to indicate how philosophy, as I conceive of it, differs from, is related to, and can contribute to and receive contributions from, other disciplines. A fundamental task of philosophy is to combat what I have called *specialism* – the doctrine that only specialized intellectual standards and disciplines are worthwhile. The basic task of philosophy is to keep alive awareness of our fundamental problem – awareness of its unsolved character, the impact that ideas about how it is to be solved, good and bad, can have on other departments of thought, and on life too: see Maxwell 1980; 2017b; 2019a. This issue will be taken up again in chapter 9 and the appendix.

4 All my work, from my first paper published in 1966, has been done in the spirit of critical fundamentalism: see Maxwell 2019a for an account of it. For an earlier exposition of the argument that this is what philosophy ought to be, see Maxwell 2014b, especially chapter 2. See also Maxwell 2019a, 145–57, where I refer explicitly to critical fundamentalism; and see Maxwell 2017b; 2019e.

5 For a brilliant account of the devastating Christian destruction of the classical world – its art, architecture, literature, philosophy, and civilization – see Nixey 2018.

6 Feynman 1963, chapter 1, 1–2.

7 Atomism solves the problem of change by segregating sharply that which does not change (the internal properties of atoms) from that which does change (the relative positions of atoms to each other). It is not a very good solution to the philosophical problem of change, however, because it is much too specific. All that is required to solve the problem of how something can both persist and change, which might be thought to be a contradiction, is the observation that we can, in any way we wish, distinguish what may be called *essential* and *accidental* properties of a thing. The essential properties are those we decide the thing must possess if it is to be this particular thing in question. Accidental properties are those the thing may lose without ceasing to be this specific thing. We can now make perfect sense of the idea that the thing changes but preserves its identity through these changes. This will be the case if only accidental properties change or are lost.

8 A slightly different translation is quoted in Guthrie 1978, 440.

9 Nicolaus Copernicus (1473–1543), Polish mathematician and astronomer, put forward the theory that the sun is at the centre of the solar system, and the planets, including the earth, go round it – a theory put forward over 1500 years earlier by Aristarchus (310–230 BCE), a Greek mathematician and philosopher. Copernicus was horrified by the complexity of the generally accepted theory due to Ptolemy (AD 100–170), which put the earth at the centre, with the sun and other planets going round the earth. Unfortunately, as Copernicus developed his own theory to take observations of the planets into account, it became increasingly complicated, and in the end, according to his theory, the planets went round, not the sun, but a point in space some distance from the sun! Copernicus published his theory more or less when on his deathbed in a book called *On the Revolutions of the Celestial Spheres*.

10 Johannes Kepler (1571–1630), a German astronomer and mathematician, discovered three key laws of planetary motion. He discovered that the

planets move in ellipses around the sun, and that the line joining a planet to the sun sweeps out equal areas in equal times. There is a wonderful account of Kepler in (Koestler 1964).

11 Galileo Galilei (1564–1642), Italian astronomer, physicist, mathematician, and philosopher, played a major role in bringing about the scientific revolution that led to the birth of modern science. He discovered the moon has craters and mountains, Jupiter has moons, and, as I mentioned in chapter 1, the milky way is made up of stars – all reported in his *The Starry Messenger* which became famous throughout Europe when first published in 1610: see Galileo 1957, 21–58. He discovered and demonstrated that objects fall with constant acceleration and projectiles trace out the path of a parabola near the earth's surface. He was accused by the Inquisition of defending Copernicus's theory, and spent the remaining years of his life under house arrest. At his trial he denied he defended the view that the earth goes round the sun, but is supposed to have muttered under his breath "And yet it moves."

12 René Descartes (1596–1650), French philosopher, mathematician, and scientist, is famous for engaging in a program of systematic doubt to discover a residue of certainty, beyond doubt, upon which the new edifice of knowledge could be built. He hit upon "I think, therefore I am." The very activity of doubting meant he could not deny that he doubted, and therefore that he himself existed. The existence of God, and that which corresponds to "clear and distinct ideas" soon followed. Descartes's physics was soon superseded by Newton's, although it continued to linger on in France until 1750, but Descartes's philosophy is still influential today. His most notable contribution to philosophy is what became known after him as Cartesian dualism: see Descartes (1949). According to David Wootton, Descartes stole most of his ideas from a Dutch natural philosopher, Isaac Beeckman: see Wootton 2016, 361–4.

13 Christiaan Huygens (1629–1695), Dutch physicist, mathematician, and astronomer, sought to develop and apply Descartes's physics. He put forward a wave theory of light.

14 Robert Hooke (1635–1703), English physicist, astronomer, biologist, paleontologist, and inventor, made major discoveries in a range of disciplines. For much of his working life, Hooke was employed as curator of experiments by the newly formed Royal Society. It was Hooke's job to prepare experiments for the society's meetings. Hooke was the first to grasp the basic principles of the solar system: objects travel with uniform velocity in straight lines unless impressed by a force; the planets move round the sun because of the attractive force of gravitation between sun

and planets. Newton got the idea from Hooke, but failed to acknowledge Hooke's role in the *Principia*. For a magnificent account of Hooke's life and work, see Inwood 2003.

15 Robert Boyle (1627–1691), Anglo-Irish chemist and physicist, is best known today for Boyle's law, which states that pressure and volume are inversely related for a given quantity of gas. Boyle all but founded modern experimental chemistry with his *The Sceptical Chymist*, published in London in 1660.

16 Isaac Newton (1642–1727), one of the greatest scientists ever, was really, like his contemporaries, a natural philosopher. It was Newton's great achievement to formulate the basic principles of what we now call "Newtonian mechanics" and then demonstrate that these principles, plus his law of gravitation, were able to predict very precisely the motions of planets, moons, and comets, and other phenomena, in his *Principia Mathematica* published in 1687. Newton claimed to have derived his law of gravitation from the phenomena by induction, but this claim is a bit dubious, especially as the phenomena amounted to applications of Kepler's laws, which Newton went on to *correct*! Newton's *Principia* is, nevertheless, a brilliant work of profound significance. Newton himself was, however, in many ways an unpleasant character. He quarrelled with both Hooke and Flamstead (astronomer royal) and did everything in his power, as President of the Royal Society, to destroy their work and scientific reputation.

17 For two excellent, recent accounts of the scientific revolution of the sixteenth and seventeenth centuries, see Cohen 2010; Wootton 2016. Both fail, however, to emphasize sufficiently the key role that empirically untestable metaphysics played in the scientific revolution; for that see Maxwell 2017b, chapters 1 and 2.

18 Newton 1952, 400.

19 Burtt 1932, 266.

20 Newton was, in many ways, at odds with most of his contemporary natural philosophers in having an almost medieval cast of mind.

21 Modern atomic physics and quantum theory require us to stretch our imaginations considerably beyond what Galileo here thought he was capable of.

22 Galileo 1957, 274.

23 Newton 1952, 124–5.

24 Zeki 1993, 238.

25 Kepler discovered that the image on the retina of the eye is upside down. Initially, there was bafflement as to how we can see the world the right

way up if this is the case. But then the thought dawned that, just as we
don't see the world external to us directly, so also we don't see the image
of the world on our retina. Only when signals transmitted along the optic
nerve have delivered their message to the brain does the miracle occur, and
we have the experience of seeing.

26 Viewed from the standpoint of critical fundamentalism, it is what physics
seems to tell us about the universe and what the causal account of perception seems to imply that go to the heart of the philosophical problem of perception. Perception constitutes a key link between the two continents of the
human world/physical universe problem, the physical universe on the one
hand, our human world on the other. Not all philosophers agree. Tim Crane
and Craig French, in their survey article "The Problem of Perception," interpret the problem to be about illusions and hallucinations, and make no
mention of the implications of physics for perception at all: see Crane and
French 2017. But other philosophers disagree. Barry Maund, in his survey
article on the related subject of colour, appreciates that a major problem
"with color has to do with fitting what we seem to know about colors into
what science (not only physics but the science of color vision) tells us about
physical bodies and their qualities": see Maund 2017. Unfortunately,
Maund fails to go on to discuss the crucial question as to what it is precisely
that physics does tell us about physical bodies: see Maxwell 2019a, 61.

27 Descartes suggested that the brain and mind interact via the pineal gland –
not a very plausible idea given our modern knowledge of the brain. For a
more recent advocacy of interactionism, see Popper and Eccles 1977.

28 Locke 1961.

29 Berkeley 1957.

30 David Hume (1711–1776), Scottish philosopher, was a leading member of
the Scottish Enlightenment. When twenty-seven, he published *A Treatise
of Human Nature* which, he said, "fell dead-born from the press." In his
lifetime he was better known for his multivolume *History of England* than
he was for his philosophical works. He is now generally regarded as one
of the greatest philosophers ever. His masterpiece, the *Treatise*, is an
unwitting *reductio ad absurdum* of extreme empiricism – the doctrine that
everything can be derived from sense impressions. The *Treatise* gets everything wrong, but with such scrupulous honesty that Hume's reputation as
one of the greatest philosophers ever is richly deserved.

31 Immanuel Kant (1724–1804) was a German philosopher of almost
impenetrable obscurity who tried to answer Hume in his most famous
and most obscure work *The Critique of Pure Reason*, first published in
1781. In his *Prolegomena to Any Future Metaphysics* Kant says that it

was Hume who awoke him from his "dogmatic slumber" in convincing him that there is a serious problem as to how there can be knowledge of the natural world: see Kant 1959, 9. Many hold Kant to be one of the very greatest philosophers, an opinion I do not share. He lacks the clarity and honesty of Hume. The problem Kant tried to solve – How can we have absolutely certain knowledge of the natural world? – is the *wrong* problem. It cannot be solved. We cannot have such knowledge: all our knowledge is ultimately conjectural, although some is more conjectural than others of it: see Maxwell 2017a. Furthermore, Kant's great idea that our experiences must have a certain order to be conscious does not achieve what Kant wants it to achieve. The world might be sufficiently orderly for us to be conscious, and yet objects might appear and disappear, from time to time, in a way that violates all physical laws. To his credit, Kant did argue for world democracy and peace, and held that persons should be treated as ends, and not as means to other ends (that is, should never be exploited).

32 John Stuart Mill (1806–1873) was an influential English philosopher and member of parliament who wrote powerfully in defence of the freedom of the individual.

33 Bertrand Russell (1872–1970) was a famous English philosopher, logician, and campaigner for peace and against nuclear weapons. He wrote with clarity and wit on a wide range of topics, but never really managed to escape from the constraints of British empiricism.

34 Ernst Mach (1838–1916) was an Austrian physicist and philosopher who criticized Newton's metaphysical ideas about space and time, and held that physics should be interpreted in terms of sense data (that is, sense impressions).

35 Albert Einstein (1879–1955) was a German natural philosopher of the modern period who put forward special and general relativity and made significant contributions to the development of quantum theory. In his paper expounding special relativity, he remarked that he had been influenced by Hume.

36 The logical positivists were a group of philosophers based mainly in Vienna between the two world wars who held that a proposition, in order to be meaningful, must be verifiable. They hoped in this way to eliminate all metaphysics as unverifiable meaninglessness, but were defeated by the realization that much of science, which they sought to defend, cannot be verified either. With the rise of Hitler, many logical positivists fled to the United States where they defended a weakened form of their doctrine, logical empiricism, which asserts merely that terms of a scientific theory, in

order to be meaningful, must be linked to observation statements by means of so-called "bridge statements." This doctrine succumbed to criticism as well.

37 A.J. Ayer (1910–1989) was a well-known English philosopher who expounded logical positivism to an English audience in a famous book *Language, Truth and Logic* (1936).

38 Johann Gottlieb Fichte (1762–1814) and Friedrich Wilhelm Schelling (1775–1854) were German idealist philosophers.

39 Friedrich Schleiermacher (1768–1834) was a German philosopher and biblical scholar.

40 Georg Wilhelm Friedrich Hegel (1770–1831) was an immensely influential German philosopher, often characterized as holding that history advances by means of a process of thesis, antithesis, synthesis. For a scathing criticism, see Popper 1962, vol. 2, chapter 12.

41 Arthur Schopenhauer (1788–1860) was an influential German philosopher who held that the world as we experience it is the outcome of a fundamental blind *will* – a view expounded in his *The World as Will and Representation* published in 1818.

42 Edmund Husserl (1859–1938) was a German idealist philosopher concerned with the nature of consciousness. He held that intentionality is a key feature of the contents of consciousness: perceptions, ideas, desires are always about some object beyond themselves.

43 Martin Heidegger (1889–1976) was a German idealist philosopher, still influential today. His best known work is *Being and Time*, published in 1927, concerned with our *Being*, characterized by *care*, and deeply affected by its relationship to *time*; it is too obscure to summarize in this brief note. Heidegger was sympathetic toward, and a member of, the Nazi party.

44 T.H. Green (1836–1882), F.H. Bradley (1846–1924), and J.M.E. McTaggart (1866–1925) were English idealist metaphysical philosophers, the first two at Oxford, the last at Cambridge.

45 Jean-Paul Sartre (1905–1980) was a famous French existentialist philosopher whose best-known philosophical work, *Being and Nothingness*, published in 1943, was massively influenced by Heidegger. Sartre was also a novelist, playwright, and political activist.

46 Maurice Merleau-Ponty (1908–1961), French idealist philosopher, was concerned with perception and how experience acquires meaning. He wrote about art, literature, and politics.

47 Michel Foucault (1926–1984) was a French philosopher and historian of ideas who wrote about the relationship between knowledge and power.

48 Jacques Derrida (1930–2004) was a French philosopher engaged in a kind of analysis called deconstructionism. He is regarded by some as a major figure in the fields of post-structuralism and postmodern philosophy.

49 Gottfried Wilhelm Leibniz (1646–1716), German philosopher and mathematician, invented the differential calculus independently of Newton. He put forward a strange view in his *Monadology*, according to which the universe is made up of point-like monads which contain, within themselves, images of what is in other monads, some monads barely conscious, others being the minds of conscious persons: see Leibniz 1956, 3–20.

50 Baruch Spinoza (1632–1677) was a Dutch philosopher who worked humbly as a lens grinder. His magnum opus, *Ethics*, published posthumously in 1677, takes as its model Euclid's *Elements*. It begins with a few definitions and axioms and then proceeds to derive theorems. Spinoza defends the two-aspect view. The mental aspect of Nature is God, the mental aspect of our brain is our consciousness.

51 Every now and again, philosophers agonize over the failure of philosophy to make progress: for a recent example, see Dietrich 2011.

52 In Maxwell 2017b I give an account of how modern science began as natural philosophy – a synthesis of what we now call science and philosophy. This synthesis then broke apart, partly as a result of Newton's claim to have derived his law of gravitation from the phenomena, but mainly because of the failure of philosophers even to formulate properly, let alone solve, two fundamental problems: the physical universe/human world problem, and the problem of induction (the problem of how scientific theories can be verified, or even selected, by means of evidence). I conclude that we need to put science and philosophy together again to create a modern version of natural philosophy. I return to these issues in the appendix.

53 See especially Popper 1962, which tackles profound problems that arise in connection with attempts to move from tribal to open, liberal, democratic societies, and criticizes major thinkers, such as Plato and Marx, who have, in different ways, opposed and argued against liberal democratic societies – the "Enemies" of the open society.

54 See Popper 1963, chapter 2.

55 Academic philosophy has not even organized itself so as to put our fundamental problem at the heart of the discipline of philosophy itself – let alone at the heart of *all* disciplines.

56 Two early defenders of Materialism in the modern period were Julien Offray de La Mettrie (1709–1751) and Baron d'Holbach (1723–1789), both members of the French Enlightenment. La Mettrie published *L'homme*

machine in 1748, in which he argued that the human being is a machine; d'Holbach published *Le Système de la Nature* in 1770, in which he defended atheism and a thoroughgoing materialism and determinism. For a twentieth-century defence of a thoroughgoing version of physicalism, see Smart 1963. For a more recent discussion of physicalism by a philosopher, together with further references on the subject, see Stoljar 2017.

57 Classic texts that can be regarded as defending aspects of naive realism are G.E. Moore, *A Defence of Common Sense*, in Moore 2002; Austin 1962; Ryle 1949; van Fraassen 1980.

58 See Spinoza 1955, *Ethics*, first published in 1677.

59 For a survey, see Maxwell 2001a, chapter 4.

60 This line of thought is further developed in Maxwell 2010a. See also Maxwell 2001a.

61 In Maxwell 2010a I argue that the fundamental problem, as I have formulated it here (the human world/physical universe problem) can be regarded as a rational development of a traditional religious formulation of the problem – one that construes human life as being created and sustained by God. Modify traditional conceptions of God to resolve problems that these traditional conceptions give rise to, and we end up with the human world/physical universe problem as formulated in this book. That, at least, is what I argue in Maxwell 2010a.

CHAPTER THREE

1 Specialization is often accompanied by the failure to give serious attention to the task of articulating, and improving the articulation of, *problems*. It is as if the assumption is made that what problems we should be trying to solve, and how they are to be understood, is entirely unproblematic, the only important task being to solve them. Nothing could be further from the truth. Often the key step required to solve a real-life problem – as opposed to a problem in an exam – is to improve the formulation of the problem, improve our understanding of it. Popper, for one, has repeatedly stressed the importance of articulating problems: see, for example, Popper 1976, chapter 29.

2 Reductionists hold that everything can, in principle, be reduced to physics. Emergentists hold that, as more complex physical systems arise, new properties or features *emerge* that cannot, even in principle, be reduced to physics.

3 I first argued for this *double comprehensibility* view in Maxwell 1984, 174–89 and 264–75, although it is hinted at earlier in Maxwell 1968b. It

is further developed in Maxwell 2000b; 2001a, chapter 5; 2010a, especially chapters 7–8; and 2019a, especially chapters 1 and 2).

4 As I have already remarked, the two-aspect conjectured solution to the physical universe/human world problem goes back to Spinoza. I first put forward elements of the version of the view I have just indicated in Maxwell 1966; 1968a; 1968b. Some of the content of these papers was subsequently put forward by Nagel 1974; Jackson 1982, 1986; Tooley 1977; Armstrong 1983; Ellis 2001; and Bird 2007 – although, unfortunately, the key tenets of what I proposed in 1966 and 1968 were lost sight of, especially the point that the mind-body problem needs to be put into the context of the broader, more fundamental physical universe/human world problem. Subsequently, I developed the two-aspect view further: see Maxwell 1974; 1980; 1984, chapters 8 and 10; 1998; 2000b; 2001a; 2004a; 2010a; 2011a; 2012a; 2014a; 2014b; 2017a; 2017b. In Maxwell 2019a I give an account of my work on the human world/physical universe problem from my first publication in 1966 onward, and go on to show that subsequent work by others on the mind-body problem and the metaphysics of science ignores my earlier work and suffers as a result. This applies to Nagel 1986; Davidson 1970; Dennett 1991b; Chalmers 2015, 2016; Sehon 2005; Ellis 2001; Bird 2007; Ladyman et al. 2007, and the work of many other contemporary philosophers.

5 See Maxwell 1966, 307.

6 Astonishingly, some philosophers have argued that physics has nothing to do with causation: see Russell 1951, chapter 9; Redhead 1990; Norton 2003; Ladyman et al. 2007, chapter 5. For a decisive refutation of this extraordinary view, see Maxwell 2019a, 122–5.

7 This cancels a possible reason for holding that objective sensory qualities do *not* exist. It does not establish that they *do* exist. J.J.C. Smart is a classic example of a philosopher who denies that anything exists over and above the physical: see Smart 1963. Most scientists, and many philosophers, do, however, tend to think that the silence of physics (and that part of science in principle reducible to physics) about *perceptual* qualities of things, their colour, sound, feel, as we experience them, *is* a good reason for holding that these perceptual qualities do not really, objectively, exist in the world around us. Actually, the silence of physics about the experiential, whether of processes going on within or without our heads, is the same: it provides no grounds whatsoever for holding that experiential qualities do not really, objectively exist – as I shall argue in what follows.

8 In practice, all sorts of limitations would arise as to what could be predicted, even if we possessed the true physical "theory of everything," T. In

all likelihood, the equations of T could be solved, if at all, only for the very simplest of physical systems. Knowledge of the instantaneous physical state of such a system would be only approximate, which would soon lead to inaccuracies in predictions we make with T. None of this means that T itself does not, in principle, make precise predictions on the basis of precise specification of instantaneous states of affairs.

9 If T is a field theory, we can put matters like this. We require that T, together with a precise specification of the state of the field throughout a spatial region R_o at some instant, implies the state of the field throughout a smaller region R_I at some later time, where R_I is such that light (and so any causal influence) that comes from outside R_o cannot enter R_I. As long as nothing can travel faster than light, this ensures that R_o and T determine the state of the field throughout R_I, given that T is a true, comprehensive, deterministic theory. A physical *field* is a physical entity spread out smoothly throughout space that varies with time. The electric field, the magnetic field, and their synthesis, the electromagnetic field, are examples.

10 For a more detailed account of this refutation of Hume on causation and the demonstration that it is possible that necessary connections between successive states of affairs exist, see Maxwell 1968a. For a more recent and more readable account, see Maxwell 2019a, chapter 1.

11 This account of the task of theoretical physics, involving the refutation of Hume on causation, was first put forward decades ago: see Maxwell 1968a. The physics community has not taken it up because of the intellectual disease of rampant specialization. The proposed realignment of the task of physics is not itself a testable idea, and does not, therefore, belong to physics. It belongs to another discipline altogether, philosophy of science. As a result, it will not reach the eyes or ears of physicists. Tooley 1977, Armstrong 1983, Ellis 2001, and Bird 2007 echo some of the argument of my 1968 paper, but miss the essential point that the fundamental laws of physics are to be interpreted as being analytic, as a result the physical state of affairs at one instant determining what exists next with *logical* (or analytic) *necessity* – as long as deterministic physicalism, appropriately interpreted, is true. The penalty for missing this basic point is that, for Tooley and company, the connection between successive states of affairs can only be that of *metaphysical necessity* – a dubious notion. For what is in my view a decisive criticism of this notion, see van Fraassen 1989; this criticism, however, fails to consider, and does not apply to, the account of physical necessity I give in Maxwell 1968a – lucidly expounded in Maxwell 2019a, chapter 1.

12 All the arguments that follow work just as well if the stronger, unorthodox version of physicalism is assumed, so that T is interpreted essentialistically, and precise specifications of instantaneous states of affairs themselves logically entail subsequent states of affairs.

13 This argument is usually attributed to Thomas Nagel 1974 and Frank Jackson 1982 and 1986, but was actually first spelled out by me several years earlier: see Maxwell 1966, especially 303–8; and Maxwell 1968b, especially 127, 134–7, and 140–1. When I drew Thomas Nagel's attention to these publications, he remarked in a letter, with great generosity, "There is no justice. No, I was unaware of your papers, which made the central point before anyone else." Frank Jackson acknowledged, however, that he had read my 1968 paper.

14 See Maxwell 2000b. This proposed solution to the problem of why physics is silent about the experiential requires there to be a good account of what it is for a physical theory to be *unified*, and so *explanatory*. This will emerge in the next chapter.

15 This way of putting it is due to J.J.C. Smart: see Smart 1963, 94–7.

16 We see here that in order to solve the philosophical part of the mind-body problem it is essential to put that problem into the broader, more fundamental context of the physical universe/human world problem.

17 I distinguished these two different distinctions between objective and subjective in Maxwell 2000b, 56. It is hinted at in Maxwell 1966, 310–1.

18 See Maxwell 1968b, 142–3.

19 Conscious head processes have both mental and physical features. Or, putting this slightly differently, conscious inner experiences are identical to brain processes. There is a famous argument due to Saul Kripke 1986 that claims to show that, if this identity holds, it must be *necessary*, not *contingent* or *factual*. That the identity is *necessary* has seemed so implausible to many philosophers that they have concluded that this identity of inner experiences and brain processes must be wrong. However, elsewhere I have shown decisively that Kripke's argument is invalid, indeed almost nonexistent: see Maxwell 2001a, 259–73 or, better, Maxwell 2019a, 189–208, which includes an additional, decisive refutation of Kripke. There is no valid objection to holding that inner experiences are contingently identical to brain processes.

20 See Maxwell 2001a, 126–31; 2011a.

21 See Kahneman 2011. Kahneman's book is very good on the illusions and self-deceptions, the irrationality, of individuals, but it says nothing about the illusions, deceptions, and irrationality of *institutions*. That lacuna

will be made good as far as academia is concerned in chapter 7 of the present book.

22 See Maxwell 1984, 181–9 and 264–7.

23 For a decisive argument establishing that purposive explanations are not reducible to physical explanations see Maxwell 2001a, 146–7; 2019a, 67–8. See also chapter 5 of the present book.

24 Sehon 2005 expounds some elements of the "double comprehensibility" view I put forward in Maxwell 1984, 174–89 and 264–75 – in ignorance, however, of my earlier and fuller account. Sehon mistakenly argues that "facts of common-sense psychology and physical science are logically independent" (12), a point repeated at the end of the book on page 230. Psychological facts are not reducible to physical facts, but that does not mean they are logically independent of all physical facts. Sehon fails to appreciate that double – or treble – comprehensibility is a miracle crying out for explanation, and explicitly rejects the version of Darwinian theory expounded here, in chapter 6, that is required to render the miracle of double and treble comprehensibility in the world itself comprehensible. See Maxwell 2019a, 65–7.

25 Physicalism, remember, is the doctrine that the universe is such that there is a true yet-to-be-discovered physical theory, T, that in principle (together with initial conditions) predicts and explains all physical phenomena. Or, more harshly, the doctrine that everything is determined (perhaps probabilistically) by necessitating physical properties specified by T essentialistically interpreted.

26 Versions of the two-aspect view have been defended by Strawson 1959; Davidson 1970; Nagel 1974, 1986; O'Shaughnessy 1980; Chalmers 1996; Hasker 1999, and many other contemporary philosophers. For a criticism of Davidson 1970, see Maxwell 2019a, 52–4.

27 Thus Nagel declares, "But while we are right to leave [the species-specific] view aside in seeking a fuller understanding of the external world, we cannot ignore it permanently, since it is the essence of the internal world, and not merely a point of view on it" (Nagel 1974, 445). "The species-specific view" here refers to perceptions and experiences specific to human beings. Nagel here denies that perceptual properties we experience really do exist out there in the external world.

28 Nagel 1986, 8.

29 Dennett 1991a.

30 Chalmers 2015; Strawson 2006a, b. For a survey article on panpsychism, see Goff et al. 2017.

31 See Chalmers 2016. For my objections to the view, see Maxwell 2019a, 57–8). Experiential physicalism is of course entirely different from panpsychism. It holds that familiar perceptual properties exist (and perceptual properties familiar to sentient creatures other than ourselves). It does not postulate the mysterious proto-mental properties of panpsychism.

32 Two further, even more serious, problems face the minimalist view. This view implies that almost everything we perceive about things around us is illusory. It is very difficult to see how the externalist account of perception can be correct. Minimalism commits one to internalism. But internalism, as we have seen, faces two serious difficulties. First, if what we directly know about in perception is our inner experience, what we know makes it very difficult to see how these inner experiences can be brain processes. Second, if what we know about when we perceive is our inner experiences, it is difficult to see how we can know anything about things external to us. Both problems arise if the minimalist two-aspect view is adopted. Neither problem faces full-blooded experiential physicalism.

33 Experiential physicalism has the additional advantage, as we have seen, that it provides an *explanation* as to why physics, even an extended physics, cannot explain the experiential: any such extended physical theory would be horribly disunified, and so nonexplanatory. Other versions of the two-aspect view of which I am aware do not include this explanation, and thus render the experiential inherently inexplicable, apparently immune as it is to scientific explanation, even when extended.

34 Put the mind-brain problem into the context of the more fundamental human world/physical universe problem and it is at once clear that the existence of *perceptual* properties in the physical universe is as much a part of the problem as the existence of *inner experiences*. Fail to put the mind-brain problem into this context, and all the attention is focused on the problem of how there can be *inner experiences* in the physical universe – just the focus that is found in so much of philosophy from Descartes to the present.

35 Chalmers 1996, xii–xiii. Actually, the so-called *hard* problem is relatively easy (although still a problem); it is the problem of what in detail goes on in the brain when we think, see, hear, imagine, talk, decide, and act that is the really hard problem. For some suggestions as to how this really hard problem may be solved, see Maxwell 2019a, chapter 2.

CHAPTER FOUR

1 Throughout this chapter, *physicalism* is to be understood as a component
   of *experiential physicalism*, the doctrine that both the physical and the
   experiential exist, the latter being incapable of being reduced to the former
   for the reasons given in the last chapter.

2 Karl Popper is famous for arguing that a theory, in order to be scientific,
   must be empirically *falsifiable*. Any theory that is not falsifiable is, for
   Popper, *metaphysical*, and not a component of scientific knowledge: see
   Popper 1963, chapter 1, 1959. Note that a *true* theory may be empirically
   falsifiable, and a *false* theory may not be. For falsifiablility, the crucial
   requirement is that the theory makes empirical predictions that could be
   false: if they are, that demonstrates that the theory is false too.

3 Standard empiricism is the common thread that runs through otherwise
   diverse views of philosophers of science, from inductivism, pragmatism,
   logical positivism, logical empiricism, conventionalism, hypothetico-
   deductivism, constructive empiricism, the views of Popper, Thomas Kuhn,
   Imre Lakatos, Bas van Fraassen, and more recent philosophers of science:
   see Popper 1959, 1963; Kuhn 1970; Lakatos 1978; van Fraassen 1980. In
   Maxwell 2005a, I demonstrate that both Kuhn and Lakatos defend versions of standard empiricism. For discussion of the point that standard
   empiricism is almost universally accepted by scientists and philosophers of
   science, see Maxwell 1998, 38–45; 2002; 2004a, 5–6, note 5. That philosophers take one or other version of standard empiricism for granted is
   very strikingly borne out by the fact that those contributing to the recently
   burgeoning field of research concerned with the metaphysics of science,
   which might be thought to reject standard empiricism, do nothing of the
   kind: see Chakravartty 2017; Mumford and Tugby 2013; Slater and
   Yudell 2017; Maxwell 2019a, chapter 4.

4 Physical theories that incorporated laws correlating physical states of
   affairs and experiential features would be horribly disunified too, and
   would not be considered for a moment whatever their empirical success
   might be: this, as we saw in the last chapter, is the key reason why all
   reference to the experiential is excluded from physics.

5 For my critical discussion of various attempts at solving the problem,
   see Maxwell 1998, 56–68; 2004b; 2004c.

6 See Einstein 1949, 23.

7 For a detailed exposition of this solution to the problem, see Maxwell
   2017a, chapter 5. Earlier expositions are to be found in Maxwell 1998,
   chapters 3 and 4; 2004a, 160–74; 2007a, 373–86; 2011b; 2013a.

8 In practice, as the number of bodies is increased, it becomes increasingly difficult to solve the equations and so make the predictions.

9 Another far less seriously disunified rival to Newton asserts that the law of gravitation is attractive between any two matter, or any two anti-matter, bodies, but is *repulsive* if one body is matter and the other body is anti-matter. This law might even be true (as far as we know at the time of writing).

10 See especially Maxwell 2019a, chapter 4. See also the appendix of the present book.

11 Scientists find unacceptable the idea that science accepts, as an item of knowledge, a metaphysical conjecture about the nature of the universe because to acknowledge this seems to amount to acknowledging that science rests on *faith*, which would seem to align science with religion. What this ignores is that there is all the difference between *rational* faith – critically scrutinized faith that one strives to improve – and irrational faith – faith dogmatically maintained. On the other hand, nonscientists find it unacceptable that science accepts the metaphysical thesis of physicalism as an item of knowledge because of the very disturbing implications that physicalism seems to have for free will, for the meaning and value of human life.

12 For a fascinating, informal account of string theory, see Greene 1999.

13 For a much more detailed argument in support of aim-oriented empiricism, see Maxwell 2017a. See also Maxwell 2017b, especially chapters 3 and 5, and appendices 1 and 2. For earlier accounts, see Maxwell 1974: 1993; 1998; 2004a; 2007a, chapter 14; 2011b; 2013a. For an entirely nontechnical account, see Maxwell 1999a.

14 For a rather more modest version of this conjecture of meta-knowability, see Maxwell 2017a, 111–21; or 2017b, 252–7.

15 See Kuhn 1970; Laudan 1980.

16 It does this by revealing that how the electromagnetic field divides up into the electric part of the field and the magnetic part differs for different reference frames moving with respect to each other. According to special relativity, any one inertial reference frame is as good as any other, so there can be no privileged division of the field into electric and magnetic fields. We are obliged to think of the electromagnetic field as one unified entity: for further discussion, see Maxwell 1998, 125–32.

17 For a more detailed discussion of theoretical unification in theoretical physics, see Maxwell 1998, chapter 4; 2017a, chapter 5 and appendix 1.

18 Maxwell 1998, 181.

19 See Maxwell 2017a. See also Maxwell 2017b, chapter 3 and appendices 1 and 2. For an earlier exposition of the argument, see Maxwell 2007a,

chapter 14. For even earlier expositions, see Maxwell 1998, chapters
3–5; 2004a, 160–74 and 205–20; 2005b. In Maxwell 1980, 46 and 74,
note 34, I make the point that the problem of induction is a product of
specialization. Standard empiricism dissociates science from philosophical speculation about what kind of world this is; it insists that science
tackles specialized empirical problems dissociated from the fundamental
problem about the nature of the universe. It is this standard empiricist
specialization, this dissociation of science from its fundamental problem,
that creates the problem of induction. See also the appendix of the
present book.

20 It may seem that the argument for aim-oriented empiricism suffers from a
well-known fatal objection: it is viciously circular. Physicalism is accepted
because it has led to the success of physical theory; physical theory is
accepted because (in part) it accords with physicalism. Each justifies
acceptance of the other – on the face of it, a blatantly invalid procedure.
Aim-oriented empiricism succeeds, however, in overcoming this well-
known difficulty. Let us call this apparently invalid procedure of allowing
choice of metaphysics to influence choice of theory, empirical success of
theory then influencing choice of metaphysics, and so on, the *positive
feedback procedure*. Three kinds of universe can now be distinguished.
The first kind is such that the *positive feedback procedure* can indeed lead
to genuine progress in knowledge, if carried out with sufficient caution.
The universe is such that if the *positive feedback procedure* is producing
merely the illusion of knowledge, this could always be discovered at any
stage by scrupulous empirical testing of theory. The second kind of universe is such that the *positive feedback procedure* can meet with great
apparent success until, abruptly, it becomes apparent that success was
illusory, and nothing that could have been done earlier would have
revealed the illusory character of the apparently successful pursuit of
knowledge. The third kind of universe is such that the *positive feedback
procedure* can meet with no success at all – not even apparent, illusory
success. The crucial point is now this. Meta-knowability, the metaphysical
thesis at level 6, asserts that this universe is not of the second kind. And
furthermore, reasons for accepting meta-knowability make no appeal to
the empirical success of knowledge. In employing the *positive feedback
mechanism*, the crucial assurance we need is that we are not in a universe
of the second kind. Meta-knowability provides that assurance. Admittedly,
the argument for accepting meta-knowability is rather weak: it is not an
argument for the truth of the thesis, but rather an argument to the effect
that proceeding as if we knew the thesis to be true can only help, and

cannot substantially hinder, progress in knowledge. For a more detailed discussion of this point, see Maxwell 2017a, chapter 9.

21 This is spelled out in much greater detail in Maxwell 2017b; see also Maxwell 2017a. And see Maxwell 2019a; and 2019c–e.

22 All this supports critical fundamentalism, as we shall see in the appendix.

CHAPTER FIVE

1 Traditionally, discussion about free will takes the form of a debate between compatibilists, who hold free will and determinism to be compatible, and incompatibilists, who hold they are not. Compatibilists argue that determinism does not imply compulsion, or lack of responsibility for one's actions or decisions, and thus does not imply there is no free will, and *indeterminism* can hardly enhance free will because it would introduce an element of chance or probability into human action. Incompatibilists argue, in opposition to this, that free will requires that there are genuinely open possible futures before us, between which we have the power to choose (not possible if determinism is true), and struggle to rebut the suggestion that indeterminism must *undermine* free will. For an excellent introduction to the debate, construed in these terms, see Kane 2005. For a lively defence of compatibilism, see Dennett 1984. The best defence of incompatibilism known to me is Kane 1998. For a critical discussion, see Maxwell 2001a, 151–4. For a defence of the view that the problem ought to be formulated in such a way that it is what science tells us about the world, or physicalism, that poses a threat to free will, not determinism, see Maxwell 2005c. In this chapter I concentrate on those issues that seem most relevant to the free will/physicalism problem rather than the traditional free will/determinism problem, although, of course, there is considerable overlap between these two formulations.

2 Physicalism, as understood here, is the doctrine that the universe is perfectly comprehensible *physically*, it being such that there is some yet-to-be-discovered, unified physical "theory of everything" that is *true*. Experiential physicalism is the version of this doctrine expounded and defended in chapters 3 and 4, according to which the experiential – sensory qualities and consciousness – exist in addition to the physical.

3 My view of the matter is that it is quite wrong to restrict free will to actions that have been premeditated. We should take the view that the proper way to act – the default mode as it were – is to act instinctively and spontaneously, thought checking action only when we get into difficulties and are confronted by problems that we cannot immediately solve.

4 For a bit more about this conception of wisdom, see Maxwell 1984, 66.

5 We shall see below, however, that values do play a crucial role in the free will version of the problem.

6 For my earlier attempts at solving the problem of free will and physicalism, see Maxwell 2001a, chapters 6–7; 2010a, chapters 7–8.

7 The terms "internalism" and "externalism" are widely used in the philosophical literature to draw distinctions between a wide variety of views. The distinction I have in mind is the one drawn in chapter 3. It should not be identified with any other distinction current in the philosophical literature.

8 For an especially powerful formulation of this argument, see van Inwagen 1986.

9 I have long argued for a fundamentally probabilistic version of quantum theory which, potentially, solves the quantum wave/particle problem and yields predictions that differ from those of orthodox quantum theory: see Maxwell 1976b; 1988; 1994b; 1998, chapter 7; 2018a. For other suggestions along these fundamentally probabilistic lines, see Gao 2018. For an exposition of the alternative, many worlds, deterministic version of quantum theory, see Wallace 2012. For a discussion of the issues, and a criticism of the many worlds view, see Maxwell 2017b, 135–51.

10 One implication of Einstein's special and general theories of relativity is that there is no such thing as an unambiguous, objective cosmic "now." What distant events are simultaneous with "here and now" is different for different observers in relative motion with one another. This means we cannot think of the universe as made up, each moment, of what exists "now," in three-dimensional space, with a past and a future. We must think of the universe as four-dimensional, stretched out in both space and time, "now" having as much objective significance as "here." Some degree of free will is perhaps possible in such a four-dimensional universe, but it is a pretty meagre kind of free will because the future is as fixed and determined as the past. But if the universe is fundamentally probabilistic, as quantum theory may be taken to suggest, then probabilistic transitions may define unambiguous, objective "nows," and the four-dimensional spacetime view of relativity theory may turn out to be false. This possibility is explored in Maxwell 2017e. See also Maxwell 2018a. In such a fundamentally probabilistic universe, a much stronger kind of free will becomes possible.

11 Here are seven increasingly substantial degrees of free will. (1) We can, at least some of the time, achieve what we desire, but we have no control over what we desire. (2) In addition, we do have control over what we

desire. (3) Both (1) and (2) hold, but our desire or intention to achieve a goal, even when successful, has no causal or productive role whatsoever in the goal being achieved. (4) Our desire or intention does have such a causal or productive role. (5) All of (1) to (4) hold, but everything we do is physically determined. (6) All of (1) to (4) holds, and probabilistic physicalism obtains, so our actions are not precisely determined physically before we were born. (7) We have the desire and the capacity to, and are actively engaged in, realizing what is of most value, potentially and actually, in the circumstances of our life.

12 How is the aim of an aim-pursuing entity to be identified? Given a variety of possible aims, the actual aim is the one that provides the best purposive explanation of what the aim-pursuing being does in a variety of circumstances. "Finding something to eat" is the aim of an animal if, in a variety of circumstances, the animal acts in ways conducive to obtaining food, given the capacities of the animal in question. What the aim is, identified in this way, may well depend crucially on what range of possible circumstances is considered – that is, on what kind of environment is considered. An animal seeking food may engage in food-seeking actions in a range of circumstances that do not include a predator; include the predator, and the animal immediately abandons food-seeking actions. In ascribing an aim, A, to a purposive being we are, explicitly or implicitly, presupposing a particular range of circumstances, a particular environment (in which the being will try to attain A).

13 In Maxwell 2019a, 41–5, I develop this hierarchical control theory of human consciousness in a little more detail and suggest it may well be true. I even suggest that it can be regarded as a scientific theory as it is empirically testable (44).

14 The notion of purposive action has been bedevilled by intellectual history, in particular by the lingering influence of Aristotle. It was Aristotle's view that the physical universe is to be explained and understood in terms of purpose. Physical things have an inherent purpose built into them, and that is the explanation as to why they behave as they do. Stones fall because they seek their natural resting place, the centre of the earth. It was one of Galileo's great battles to oppose this purposive metaphysics with the idea that "the book of nature is written in the language of mathematics" – an early version of physicalism. One outcome of this battle has been that scientists after Galileo have tended to take for granted that the Aristotelian notion of purposiveness is incompatible with modern physics, incompatible indeed with modern science. Even biologists have made this assumption, holding that it cannot be correct to attribute purpose to

animals, to living things. The all-important point is to note that there are two notions of purposive action, the Aristotelian, incompatibilist one, and a feedback-mechanism, compatibilist one. The first holds that purposiveness is incompatible with physicalism, whereas the second holds that it is compatible. Both notions are legitimate. The crucial question, however, is: Is there anything that is purposive in the Aristotelian, incompatibilist sense? Those who hold that we have free will, and free will is incompatible with physicalism, in effect hold that we are purposive beings in the Aristotelian sense. My view, of course, is that we are *not* Aristotelian beings, and there are none in existence.

15 In practice, consciousness often does not have this status. Instead of determining goals and actions, it is pushed into adopting specific goals and actions by unconscious desires and feelings: see, for example, Kahneman 2011 for a mass of evidence that unconscious processes influence conscious thinking and decision making. Some experts on the brain argue that this is *always* the case. Thus, George Miller declares, "No activity of mind is ever conscious. In particular, the mental processes involved in our desires and emotions are never conscious. Only the end product of these motivational processes can ever become known to us directly" (Miller, 1962, 72). But if the brain has the kind of hierarchical structure I have indicated, with consciousness as the master control system, the mere fact that much that goes on is unconscious just means that many subordinate control systems, subordinate to consciousness, are themselves unconscious. It would be a disaster for conscious control if all these subordinate control systems were themselves conscious.

16 Here, *head process* is used to refer to a process going on inside the head of a conscious person, leaving it open as to whether it is just a *neurological* process, or whether it is a *conscious* process as well.

17 First formulated in Maxwell 2010b. For a more elaborate discussion, see Maxwell 2019a, 68–77.

18 I have simplified things enormously, for the sake of clarity. Strictly speaking, and from the standpoint of physics, the cause of my body moving is not just the specific brain process that triggers and controls my actions; it includes the persistent state of the rest of my brain, my body, and my environment. The common sense notion of cause (as opposed to the notion in physics) concentrates on that prior change that brought about the caused event in question. Furthermore, the brain processes in question do not merely "cause" my bodily motions; they control them. I am, consciously or unconsciously, aware of what I do, and that awareness feeds back into the controlling brain processes.

19 Chapter 3, note 19.

20 See Kripke 1986.

21 Jaegwon Kim has repeatedly argued against any view which, like the one defended here, upholds both physicalism and the thesis that mental features exist that cannot be reduced to, or explained in terms of, the physical. His basic objection is that any such view cannot account for mental causation – the capacity of our desires, intentions, and decisions to act to produce or cause our actions. If physicalism is true, then everything we do is determined by *physics*, and that leaves no room whatsoever for *consciousness*, for anything *mental*, to have a role: see Kim 1998a; 2005. But Kim makes the fatal mistake of assuming that Kripke is correct in holding that mental events cannot be contingently identical to physical events: see Kim 1998a, 98. Reject Kripke's views on identity, accept that mental events are contingently identical to neurological (ultimately, physical) events in the brain, and it becomes a platitude that mental events cause, or are a part of the cause of, what we do, our bodily movements.

22 See Maxwell 2001a, 259–73, or better, Maxwell 2019a, 189–208, which includes an additional, decisive refutation of Kripke.

23 See Maxwell 2001a, 123 and 137, note 53.

24 See, for example, Smith and Jones 1986.

25 Adopt the internalist theory of perception, and we are driven to adopt a view not so very different from epiphenomenalism, vulnerable to the criticism that, given this view, there can be no free will. (Epiphenomenalism holds that brain processes cause distinct mental events, but not vice versa.) For the internalist theory, in contrast to the externalist theory, implies that our perceptual experiences are very different from brain processes, and thus suggests that mental processes, in general, are distinct from brain processes and thus cannot have a role in producing action unless they interact with brain processes, which would involve a violation of physical law and physicalism. Adopt the external theory of perception, and experiential controllism more generally, and these implications are avoided.

26 See Smart 1963, 94.

27 It is this kind of detailed self-knowledge that orthodox functionalists tend to deny – apparent, for example, in Daniel Dennett's 1991a denial of the meaningfulness of the question of where, in the brain, consciousness is to be located. This is, in my view, a meaningful and important question, one to which I have given a conjectural answer: see Maxwell 2001a, chapter 8.

28 This requires qualification. Such a causal, physical explanation could only be given of a control feature *depicted in terms that are reducible to, and thus explicable in terms of, the physical*.

29 It is compatible with the view, indicated above, that what we ordinarily
know about neurological processes going on inside our skulls is the
control aspect of these processes.

30 A future theory of sentience and consciousness may well explain why beings
who have brains, like mammals and humans, are sentient, and even, in the
case of humans and some mammals perhaps, conscious. It may be that once
a living brain is such that neurological processes associated with controlling
action embody awareness of the control aspects of other neurological processes, especially those associated with feelings, desires, and perceptions, in
at least a zombie-like sense of "awareness," then inevitably zombie-like
"awareness" becomes *real* awareness, and authentic sentience and, ultimately, consciousness emerge. In developing any such theory of sentience
and consciousness, it will be vital to look at the matter from an evolutionary
standpoint. How and why did sentience and consciousness first evolve? I
have suggested that they emerged when the actions of animals began to be
controlled by means of feelings and desires: see Maxwell 2001a, 162–201;
or 2001b. The theory I sketched in chapter 3 – see Maxwell 2001a, 126–31;
2011 – which provides an explanation as to why inner experiences and neurological processes are correlated in the ways that they are, carries the implication that philosophical zombies do not exist. If a person, a putative
zombie, has a brain sufficiently similar to mine, then, according to this theory, that person has inner experiences (more or less) like mine. The specific
theory I have put forward may not be correct, but a modified version of it
might well be correct.

31 This elaborates a bit on my remark at the beginning of chapter 3 that we
are *doubly* comprehensible.

32 This is a conjecture, of course, but one argued for in chapters 3 and 4.

33 Quotation marks around desire, perception, etc. indicate that these are
experientially denuded versions of these familiar notions.

34 Jaegwon Kim has cast doubt on the idea that it is possible for there to be
two different, true explanations of the same phenomena, neither reducible
to the other: see Kim 1998. But that it is possible, and happens all the
time, should be obvious from the following consideration. Endless examples of nonsentient goal-seeking devices exist, such as guided missiles,
robots, chess-playing programs, and nonsentient creatures. It is entirely
unproblematic to hold that the actions of such devices or creatures can (in
principle) be explained in two kinds of ways: physically and purposively.
The only questionable point, perhaps, is whether purposive explanations
really cannot be reduced to physical explanations. I have already given
reasons for holding that purposive explanations cannot be so reduced.

35 For a definition of epiphenomenalism, see note 25.

36 In other words, physical features of head processes play a crucial role in producing human action because these features play a vital role in true physical explanations of these human actions.

37 What precisely does this mean? It means at least that the structure and functioning of the brain of a conscious person is so delicately and intricately contrived that physical processes occurring in it cause, or better, control, the person to do what that person decides to do, so that the person acts in accordance with his or her desires, feelings, beliefs, perceptions, intentions – these all being brain states and processes (ultimately, physical states and processes).

38 I first put a version of this argument forward in Maxwell 1984, 274; 2nd ed., 2007a, 295.

CHAPTER SIX

1 See Lane 2009, chapter 1.

2 Monod 1974.

3 Evolution does not have a purpose, but mechanisms responsible for evolution, although initially purposeless, do gradually come to involve purposive action of living things, as we shall see.

4 To say that is not to say, however, that purposive explanations can be reduced to physical explanations. They cannot. Purposive explanations for actions performed, couched in terms of goals, actions designed to attain goals, beliefs, decisions, reasons for action, etc., make sense of things in a way that is different from, and not reducible to, physical explanation. Purposive things exhibit double comprehensibility, as we saw in the last chapter.

5 For my earlier advocacy of the purposive version of Darwinism, see Maxwell (1984, 267–75; 2001a, chapter 7; 2010a, chapter 8; 2017b, 192–200. I was much influenced by Hardy 1965; and by remarks of Karl Popper in his lectures: see text below, and Popper 1976, chapter 37. Aspects of the purposive view have been expounded by Jablonka and Avital 2000; Jablonka and Lamb 1995; Odling-Smee et al. 2003.

6 Leland et al. 2014.

7 Ibid., 162.

8 Jean-Baptiste Lamarck, who was born in 1744 and died in 1829, was a French biologist and an early proponent of the view that evolution occurred in accordance with natural laws.

9 A young proto-giraffe that acquires a long neck is unlikely to use it to eat leaves high up in trees unless fellow, adult proto-giraffes are already striving to do this.

10 A basic task of Darwinian theory is to help explain how and why the
    pattern of purposive comprehensibility has become superimposed on the
    pattern of physical comprehensibility. In order to make this intelligible,
    Darwinian theory needs to exploit both kinds of patterns of comprehensi-
    bility – both modes of explanation, physical and purposive. This threatens
    to sabotage the capacity of Darwinian theory to explain how purposive-
    ness has evolved in a purposeless universe (by presupposing the very thing
    to be explained). But as long as the principle of noncircularity is observed,
    this threat is kept at bay.

11 The term "Darwin's finches" was first employed by Percy Lowe in 1936
    and popularized by David Lack in his book *Darwin's Finches*, first pub-
    lished in 1947.

12 In reality, many mutations would be required, over a period of time, to
    change legs into flippers (and to make other changes), mutations and
    changes in behaviour being incremental during this time. These complica-
    tions do not change the basic point that a change in purposive action is
    the key initial change, and this has nothing to do with anything genetic.

13 Margulis 1999.

14 It has also been suggested that the Cambrian explosion – the sudden
    appearance of a multitude of diverse many-celled creatures some 540
    million years ago – was in part the result of purposive action of early
    creatures, for example "the action of sponges in facilitating the oxygen-
    ation of the oceans" (Erwin and Valentine 2013, 337).

15 See Odling-Smee et al. 2003.

16 Dawkins 1978, chapter 11. This meme view has been endorsed by Daniel
    Dennett 1996, chapter 12) and criticized by Holdcroft and Lewis 2000.
    For a discussion, see Maxwell 2001a, 175–9.

17 But could not one have a version of Darwinism that is interpreted to be
    about things that are replicated, with inheritable variations, wherever they
    may be in the universe, whether purposive or not? One can indeed have
    such a theory; but applications of the theory to entities that are replicated
    without purposive action being involved in any way whatsoever are likely to
    be very limited indeed. The beginnings of life on earth might be a case in
    point. Genes and memes are only replicated because of the involvement of
    purposive life. Instead of thinking of the human being as the means whereby
    genes replicate themselves, we need rather to think of genes merely as being
    a part of the processes whereby human beings reproduce themselves. The
    basic task of Darwinian theory is to help us understand the evolution of
    purposive *life*, not purposeless genes – or memes for that matter.

18 The significance of this point will, I hope, become clearer in chapter 7. There, I distinguish two kinds of inquiry, knowledge-inquiry and wisdom-inquiry, and argue that the latter is more rigorous and, potentially, of greater human value. Wisdom-inquiry holds that thought, at its most fundamental, is associated with and guides our actions. Granted wisdom-inquiry, it is abundantly clear that cultural artifacts – Dawkins's memes – only make sense when related to human action, a point that is perhaps not so obvious when matters are viewed from the perspective of knowledge-inquiry. For an earlier discussion of this issue, see Maxwell 1984, 174–81.

19 Lumsden and Wilson 1981; Durham 1991.

20 See Maxwell 1984, 174–81 and 265–75; 2001a, chapters 7–8; 2010a, chapter 8.

21 See chapter 3, pp. 46–9 and note 13.

22 Motivational control is a necessary, but not a sufficient, condition for sentience.

23 I put forward this theory of imagination in Maxwell 1984, 175–8, somewhat before current brain imaging techniques had been developed. I was delighted to learn subsequently that these techniques, such as MRI scanning, had verified my theory.

24 See chapter 3 for the introduction of the notion of "personalistic understanding." The terminology is a bit unfortunate in one respect: it suggests that it is a kind of understanding that only persons, or human beings, can have. In fact animals acquire "personalistic understanding" of each other, in that they can guess the intentions of other animals, and can even use their personalistic understanding of others to manipulate those others. Jane Goodall tells the story of two chimpanzees eating bananas: suddenly, one of them stares into the undergrowth and emits the cry that means "tiger." The other chimpanzee flees in terror, but the first one remains at ease and calmly eats up all the remaining bananas himself. Our human personalistic understanding of each other has evolved from personalistic understanding that our animal ancestors acquired of each other.

25 Grice 1957, reprinted in Grice 1989, chapter 14. Grice makes no attempt, however, to indicate, as I have done here, the manner in which the multilayered character of human communication can be seen as having emerged gradually as a result of Darwinian evolution.

26 For an earlier discussion of the evolution of the hierarchy of mutual understanding involved in human communication and the use of language, see Maxwell 2001a, 189–90.

27 The master control system could be a number of control systems operating more or less independently of one another.

28 For a fascinating account of hunting and gathering life, as lived by the Pygmies of the rain forests of central Africa, see Turnbull 1976. Turnbull describes what he considers to be the consequences of abandoning the day-to-day hunting and gathering way of life, and taking up the agricultural way of life of the Bantu.

29 A sentient animal is one that experiences sensations, whether of touch, taste, smell, vision, sound, or pain, fear, repugnance, desire, or pleasure.

30 Hillel the Elder.

31 In producing offspring, plants act by means of growth – the production of seeds, fruit, flowers.

32 According to the aquatic ape hypothesis, first put forward by Alister Hardy, and subsequently very substantially developed by Elaine Morgan (1990), many of our present bodily features can be explained by the theory that our distant ancestors spent much time in rivers, estuaries, or the sea. This theory, if correct, dramatically illustrates how changes in ways of life (in this case taking to the sea) can have substantial consequences for subsequent evolution.

CHAPTER SEVEN

1 For an upbeat view of human progress that has been achieved since the scientific revolution, see Pinker 2018. For a criticism, see Maxwell 2018b.

2 "[O]ne of the most remarkable features of pygmy life [is] the way everything settles itself with apparent lack of organization. Co-operation is the key to pygmy society" (Turnbull 1961, 115). How different from our world! In our vast, complex, diverse, rapidly changing modern world, charged with inequality and conflict, cooperation without organization is almost inconceivable, and in any case usually seems difficult to attain even with organization.

3 See Maxwell 1976a; 1980; 1984; 1991; 1992; 1994a; 2000a; 2001a, chapter 9; 2001c; 2003; 2004a; 2005d; 2006b; 2009; 2010a, chapter 9; 2010c; 2010d; 2011c; 2012a–e; 2013b; 2014a; 2015; 2016b; 2017a–d; 2017f; 2018b; 2019a–b; 2019f–h. The argument was first spelled out in detail in Maxwell 1984. Detailed expositions of further developments are to be found in Maxwell 1998; 2004a; 2014a; 2016b; 2017a; 2017b. For summaries of the argument, see Maxwell 1991; 1992; 1994a; 2000a; 2007b; 2012a; 2017d; 2019f–h. In Maxwell 2019a, I give an account of my life's work, beginning with my earliest publications in

1966 and 1968, and examine in detail subsequent work of over 150 philosophers – work that suffers from neglect of my earlier work in the field. I have been profoundly shocked at the lack of interest over the decades in an argument that reveals that academia is irrational and dysfunctional when judged from the standpoint of helping to promote human welfare.

4 This assumption may be challenged. Does not academic inquiry seek knowledge for its own sake, it may be asked, whether it helps promote human welfare or not? Later on, I will argue that the conception of inquiry I am arguing for, wisdom-inquiry, does better justice than knowledge-inquiry to *both* aspects of inquiry, pure and applied. The basic aim of inquiry, according to wisdom-inquiry, is to help us realize what is of value in life, "realize" meaning both "apprehend" and "make real." "Realize" thus accommodates both aspects of inquiry, "pure" research or "knowledge pursued for its own sake" on the one hand, and technological or "mission-oriented" research on the other – both, ideally, seeking to contribute to what is of value in human life. Wisdom-inquiry, like sight, is there to help us find our way around. And like sight, wisdom-inquiry is of value to us in two ways: for its intrinsic value, and for practical purposes. The first is almost more precious than the second.

5 For a more detailed development of this argument, see especially Maxwell 1980, 1984, 2004a, 2014a – and other works referred to in note 3.

6 Funds devoted, in the United States, United Kingdom, and some other wealthy countries, to military research are especially disturbing: see Langley 2005 and Smith 2003.

7 See Maxwell 1984, chapter 3 for a much more detailed discussion of the damaging social repercussions of knowledge-inquiry.

8 Wisdom-inquiry was first expounded and argued for in detail in Maxwell 1984, where it was dubbed "the philosophy of wisdom." I later modified the name. "Wisdom-inquiry" stands for both a specific kind of inquiry, and the corresponding view (or philosophy) as to what the aims and methods of inquiry ought to be. An even earlier exposition of wisdom-inquiry is to be found in Maxwell 1976a. My first exposition of aim-oriented empiricism, a key component of wisdom-inquiry, as we shall see, is to be found in Maxwell 1974.

9 It is the vision of the world, revealed to us by modern science, that poses the problems for the existence and value of our human world that this book tackles. On the other hand, the astonishing success of modern science in establishing this vision as scientific knowledge may well have vital clues as to how we can best go about enhancing life of value in our human

world. That this may be possible was the profound discovery of the Enlightenment.

10 For excellent accounts of the Enlightenment, see Gay 1973; Israel 2013.

11 See Aron 1968; 1970; Farganis 1993, introduction; Hayek 1979.

12 The blunders of the philosophes are not entirely undetected. Karl Popper, in his first four works, makes substantial improvements to the traditional Enlightenment program (although Popper does not himself present his work in this fashion). Popper first improves traditional conceptions of the progress-achieving methods of science (Popper 1959). This conception, *falsificationism*, is then generalized to become *critical rationalism*. He then applied critical rationalism to social, political, and philosophical problems (Popper 1961, 1962, 1963). The version of the Enlightenment program about to be outlined here can be regarded as a radical improvement of Popper's version: see Maxwell 2004a, chapter 3; 2006b; 2017c. Falsificationism is the doctrine that science makes progress, not by verifying theories (which cannot be done), but by subjecting theories to sustained attempted empirical refutation. When a theory is falsified, scientists are provoked to think up an even better theory that is not falsified. Critical rationalism is the doctrine that to be rational is to be critical.

13 The allegiance of the scientific community to standard empiricism prevents it from putting AOE into scientific practice explicitly. AOE can be implemented only in a partial, curtailed fashion. That is enough, however, for the positive feedback feature of AOE to have some impact on science itself. Thus, ideas about nonempirical factors that should influence choice of theory in physics have evolved since Newton's time. This kind of positive feedback effect would have even more of an impact on science if standard empiricism was repudiated, and AOE explicitly accepted and implemented instead: see Maxwell 2017b, chapter 5.

14 For more detailed expositions of this step in the overall argument, from standard to aim-oriented empiricism, see Maxwell 1974; 1976a; 1984; 1998; 2004a; 2005a–b; 2006; 2011b; 2017a–c; 2019a–b. And of course chapter 4 of the present book – as well as the appendix.

15 The inherently problematic character of the aim of creating civilization can be highlighted in a number of ways. People have very different ideas as to what does constitute civilization. Most views about what constitutes Utopia, an ideally civilized society, have been unrealizable *and* profoundly undesirable. People's interests, values, and ideals clash. Even values that, one may hold, ought to be a part of civilization may clash. Thus freedom and equality, even though interrelated, may nevertheless clash. It would be an odd notion of individual freedom that held that freedom was for some

and not for others; and yet if equality is pursued too single-mindedly, this
will undermine individual freedom, and will even undermine equality, in
that a privileged class will be required to enforce equality on the rest, as in
the old Soviet Union. A basic aim of legislation for civilization, we may
well hold, ought to be to increase freedom by restricting it: this brings out
the inherently problematic, paradoxical character of the aim of achieving
civilization. One thinker who has stressed the inherently problematic,
contradictory character of the idea of civilization is Isaiah Berlin; see, for
example, Berlin 1980, 74–9. Berlin thought the problem could not be
solved; I, on the contrary, hold that the hierarchical methodology indicated here provides us with the means to learn how to improve our
solution in real life.

16 See Maxwell 1984, chapters 3, 6, and 7; 2014a, chapter 2.

17 "Aims," here, refers to the actual aims of what we do, what our actions
will produce in the given environment, not aims we declare, or believe we
are pursuing.

18 The fundamental importance of putting aim-oriented rationality into practice is still unknown despite it having been argued for repeatedly over the
decades since 1976: see note 3.

19 Aim-oriented rationality might be summed up in a little more detail as
involving the following methods: (1) Articulate, and try to improve the
articulation of, problems associated with aims-and-methods. (2) Propose
and critically assess possible solutions, possible aims-and-methods. (3)
Assess these with respect to experience when they are put into practice in
life. (4) Given a long-term, inherently highly problematic aim, represent
this at a number of levels of specificity and generality, in an attempt to
arrive at a relatively unproblematic representation of the aim that can
provide a framework within which problems associated with more specific
versions of the aim may be resolved. (5) Adapt this to the case of
cooperative resolution of conflicts. (6) Whenever rationality appears to be
a liability, and irrationality seems to be required for success, conjecture
that aims are being misrepresented and try to articulate repressed, problematic aims. (7) Interconnect thought about problematic aims-and-methods and actions in such a way as to promote the improvement of aims and
methods in life. (8) Try to discover *why* a problematic aim is being pursued, both in the historical or causal sense of how the aim came to be pursued in the first place, and in the rationalistic sense of for what further aim
(if any) the given aim is being pursued.

20 Maxwell 1976a, 5.

21 Einstein 1973, 80.

22 Ibid., 11.

23 Einstein 1949, 17.

24 A remarkable exception is Penrose 2004.

25 I might add that the hierarchical conception of science indicated here does better justice to the scientific quest for understanding than does orthodox standard empiricist views: see Maxwell 1998, chapters 4 and 8; 2004a, chapter 2; 2017b, chapter 5.

26 These considerations are developed further in Maxwell 1976a; 1984; 2004a; 2014b; 2016a, 200–1; and 2019b, 64–7.

27 For a fuller exposition of such an account of empathic understanding, see Maxwell 1984, 171–89 and chapter 10; and 2001a, chapters 5–7 and 9.

28 Maxwell, 1984, 183–5.

29 For a list of twenty-three structural changes that need to be made to knowledge-inquiry to convert it into wisdom-inquiry, see Maxwell 2017b, 235–9.

30 For example, at University College London (my own university), there is a new, very successful initiative called "UCL Grand Challenges": this brings specialists together to tackle global problems. See https://www.ucl.ac.uk/grand-challenges/.

CHAPTER EIGHT

1 The evolutionary aims of survival and reproductive success can become transformed as a result of cultural reinterpretation. Thus the suicide bomber may be pursuing survival: he may believe that eternal life in paradise awaits. The entrepreneur creating a business, the politician promoting laws or a political movement, the scientist contributing to science, the author publishing books: these and other such activities may be reinterpretations of reproductive success, the production of offspring. But that evolutionary aims are open to these kinds of reinterpretation does not mean that people consciously evolve their aims in these ways. It does not mean that people are in control of the basic aims they pursue in life.

2 Popper 1962.

3 A society and culture that helped us to learn and grow as a result of exposure to the diversity of the open society would be one that put aim-oriented rationality and wisdom-inquiry into practice.

4 When it comes to human beings, we need to distinguish (a) what we *say* we value; (b) what we *believe* we value; (c) what we *actually* value (based on our actions); and (d) what is actually of value to us. It is customary, furthermore, to speak not just of what is of value to some person, but also of the *values* of that person. These latter amount to a broad

characterization of the aims of that person, sufficiently open-ended not to be tied to the specific context of that person's life, here and now. Furthermore, a person's values may well be aims characterized in a sufficiently broad way to be, in that person's view, values that everyone should uphold and live by. Personal happiness, fame, success, a quiet life, love, fulfillment; any of these might be constitutive of the values of someone.

5 Moral relativism is defended by Harman 2000, and in a modified form by Wong 2006 and Velleman 2015.

6 One might seek to provide reasons for rejecting obnoxious values, such as Hitler's, on the grounds that they violate the law. But obnoxious values, once they become dominant, can all too easily lead to correspondingly obnoxious laws, as the example of Hitler's Germany indicates.

7 In this vein, Edvard Westermarck wrote, "Could it be brought home to people that there is no absolute standard in morality, they would perhaps be on the one hand more tolerant and on the other more critical in their judgments" (Westermarck 1932, 59).

8 Liberalism should lead us to value people equally – before the law, I would add. But it should not lead us to value equally the *opinions* of people about what is of value. To do so leads straight to the destruction of liberalism as anything other than a personal opinion, no better than any rival.

9 See chapter 7, note 3, for Turnbull's remark about the instinctive cooperation of the Pygmies.

10 For an excellent defence of moral realism, see Brink 1989. See also Maxwell 1999b and Shafer-Landau 2003.

11 Hume argues that nothing about what *ought* to be can be derived from what *is*: see Hume 1959, vol. 2, book III, part 1, section 1.

12 See Moore 1993.

13 In his philosophical novel *Zen and the Art of Motorcycle Maintenance*, Pirsig argues, influenced by Lao Tzu, that quality is the basic stuff out of which everything else, both matter and mind, is composed.

14 See Popper 1963, introduction.

CHAPTER NINE

1 Darwin's problem was evolution: How and why it occurs, what the mechanism is for its occurrence. That is not at all the same as the problem: How life of value can exist and best flourish embedded as it is in the physical universe. Nevertheless, Darwin's solution to his problem has profound implications for our problem – the problem of this book – as I have tried to show in chapter 6.

2 Fullerton 2015, first published 1906; Russell 1982, first published 1912;
   Sinclair 1945; Nagel 1987; Hospers 1997; Blackburn 1999; Hollis 2001;
   Ragland and Heidt 2001; Craig 2002; Nuttall 2002; Shand 2002; Pojman
   2004; Scruton 2012; Hales 2013.

3 I gave an example in chapter 3. There, I made the point that, in order to
   solve the philosophical part of the mind-body problem it is essential to do
   what orthodox philosophy does not do, put the problem into the context
   of the broader, more fundamental human world/physical universe
   problem.

4 Pojman 2004.

5 Although quite a lot of academic philosophy has no implications for
   anything outside philosophy, good or bad, some philosophy would have
   bad implications, if taken seriously. Idealism, solipsism, anti-rationalist
   philosophies such as phenomenology, existentialism, social constructiv-
   ism, and postmodernism, and hardline physicalism (everything is just
   physics) are examples. Marxism is an obvious example of a philosophy
   that actually has had bad implications in the real world, as a result of its
   advocacy of the dictatorship of the proletariat (which in practice means
   the dictatorship of those who elect themselves to represent them). Most
   philosophies of science, if put into scientific practice, would have bad
   implications for science itself. This is true of inductivism, logical positivism, logical empiricism, conventionalism, and even Karl Popper's falsifi-
   cationist philosophy of science. In the main, philosophers of science do
   not have sufficient confidence in their doctrines to try to convince the
   scientific community that they ought to put their ideas into scientific
   practice. This is perhaps the saving grace of philosophy: in the main its
   ideas are not taken sufficiently seriously for anyone to think of putting
   its ideas into practice in life. One striking exception to all this is the
   work of Karl Popper, which has fruitful implications for a wide range of
   human endeavours, as I have sought to make clear in Maxwell 2017c,
   chapter 1 and elsewhere. Popper himself argued that philosophical
   problems have their roots outside philosophy: see Popper 1963, chapter
   2. He clearly thought that philosophical ideas, if they are any good,
   ought to have fruitful implications for endeavours outside philosophy.
   And he successfully practised what he preached: see especially Popper
   1959; 1962; 1963; 1976. This book, and my work more generally, treads
   in his footsteps (or on a path close to his footsteps) as I make clear in
   Maxwell 2012a. See also Maxwell 2016a; 2017c.

6 Wittgenstein 1958, 49ᵉ, 124. Wittgenstein, one should note, has exerted an
   immense influence on modern analytic philosophy.

7 Chapter 7 has implications for the nature of mathematics, as I have shown in Maxwell 2010e. The attempt to make sense of mathematics as a branch of *knowledge*, within the framework of knowledge-inquiry, meets with long-standing, insuperable problems. All the standard attempted solutions fail: Platonism, logicism, formalism, intuitionism, mathematics as an elaboration of set theory. Furthermore, these standard views do not even recognize – and certainly fail to solve – a key problem in the philosophy of mathematics: How is significant mathematics to be distinguished from what is trivial? All these problems are readily solved within the framework of wisdom-inquiry. Mathematics can be held to be the development and systematization of problem-solving methods, the exploration and characterization of problematic possibilities. A piece of mathematics, in order to be significant, must, when appropriately interpreted (1) provide solutions to a range of problems in the real world (outside mathematics), and/or (2) facilitate solutions to problems in a range of other branches of mathematics (the wider the range the better). Mathematics seeks (a) diversity of problems and problem-solving methods, (b) systematization – the interconnection of diverse problem-solving methods, and (c) to provide help with solving problems outside mathematics in as wide a range of important areas of human endeavour as possible. For details, see Maxwell 2010e.

8 Once it is acknowledged that a physical theory, in order to be acceptable, must be both (1) sufficiently empirically successful and (2) sufficiently unified, it is clear that orthodox quantum theory, despite its immense empirical success, is unacceptable because it is appallingly disunified. It is a disunified jumble of quantum postulates, and some part of classical physics for a treatment of measurement: see Maxwell 1976b; 1988; 1994b; 1998, chapter 7; 2017e; 2018a. In order to avoid referring to measurement, quantum theory must have its own physical ontology, which means a solution must be found to the quantum wave/particle problem. I have put forward a testable, fundamentally probabilistic version of quantum theory that does, potentially, solve the wave/particle problem. This work on quantum theory is directly related to my work on the fundamental problem.

9 Elsewhere I have argued that philosophy devoted to tackling the human world/physical universe problem has implications for neuroscience: see Maxwell 1985; 2001a, chapter 8.

10 See Maxwell 2005e, republished in Maxwell 2014b.

11 Maxwell 2017b, chapter 5.

12 This is, in my view, very convincingly established in Maxwell 2017a; see also Maxwell 2017b, especially chapters 3 and 5. But the argument for

aim-oriented empiricism goes back to Maxwell 1974; it is even hinted at in Maxwell 1972.

13 See Maxwell 2002; 2019a; 2019c–d.

14 See Maxwell 1984 or, better, 2007a; and works referred to in note 3, chapter 7.

15 See chapter 7, note 3.

APPENDIX

1 "Specialization may be a great temptation for the scientist. For the philosopher it is the mortal sin" (Popper 1963, 136). Critical fundamentalist philosophers will, however, have to come to grips with the specialized techniques of other disciplines.

2 For an exposition and criticism of specialized intellectual standards and a defence of critical fundamentalism, see Maxwell 1980. A slightly modified version of this article can be found in Maxwell 2017c, chapter 9.

3 Leibniz, Spinoza, Locke, Berkeley, Hume, and Kant all disagreed more or less radically with Descartes.

4 What, it may be asked, is the big difference between the problems generated by Cartesian dualism and the human world/physical universe problem? The former are those I have just indicated in the text – insoluble, but illusory as a result of being the product of a false doctrine. The human world/physical universe problem, by contrast, encompasses all our problems of thought and life. Its initial formulation presupposes, as an initial conjecture, that the world we experience really does exist – just what Cartesian dualism, and modern philosophers and scientists, deny. Acknowledge that physics is about only a highly restricted aspect of everything, and it at once becomes possible to hold that the silence of physics about perceptual qualities does not mean that they do not exist – just what Cartesian dualism denies. Grant that perceptual qualities do really exist, and it at once it becomes possible to uphold what I have called the "externalist" account of perception. We see most directly what we ordinarily think we see: what is external to us, not our inner experiences. Immediately, two insuperable problems generated by Cartesian dualism vanish. We do indeed ordinarily acquire knowledge about the world around us in perception; but we don't ordinarily know enough about our inner experiences to exclude the obvious hypothesis that they are brain processes. By contrast, the "internalist" account of perception, to which Cartesian dualism is committed, implies that both points are appallingly problematic. How can we know anything about the world around us

if what we really directly *see* and *know about* are invariably our inner experiences? Granted we do directly see and know our inner experiences whenever we perceive, it is clear that what we know makes it impossible that these inner experiences could be brain processes. The "internalist" theory generates both the problem of how we can know anything about the external world, and the problem of how mental entities, that we "know" to be distinct from brain processes, can be related to the latter. By contrast, the "externalist" theory demolishes both problems simultaneously. Thus, begin with the human world/physical universe problem, and we quickly reach a view – experiential physicalism – that reconciles what physics tells us about the world with the world as we experience it, both without us and within us. A major chunk of the philosophical part of the mind-body problem is essentially solved, and one is released to tackle a multitude of further problems concerning the existence and flourishing of life of value in the physical universe. By contrast, stick with the problems generated by Cartesian dualism (even if one has rejected the view itself) and one will be stuck with them forever, for they are insoluble, the product of a false doctrine in the first place. The fundamental error of Cartesian dualism and philosophy since Descartes up to the present is the one I pointed out in my first published paper of 1966, the failure to recognize that physics is about only a highly restricted aspect of everything, the silence of physics about perceptual qualities thus in no way implying that these qualities do not really exist out there in the world.

5 See Berkeley 1957.

6 See Hume 1959.

7 See Kant 1961, 292.

8 The human world/physical universe problem only arises if it is acknowledged that the physical universe exists, is partly known by physics, and is such that we have no – or almost no – direct experience of it in perception. This was denied by Berkeley, Hume, Kant, and many philosophers and scientists who came after them.

9 See Mill 1963–91, 9:183.

10 See Ayer 1936 for a classic statement of logical positivism.

11 Only when this is done can one begin to see that key points, discussed in chapter 3 – such as that physics is about a highly restricted aspect of the world, and thus that the silence of physics about perceptual qualities does not mean they do not exist – are crucial steps toward the solution to the philosophical mind-body problem. See note 4.

12 See Maxwell 2019a, chapters 2 and 4 for a critical survey of recent work of this kind.

13 See Sellars 1963, 1–40. Sellars failed, however, to include, let alone discuss, that aspect of the problem that concerns the *flourishing* of what is of value in life: how we can best go about tackling problems of living, including global problems, so that we may realize what is of value. He failed to present the problem as our fundamental problem.

14 See Smart 1963; Nagel 1986; Dennett 1991a; and Chalmers 1996.

15 Daniel Kaufman, in a recent article, declares "philosophy's decline within the Academy is already well underway," and goes on to say "Daniel Dennett recently said that 'a great deal of philosophy doesn't really deserve much of a place in the world' and has become 'self-indulgent, clever play in a vacuum that's not dealing with problems of any intrinsic interest.' Jerry Fodor wondered why 'no one reads philosophy' and could not 'shake the sense that something has gone awfully wrong.' Just last year, Susan Haack went so far as to publish an essay entitled 'The Real Question: Can Philosophy Be Saved?' She is not hopeful" (Kaufman 2019).

16 Just this is argued in a recent article: see Lycan 2019. The main points of this book are, I believe, undeniable and really important but this is not, as yet, generally recognized (at the time of writing).

17 Bertrand Russell tells this story briefly in Russell 1982, 90, although he goes on to suggest that philosophy has the task of tackling fundamental problems even though truth may here be unattainable. Versions are also told in Kuhn 1970, chapter 2; Ayer 1982, 14; Papineau 2017; and Lycan 2019. I tell the story, and criticize it, in Maxwell 2017b, chapters 2–4.

18 Elsewhere I have argued that conceptual analysis is a kind of anti-philosophy, damagingly irrational: see Maxwell 2010b; 2019a, 145–7.

19 Lycan 2019, 200. It is significant that Lycan's paper is devoted to finding out whether there have been any permanent contributions in philosophy: putting on one side the successful disciplines that have broken away from philosophy, the contributions that Lycan discerns are pretty thin on the ground!

20 Scientists who take standard empiricism for granted may deny they make any philosophical assumptions, but nevertheless such assumptions inevitably lurk implicitly in their work. Standard empiricism is itself a philosophical view.

21 Standard empiricism holds that in science theories are accepted on the basis of *evidence*, considerations that have to do with the simplicity, unity, or explanatory character of a theory being taken into account as well, but no thesis about the world being accepted permanently as a part of scientific knowledge independently of evidence: see chapter 4.

22 For a recent, informal, and entertaining account of the confusion that results when theoretical physics fails to make explicit and criticize problematic, implicit metaphysical assumptions of underlying unity, see Hossenfelder 2018.

23 See Maxwell 2014a, chapter 2 for a more detailed discussion of empirical research in social inquiry as it ought to be conducted within the framework of wisdom-inquiry.

24 Maxwell 1974; 1984, chapters 5 and 9; 1993, 61–79; 1998; 1999a; 2002; 2004a, appendix; 2004b; 2005a; 2005b; 2006a; 2007, chapters 5, 9, and 14; 2009; 2010a, chapter 5; 2011b; 2012f; 2013; 2016a; 2017a–c; 2019a; 2019c–e).

25 Newton 1962, 400.

26 Ibid., 547.

27 For a much more detailed account of the way Newton's work led to the eclipse of natural philosophy and the establishment of empirical science, see Maxwell 2017b, especially chapters 1–2.

28 See Harman 1965.

29 For Newton's rules of reasoning, see Newton 1962, 398–400.

30 It was refuted in 1974: see note 24.

31 See Hume 1959, Book 1, Part III. Hume did not explicitly formulate his argument as a refutation of the Newtonian conception of science but that is what it amounts to. Hume did not get everything right. As I pointed out in chapter 3, pp. 42–5, he was wrong to argue that there cannot be necessary connections between successive events or, as he put it, that "necessity is something that exists in the mind, not in objects" (163). We must be more modest. For all we can know for certain, necessity may exist in objects – and given the astonishing regularities we observe in nature, it is not unreasonable to conjecture that necessary connections between successive states of affairs do exist in reality – necessary connections that are responsible for the regularities that we observe. For a defence of this view, see Maxwell 1968a. For a more recent, readable, and perhaps more lucid exposition, see Maxwell 2019a, 10–18. And see too, of course, chapter 3, pp. 42–5 of the present book. Hume did, however, get right the crucial point that, for all that we can know for certain, the course of nature may suddenly change, and laws and theories hitherto apparently well-established empirically may abruptly be falsified by what occurs. "We can at least conceive a change in the course of nature; which sufficiently proves that such a change is not absolutely impossible" (Hume 1959, 91). Hume should have added, "as far as we can know for certain."

32 For a detailed exposition of the argument that we need to put science and philosophy back together again and recreate a modern version of natural philosophy that puts aim-oriented empiricism into practice, see Maxwell 2017b. See also works referred to in note 24.

33 One philosopher who has grasped that Hume is right, and that the Newtonian conception of science must be rejected is Karl Popper. He has argued that, even though evidence cannot verify theories, it can falsify them. And that makes scientific progress possible. We can, in science, put forward empirically falsifiable conjectures and do everything we can to refute them empirically so that, when we succeed, we are forced to think up something better. In this way, we learn from our mistakes. Science is a process of conjecture and refutation. Popper claims in this way to solve Hume's problem of induction: see Popper 1972, 1–2. There can be no doubt that this is a major step forward. It construes the basic problem in the correct way, in that it holds Hume's argument to be valid and takes the task to be to develop an adequate conception of science that is *not* refuted by Hume. But Popper's attempted solution fails. His "conjecture and refute" conception of science, even though it abjures verification, is still refuted by Hume. Popper cannot justify, or provide a rationale for, the rejection of empirically successful theories of high empirical content that are disunified: see Maxwell 1972; 1974, 133–4; 2005a.

34 For attempts to solve Hume's problem along these lines, and extensive references to other such attempts, see Kyburg 1970; Swain 1970; Howson 2000. For a recent survey article of such approaches to the problem, and further references, see Henderson 2019.

35 In recent years, serious attempts to solve Hume's problem of induction (as traditionally conceived) seem to have become more and more infrequent. It seems that repeated failure in the past has finally produced exhaustion. Few, it seems, still believe that a solution to Hume's problem is possible. What is so astonishing about this attitude is that there seems to be not a glimmering of an awareness that the traditional way of formulating Hume's problem ought to be seen from the outset *as the wrong way to formulate it*. Of course the problem, formulated in that way, is insoluble. But no one should have formulated it like that in the first place. Or, if they did, they should have quickly come to their senses, and thought again.

36 Bertrand Russell went further. He said that if Hume's problem cannot be solved, "there is no intellectual difference between sanity and insanity" (Russell 1946, 699).

37 It almost seems as if Newton's personal neurosis was responsible for casting a long methodological shadow of neurosis over science down the

centuries. One of my books does have, in fact, the title *Is Science
Neurotic?* The answer is "yes." Science suffers from what I call "rationalistic neurosis" because it represses the real but profoundly problematic aim
of seeking *explanatory truth* (truth presupposed to be explanatory or
unified), and replaces it with the declared, token aim of truth per se.

38 By far the best account I have given of the solution to Hume's problem is
to be found in Maxwell 2017a. For earlier expositions of the argument,
see note 24.

39 The Newtonian conception of science creates the illusion of a gulf between
science and philosophy in two ways. First, the Newtonian view excludes
metaphysics from scientific knowledge; and second, it claims that scientific
knowledge is verified by evidence. Philosophy, by contrast, is full of
metaphysics and does not claim to verify any philosophical doctrine by
evidence. Adopt the conjectural, natural philosophy view of science based
on AOE, and both reasons for a gulf between science and philosophy
disappear. Scientific knowledge includes metaphysics at a fundamental
level and is irredeemably conjectural in character.

40 van Fraassen 1985, 259–60.

41 See Maxwell 2017a, 111–20 and 129–38. See also Maxwell 2006a;
2019a, 104–6.

42 Aim-oriented empiricism is not alone in seeking to solve Hume's problem
by means of metaphysical principles. Bertrand Russell tried this approach,
as the van Fraassen quote indicates. See Russell 1948, Part VI. It has been
attempted by Braithwaite 1953, 255–92; Salmon 1974, 85–7; Mellor
1991, 254–68; McAllister 1996, 100–1. These attempts all fail essentially
because they put the metaphysical presuppositions of physics on one level
and do not recognize the conjectural and fallible character of these
presuppositions, the need to improve them as physics proceeds. In order to
solve Hume's problem, it is essential to recognize the fallible character of
the metaphysical presuppositions of physics, the need, as a result, to distinguish at least five distinct levels of presuppositions to facilitate the
improvement of those most likely to be false and in need of improvement,
at and near the bottom of the hierarchy. Distinguishing these five levels
makes it possible to provide different justifications for acceptance, at different levels, from the narrowly pragmatic for the top two theses to quasi-
empirical for the bottom three. For details, see Maxwell 2017a, chapter 9.
See also Maxwell 2019a, 104–6.

43 See Maxwell 2006a.

44 How does aim-oriented empiricism account for the simulacrum of verification of laws and theories in other branches of natural science, such as

chemistry? As in physics, so in chemistry, laws and theories deemed to be "verified" must satisfy *two* requirements; they must be sufficiently empirically successful, and sufficiently in accord with results of physics, in turn deemed to be "verified" because they are sufficiently in accord with both evidence and physicalism.

45 See Maxwell 1998, 4–6, for this point. See also Maxwell 1984, chapter 9. Chapter 9 of this latter work is entitled "Refutation of Minimal Standard Empiricism: From Science to Natural Philosophy."

46 Republished as chapter 9 of Maxwell 2017c: see pages 261–3 and 345n32.

References

Al-Khalili, J. 2003. *Quantum: A Guide for the Perplexed*. London: Weidenfield & Nicholson.

Armstrong, D. 1983. *What Is a Law of Nature?* Cambridge: Cambridge University Press.

Aron, R. 1968–70. *Main Currents in Sociological Thought*. 2 vols. Harmondsworth: Penguin.

Austin, J.L. 1962. *Sense and Sensibilia*. Oxford: Oxford University Press.

Ayer, A.J. 1936. *Language, Truth and Logic*. London: Gollancz.

– 1982. *Philosophy in the Twentieth Century*. London: Weidenfeld and Nicolson.

Berkeley, G. 1957. *A New Theory of Vision and Other Writings*. London: Dent (first published 1709, 1710, and 1713).

Berlin, I. 1980. *Against the Current*. London: Hogarth Press.

Bird, A. 2007. *Nature's Metaphysics: Laws and Properties*. Oxford: Clarendon Press.

Blackburn, S. 1999. *Think: A Compelling Introduction to Philosophy*. Oxford: Oxford University Press.

Braithwaite, R.B. 1953. *Scientific Explanation*. Cambridge: Cambridge University Press.

Brink, D.O. 1989. *Moral Realism and the Foundations of Ethics*. Cambridge: Cambridge University Press.

Burtt, E.A. 1932. *The Metaphysical Foundations of Modern Science*. London: Routledge and Kegan Paul.

Chakravartty, A. 2017. *Scientific Ontology: Integrating Naturalized Metaphysics and Voluntarist Epistemology*. Oxford: Oxford University Press.

Chalmers, D. 1996. *The Conscious Mind*. Oxford: Oxford University Press.

– 2015. "Panpsychism and Panprotopsychism." In *Consciousness in the Physical World: Perspectives on Russellian Monism*, edited by T. Alter and Y. Nagasawa, 246–76. New York: Oxford University Press.

– 2016. "The Combination Problem for Panpsychism." In *Panpsychism*, edited by G. Brüntrup and L. Jaskolla, 179–214. New York: Oxford University Press.

Cohen, H.F. 2010. *How Modern Science Came into the World*. Amsterdam: Amsterdam University Press.

Craig, E. 2002. *Philosophy: A Very Short Introduction*. Oxford: Oxford University Press.

Crane, T., and C. French. 2017. "The Problem of Perception." In Zalta, *The Stanford Encyclopedia of Philosophy*. https://plato.stanford.edu/archives/spr2017/entries/perception-problem/.

Davidson, D. 1970. "Mental Events." In *Experience and Theory*, edited by L. Foster, and J.W. Swanson, 79–101. London: Duckworth.

Dawkins, R. 1978. *The Selfish Gene*. London: Paladin.

Dennett, D. 1984. *Elbow Room: The Varieties of Free Will Worth Wanting*. Oxford: Clarendon Press.

– 1991a. *Consciousness Explained*. London: Allen Lane.

– 1991b. "Real Patterns." *Journal of Philosophy* 88, 27–51.

– 1996. *Darwin's Dangerous Idea*. London: Penguin Books.

Descartes, R. 1949. *A Discourse on Method, etc.* London: Everyman.

Dietrich, E. 2011. "There Is No Progress in Philosophy." *Essays in Philosophy* 12, 329–44.

Durham, W.H. 1991. *Coevolution: Genes, Culture and Human Diversity*. Stanford: Stanford University Press.

Einstein, A. 1949. "Autobiographical Notes." In *Albert Einstein: Philosopher-Scientist*, edited by P.A. Schilpp, 3–94. Illinois: Open Court.

– 1973. *Ideas and Opinions*. London: Souvenir Press.

Ellis, B. 2001. *Scientific Essentialism*. Cambridge: Cambridge University Press.

Erwin, D.H., and J.W. Valentine. 2013. *The Cambrian Explosion: The Construction of Animal Diversity*. Greenwood Village, CO: Roberts and Company.

Farganis, J., ed. 1993. *Readings in Social Theory: The Classic Tradition to Post-Modernism*. New York: McGraw-Hill.

Feynman, R., R.B. Leighton, and M. Sands. 1963. *The Feynman Lectures on Physics*, vol. 1. Reading, MA: Addison-Wesley.

Fullerton, G.S. 2015. *An Introduction to Philosophy*. Aeterna Press (first published 1906).

Galileo. 1957. *Discoveries and Opinions of Galileo*. Translated and edited by S. Drake. New York: Doubleday.

Gao, S., ed. 2018. *Collapse of the Wave Function*. Cambridge: Cambridge University Press.

Gay, P. 1973. *The Enlightenment: An Interpretation*. London: Wildwood House.

Goff, P., W. Seager, and S. Allen-Hermanson. 2017. "Panpsychism." In Zalta, *The Stanford Encyclopedia of Philosophy*. https://plato.stanford.edu/archives/win2017/entries/panpsychism/.

Greene, B. 1999. *The Elegant Universe*. New York: Norton.

Grice, H.P. 1957. "Meaning." *Philosophical Review* 66, 377–88.

– 1989. *Studies in the Way of Words*. Cambridge: Harvard University Press.

Guthrie, W.K.C. 1978. *A History of Greek Philosophy*. Vol. 2, *The Presocratic Tradition from Parmenides to Democritus*. Cambridge: Cambridge University Press.

Hales, S. 2013. *This Is Philosophy: An Introduction*. Oxford: Wiley-Blackwell.

Hardy, A. 1965. *The Living Stream*. London: Collins.

Harman, G. 1965. "The Inference to the Best Explanation." *Philosophical Review* 74, 88–95.

– 2000. *Explaining Value*. Oxford: Clarendon Press.

Hasker, W. 1999. *The Emergent Self*. Ithaca: Cornell University Press.

Hayek, F.A. 1979. *The Counter-Revolution of Science*. Indianapolis: LibertyPress.

Heidegger, M. 1962. *Being and Time*. Translated by J. Macquarrie and E. Robinson. Oxford: Blackwell (first published in 1927).

Henderson, L. 2019. "The Problem of Induction." In Zalta, *The Stanford Encyclopedia of Philosophy*. https://plato.stanford.edu/archives/spr2019/entries/induction-problem/.

d'Holbach, Paul-Henri Thiry, Baron. 1820. *The System of Nature*. London: Thomas Davison (first published in French as *Le Système de la nature* in 1770) http://www.ftarchives.net/holbach/system/osyscontents.htm.

Holdcroft, D., and H. Lewis. 2000. "Memes, Minds and Evolution." *Philosophy* 75, 161–82.

Hollis, M. 2001. *Invitation to Philosophy*. Oxford: Blackwell.

Hospers, J. 1997. *An Introduction to Philosophical Analysis*. London: Routledge.

Hossenfelder, S. 2018. *Lost in Math: How Beauty Leads Physics Astray.*
New York: Basic Books.

Howson, C. 2000. *Hume's Problem.* Oxford: Oxford University Press.

Hume, D. 1959. *A Treatise of Human Nature.* London: Everyman
(first published in 1738).

Inwood, S. 2003. *The Man Who Knew Too Much.* London: Pan Books.

Israel, J.I. 2013. *Democratic Enlightenment.* Oxford: Oxford University Press.

Jablonka, E., and E. Avital. 2000. *Animal Traditions: Behavioural
Inheritance in Evolution.* Cambridge: Cambridge University Press.

– and M.J. Lamb. 1995. *Evolution in Four Dimensions.* Cambridge: MIT
Press.

Jackson, F. 1982. "Epiphenomenal Qualia." *Philosophical Quarterly* 32,
127–36.

– 1986. "What Mary Didn't Know." *Journal of Philosophy* 3, 291–5.

Kahneman, D. 2011. *Thinking, Fast and Slow.* London: Allen Lane.

Kane, R. 1998. *The Significance of Free Will.* Oxford: Oxford University
Press.

– ed. 2005. *A Contemporary Introduction to Free Will.* Oxford: Oxford
University Press.

Kant, I. 1961. *Critique of Pure Reason.* London: Macmillan
(first published in 1781).

– 1959. *Prolegomena to any Future Metaphysics.* Manchester: Manchester
University Press (first published in German in 1783).

Kaufman, D. 2019. "The Decline and Rebirth of Philosophy." *Philosophy
Now* 130, February/March https://philosophynow.org/issues/130/
The_Decline_and_Rebirth_of_Philosophy.

Kim, J. 1998a. *Mind in a Physical World.* Cambridge: MIT Press.

– 1998b. "Mechanism, Purpose, and Explanatory Exclusion."
Philosophical Perspectives 3, 77–108.

– 2005. *Physicalism, or Something Near Enough.* Princeton: Princeton
University Press.

Koestler, A. 1964. *The Sleepwalkers.* Harmondsworth: Penguin.

Kripke, S. 1986. *Naming and Necessity.* Oxford: Blackwell.

Kuhn, T.S. 1970. *The Structure of Scientific Revolutions.* Chicago:
University of Chicago Press (first edition 1962).

Kumar, M. 2008. *Quantum: Einstein, Bohr, and the Great Debate about
the Nature of Reality.* Cambridge: Icon Books.

Kyburg, H. 1970. *Probability and Inductive Logic.* London:
Collier-Macmillan.

Lack, D. 1983. *Darwin's Finches.* Cambridge: Cambridge University Press.

Ladyman, J., D. Ross, D. Spurrett, and J. Collier. 2007. *Every Thing Must Go: Metaphysics Naturalized*. Oxford: Oxford University Press.

Lakatos, I. 1978. *The Methodology of Scientific Research Programmes: Philosophical Papers*, vol. 1. Cambridge: Cambridge University Press.

La Mettrie, J.O. 1912. *Man a Machine*. La Salle, IL: Open Court (first published in French as *L'homme machine* in 1748).

Lane, N. 2009. *Life Ascending*. London: Profile Books.

Langley, C. 2005. *Soldiers in the Laboratory*. Folkstone: Scientists for Global Responsibility.

Laudan, L. 1980. "A Confutation of Convergent Realism." *Philosophy of Science* 48, 19–48.

Leibniz, G.W. 1956. *Philosophical Writings*. London: Everyman.

Leland, K., et al. 2014. "Does Evolutionary Theory Need a Rethink?" *Nature* 514 (9 October): 162–4.

Locke, J. 1961. *An Essay Concerning Human Understanding*. London: Everyman (first published in 1690).

Lumsden, C.J., and E.O. Wilson. 1981. *Genes, Mind, and Culture: The Coevolutionary Process*. Cambridge: Harvard University Press.

Lycan, W.G. 2019. "Permanent Contributions in Philosophy." *Metaphilosophy* 50, no. 3, 199–211.

Margulis, L. 1999. *The Symbiotic Planet*. London: Phoenix.

Maund, B. 2019. "Color." In Zalta, *The Stanford Encyclopedia of Philosophy*. https://plato.stanford.edu/archives/spr2019/entries/color/.

Maxwell, N. 1965. "Physics and Common Sense: A Critique of Physicalism." Master's thesis, Manchester University.

– 1966. "Physics and Common Sense." *British Journal for the Philosophy of Science* 16, 295–311.

– 1968a. "Can There Be Necessary Connections between Successive Events?" *British Journal for the Philosophy of Science* 19, 1–25.

– 1968b. "Understanding Sensations." *Australasian Journal of Philosophy* 46, 127–46.

– 1972. "A Critique of Popper's Views on Scientific Method." *Philosophy of Science* 39, 131–52.

– 1974. "The Rationality of Scientific Discovery." *Philosophy of Science* 41, 123–53 and 247–95.

– 1976a. *What's Wrong with Science?* Hayes: Bran's Head Books.

– 1976b. "Towards a Micro Realistic Version of Quantum Mechanics. Parts I and II." *Foundations of Physics* 6, 275–92 and 661–76.

– 1980. "Science, Reason, Knowledge and Wisdom: A Critique of Specialism." *Inquiry* 23, 19–81.

– 1984. *From Knowledge to Wisdom: A Revolution in the Aims and Methods of Science.* Oxford: Blackwell.

– 1985. "Methodological Problems of Neuroscience." In *Models of the Visual Cortex,* edited by D. Rose and V.G. Dobson, 11–21. Chichester: John Wiley and Sons. http://discovery.ucl.ac.uk/1345060/.

– 1988. "Quantum Propensiton Theory: A Testable Resolution of the Wave/Particle Dilemma." *British Journal for the Philosophy of Science* 39, 1–50.

– 1991. "How Can We Build a Better World?" In *Einheit der Wissenschaften: Internationales Kolloquium der Akademie der Wissenschaften zu Berlin, 25–27 June 1990,* edited by J. Mittelstrass, 388–427. Berlin and New York: Walter de Gruyter.

– 1992. "What Kind of Inquiry Can Best Help Us Create a Good World?" *Science, Technology and Human Values* 17, 205–27.

– 1993. "Induction and Scientific Realism: Einstein versus van Fraassen." *British Journal for the Philosophy of Science* 44, 61–79, 81–101, and 275–305.

– 1994a. "Towards a New Enlightenment: What the Task of Creating Civilization Has to Learn from the Success of Modern Science." In *Academic Community: Discourse or Discord?,* edited by R. Barnett, 86–105. London: Jessica Kingsley.

– 1994b. "Particle Creation as the Quantum Condition for Probabilistic Events to Occur." *Physics Letters* A 187, 351–5.

– 1998. *The Comprehensibility of the Universe.* Oxford: Clarendon Press.

– 1999a. "Has Science Established That the Universe Is Comprehensible?" *Cogito* 13, no. 1, 139–145.

– 1999b. "Are There Objective Values?" *The Dalhousie Review* 79, no. 3, 301–17.

– 2000a. "Can Humanity Learn to Become Civilized? The Crisis of Science without Civilization." *Journal of Applied Philosophy* 17, 29–44.

– 2000b. "The Mind-Body Problem and Explanatory Dualism." *Philosophy* 75, 49–71.

– 2001a. *The Human World in the Physical Universe: Consciousness, Free Will and Evolution.* Lanham, MD: Rowman and Littlefield.

– 2001b. "Evolution of Sentience, Consciousness and Language Viewed from a Darwinian and Purposive Perspective." http://philpapers.org/rec/MAXEOS (Maxwell 2001a, pp. 162–201).

– 2001c. "Can Humanity Learn to Create a Better World? The Crisis of Science without Wisdom." In *The Moral Universe,* edited by T. Bentley and D.l. Stedman Jones, *Demos Collection* 16, 149–156.

– 2002. "The Need for a Revolution in the Philosophy of Science." *Journal for General Philosophy of Science* 33, 381–408.

– 2003. "Science, Knowledge, Wisdom and the Public Good." *Scientists for Global Responsibility Newsletter* 26, February, 7–9.

– 2004a. *Is Science Neurotic?* London: Imperial College Press.

– 2004b. "Non-empirical Requirements Scientific Theories Must Satisfy: Simplicity, Unification, Explanation, Beauty." http://philsci-archive.pitt. edu/archive/00001759/.

– 2004c. "Comprehensibility rather than Beauty." http://philsci-archive. pitt.edu/archive/00001770/.

– 2005a. "Popper, Kuhn, Lakatos and Aim-Oriented Empiricism." *Philosophia* 32, nos. 1–4, 181–239.

– 2005b. "A Mug's Game? Solving the Problem of Induction with Metaphysical Presuppositions." http://philsci-archive.pitt.edu/2230/.

– 2005c. "Science versus Realization of Value, not Determinism versus Choice." *Journal of Consciousness Studies* 12, no. 1, 53–8.

– 2005d. "A Revolution for Science and the Humanities: From Knowledge to Wisdom." *Dialogue and Universalism* 15, no. 1–2, 29–57.

– 2005e. "Philosophy Seminars for Five-Year-Olds." *Learning for Democracy: An International Journal of Thought and Practice* 1, no. 2, 71,–7.

– 2006a. "Practical Certainty and Cosmological Conjectures." In *Is There Certain Knowledge?* edited by M. Rahnfeld, 44–59. Leipzig: Leipziger Universitätsverlag.

– 2006b. "The Enlightenment Programme and Karl Popper." In *Karl Popper: A Centenary Assessment*. Vol. 1, *Life and Times, Values in a World of Facts*, edited by I. Jarvie, K. Milford, and D. Miller, chapter 11, 177–190. London: Ashgate.

– 2007a. *From Knowledge to Wisdom: A Revolution for Science and the Humanities*. London: Pentire Press (2nd edition of Maxwell 1984).

– 2007b. "From Knowledge to Wisdom: The Need for an Academic Revolution." *London Review of Education* 5, no. 2, 97–115.

– 2009. "How Can Life of Value Best Flourish in the Real World?" In *Science and the Pursuit of Wisdom: Studies in the Philosophy of Nicholas Maxwell*, edited by Leemon McHenry, 1–56. Frankfurt: Ontos Verlag.

– 2010a. *Cutting God in Half – and Putting the Pieces Together Again*. London: Pentire Press.

– 2010b. "Reply to Comments on *Science and the Pursuit of Wisdom*." *Philosophia* 38, no. 4, 667–90.

– 2010c. "The Urgent Need for an Academic Revolution: The Rational Pursuit of Wisdom." In *Death and Anti-Death*. Vol. 7, *Nine Hundred Years after St Anselm (1033–1109)*, edited by C. Tandy, chapter 7, 211–38. Palto Alto, CA: Ria University Press.

– 2010d. "Universities: From Knowledge to Wisdom." *Scientists for Global Responsibility Newsletter* issue 38, 18–20.

– 2010e. "Wisdom Mathematics." *Friends of Wisdom Newsletter* no. 6, 1–6. http://www.knowledgetowisdom.org/Newsletter%206.pdf.

– 2011a. "Three Philosophical Problems about Consciousness and Their Possible Resolution." *Open Journal of Philosophy* 1, issue 1, 1–10.

– 2011b. "A Priori Conjectural Knowledge in Physics." In *What Place for the A Priori?*, edited by M. Shaffer and M. Veber, 211–40. Chicago: Open Court.

– 2011c. "We Need an Academic Revolution." *Oxford Magazine* no. 309, 15–18.

– 2012a. "Arguing for Wisdom in the University: An Intellectual Autobiography." *Philosophia* 40, no. 4, 663–704.

– 2012b. "Creating a Better World: Towards the University of Wisdom." In *The Future University: Ideas and Possibilities*, edited by R. Barnett, 123–38. New York: Routledge.

– 2012c. "How Universities Can Help Humanity Learn How to Resolve the Crises of Our Times – From Knowledge to Wisdom: The University College London Experience." *Handbook on the Knowledge Economy* 2, edited by G. Heam, T. Katlelle, and D. Rooney, 158–79. Cheltenham: Edward Elgar.

– 2012d. "Our Global Problems and What We Need to Do about Them." In *Death and Anti-Death Anthology*. Vol. 10, *Ten Years after John Rawls (1921–2002)*, edited by C. Tandy and J. Lee, chapter 7, 131–74. Palo Alto, CA: Ria University Press.

– 2012e. "The Menace of Science without Civilization: From Knowledge to Wisdom, Text of Keynote Lecture given in Warsaw 20 May 2011." *Dialogue and Universalism* no. 3, 39–63.

– 2012f. "In Praise of Natural Philosophy: A Revolution for Thought and Life." *Philosophia* 40, no. 4, 705–15.

– 2013a. "Has Science Established That the Cosmos Is Physically Comprehensible?" In *Recent Advances in Cosmology*, edited by A. Travena and B. Soen, chapter 1, 1–56. New York: Nova Science Publishers Inc.

– 2013b. "Knowledge or Wisdom?" *The Philosophers' Magazine*, issue 62, 3rd quarter, 17–18.

– 2014a. *How Universities Can Help Create a Wiser World: The Urgent Need for an Academic Revolution*. Exeter: Imprint Academic.

– 2014b. *Global Philosophy*. Exeter: Imprint Academic.

– 2015. "Can the World Learn Wisdom?" *Philosophy Now* (June/July): 32–5.

– 2016a. "Popper's Paradoxical Pursuit of Natural Philosophy." In *The Cambridge Companion to Popper*, edited by J. Shearmur and G. Stokes, chapter 7, 170–207. Cambridge: Cambridge University Press.

– 2016b. "Can Scientific Method Help Us Create a Wiser World?" In *Practical Wisdom in the Age of Technology: Insights, Issues and Questions for a New Millennium*, edited by N. Dalal, A. Intezari, and M. Heitz, chapter 11, 147–61. London: Routledge.

– 2017a. *Understanding Scientific Progress*. Saint Paul, MN: Paragon House.

– 2017b. *In Praise of Natural Philosophy: A Revolution for Thought and Life*. Montreal & Kingston: McGill-Queen's University Press.

– 2017c. *Karl Popper, Science and Enlightenment*. London: UCL Press.

– 2017d. "Do We Need an Academic Revolution to Create a Wiser World?" In *The Idea of the University*. Vol. 2, *Contemporary Perspectives*, edited by R. Barnett and M.A. Peters, chapter 28. New York: Peter Lang.

– 2017e. "Relativity Theory May not Have the Last Word on the Nature of Time: Quantum Theory and Probabilism." In *Space, Time and the Limits of Human Understanding*, edited by G. Ghirardi and S. Wuppuluri, 109–24. Cham, Switzerland: Springer.

– 2017f. "Can Universities Save Us from Disaster?" *On the Horizon* 25, no. 2, 115–30. http://www.emeraldinsight.com/doi/full/10.1108/OTH-04-2016-0019.

– 2018a. "Could Inelastic Interactions Induce Quantum Probabilistic Transitions?" In Gao 2018, chapter 14, 257–73.

– 2018b. "We Need Progress in Ideas about How to Achieve Progress." *Metascience*. https://doi.org/10.1007/s11016-018-0312-4.

– 2019a. *The Metaphysics of Science and Aim-Oriented Empiricism: A Revolution for Science and Philosophy*. Sythese Library. Cham, Switzerland: Springer.

– 2019b. *Science and Enlightenment: Two Great Problems of Learning*. Cham, Switzerland: Springer.

– 2019c. "A New Task for Philosophy of Science." *Metaphilosophy* 50, no. 3, 316–38.

– 2019d. "Aim-Oriented Empiricism and the Metaphysics of Science." *Philosophia* 1–18.https://link.springer.com/article/10.1007%2Fs11406-019-00064-w.

– 2019e. "Natural Philosophy Redux." *Aeon* 13 May. https://aeon.co/essays/bring-back-science-and-philosophy-as-natural-philosophy.

– 2019f. "The Urgent Need for Social Wisdom." In *The Cambridge Handbook of Wisdom*, edited by R. Sternberg and J. Glück, chapter 33, 754–80. Cambridge: Cambridge University Press.

– 2019g. "How Wisdom Can Help Solve Global Problems." In *Applying Wisdom to Contemporary World Problems*, edited by R. Sternberg, H. Nusbaum, and J. Glück, chapter 13, 337–80. London: Palgrave Macmillan.

– 2019h. "The Scandal of the Irrationality of Academia." *Philosophy and Theory in Higher Education*, special issue, "The Anthropocene and Higher Education" 1, no. 1, 105–28.

McAllister, J. 1996. *Beauty and Revolution in Science*. Ithaca: Cornell University Press.

Mellor, D.H. 1991. *Matters of Metaphysics*. Cambridge: Cambridge University Press.

Mill, J.S. 1963–91. *The Collected Works of John Stuart Mill: An Examination of Sir William Hamilton's Philosophy*, vol. 9, edited by J.M. Robson. London: Routledge and Kegan Paul.

Miller, G. 1962. *Psychology: The Science of Mental Life*. Gretna, LA: Pelican Books.

Monod, J. 1974. *Chance and Necessity*. Glasgow: Fontana.

Moore, G.E. 1993. *Principia Ethica*. Cambridge: Cambridge University Press (first published 1903).

– 2002. *Philosophical Papers*. London: Routledge.

Morgan, E. 1990. *The Scars of Evolution*. London: Penguin.

Morton, A. 2009. *Eating the Sun*. London: Fourth Estate.

Mumford, S., and M. Tugby, eds. 2013. *Metaphysics and Science*. Oxford: Oxford University Press.

Nagel, T. 1974. "What Is It Like to Be a Bat?" *Philosophical Review* 83, 435–50.

– 1986. *The View from Nowhere*. Oxford: Oxford University Press.

– 1987. *What Does It All Mean? A Very Short Introduction to Philosophy*. Oxford: Oxford University Press.

Newton, I. 1952. *Opticks*, London: Constable (first published in 1704; this edition in 1730).

– 1962. *Principia*, vol. 2, *The System of the World*, translated by Andrew Motte. Berkeley: University of California Press.

Nixey, C. 2018. *The Darkening Age: The Christian Destruction of the Classical World*. London: Pan Books.

Norton, J. 2003. "Causation as Folk Science." *PhilSci Archive*, www.philsci-archive.pitt.edu/archive/00001214.

Nuttall, J. 2002. *An Introduction to Philosophy*. Cambridge: Polity.

Odling-Smee, F.J., K.N. Leland, and M.W. Feldman. 2003. *Niche Construction*. Princeton: Princeton University Press.

O'Shaughnessy, B. 1980. *The Will*. Cambridge: Cambridge University Press.

Papineau, D. 2017. "Is Philosophy Simply Harder than Science?" *Times Literary Supplement*, 1 June. https://www.the-tls.co.uk/articles/public/philosophy-simply-harder-science/.

Penrose, R. 2004. *The Road to Reality*. London: Jonathan Cape.

Pinker, S. 2018. *Enlightenment NOW*. London: Allen Lane.

Pirsig, R. 1974. *Zen and the Art of Motorcycle Maintenance*. London: Bodley Head.

Plato. 1970. *The Republic*. Translated by B. Jowett. London: Sphere Books (first published around 380 BCE).

Pojman, L.P., ed. 2004. *Introduction to Philosophy: Classical and Contemporary Readings*. Oxford: Oxford University Press.

Popper, K.R. 1959. *The Logic of Scientific Discovery*. London: Hutchinson.

– 1961. *The Poverty of Historicism*. London: Routledge and Kegan Paul.

– 1962. *The Open Society and Its Enemies*. London: Routledge and Kegan Paul.

– 1963. *Conjectures and Refutations*. London: Routledge and Kegan Paul.

– 1972. *Objective Knowledge*. Oxford: Clarendon Press.

– 1976. *Unended Quest*. Glasgow: Fontana.

– Popper, K.R., and J. Eccles. 1977. *The Self and Its Brain: An Argument for Interactionism*. Berlin: Springer.

Rae, A. 1992. *Quantum Physics: Illusion or Reality?* Cambridge: Cambridge University Press.

Ragland, C.P., and S. Heidt, eds. 2001. *What Is Philosophy?* New Haven: Yale University Press.

Redhead, M.L.G. 1990. "Explanation." In *Explanation and Its Limits*, edited by D. Knowles, 135–54. Cambridge: Cambridge University Press.

Russell, B. 1946. *A History of Western Philosophy*. London: George Allen and Unwin.

– 1951. *Mysticism and Logic.* London: George Allen and Unwin.

– 1982. *The Problems of Philosophy.* Oxford: Oxford University Press (first published in 1912).

Ryle, G. 1949. *The Concept of Mind.* London: Hutchinson.

Salmon, W.C. 1974. "The Pragmatic Justification of Induction." In *The Justification of Induction,* edited by R. Swinburne, 85–97. Oxford: Oxford University Press.

Sartre, J.-P. 1958. *Being and Nothingness.* Translated by H.E. Barnes. London: Methuen (first published in French in 1943).

Schopenhauer, A. 1965. *The World as Will and Representation.* Edited and translated by J. Norman, A. Welchman, and C. Janaway. Cambridge: Cambridge University Press (first published in 1818).

Scruton, R. 2012. *Modern Philosophy: An Introduction and Survey.* London: Bloomsbury.

Sehon, S. 2005. *Teleological Realism: Mind, Agency, and Explanation.* Cambridge: MIT Press.

Sellars, W. 1963. *Science, Perception and Reality.* London: Routledge and Kegan Paul.

Shafer-Landau, R. 2003. *Moral Realism: A Defence.* Oxford: Clarendon Press.

Shand, J. 2002. *Philosophy and Philosophers: An Introduction to Western Philosophy.* Chesham: Acumen.

Sinclair, W.A. 1945. *An Introduction to Philosophy.* Oxford: Oxford University Press.

Slater, M., and S. Yudell, eds. 2017. *Metaphysics and the Philosophy of Science.* Oxford: Oxford University Press.

Smart, J.J.C. 1963. *Philosophy and Scientific Realism.* London: Routledge and Kegan Paul.

Smith, D. 2003. *The Atlas of War and Peace.* London: Earthscan.

Smith, P., and O.R. Jones. 1986. *The Philosophy of Mind: An Introduction.* Cambridge: Cambridge University Press.

Snow, C.P. 1986. *The Two Cultures: And a Second Look.* Cambridge: Cambridge University Press.

Spinoza, B. 1955. *On the Improvement of the Understanding, The Ethics, Correspondence.* New York: Dover.

Squires, E. 1986. *The Mystery of the Quantum World.* Bristol: Adam Hilger.

Stoljar, D. 2017. "Physicalism." In Zalta, *The Stanford Encyclopedia of Philosophy.* https://plato.stanford.edu/archives/win2017/entries/physicalism/.

Strawson, G. 2006a. "Realistic Materialism: Why Physicalism Entails Panpsychism." *Journal of Consciousness Studies* 13 (10–11): 3–31.
– 2006b. "Panpsychism? Replies to Commentators and a Celebration of Descartes." *Journal of Consciousness Studies* 13 (10–11): 184–208.
Strawson, P.F. 1959. *Individuals*. London: Methuen.
Swain, M., ed. 1970. *Induction, Acceptance and Rational Belief*. Dordrecht: Reidel.
Tooley, M. 1977. "The Nature of Law." *Canadian Journal of Philosophy* 7, 667–98.
Turnbull, C. 1961. *The Forest People*. New York: Simon and Schuster.
van Fraassen, B. 1980. *The Scientific Image*. Oxford: Clarendon Press.
– 1985. "Empiricism in the Philosophy of Science." In *Images of Science*, edited by P.M. Churchland and C.A. Hooker, 245–308. Chicago: University of Chicago Press.
– 1989. *Laws and Symmetry*. Oxford: Clarendon Press.
van Inwagen, P. 1986. *An Essay on Free Will*. Oxford: Clarendon Press.
Velleman, J.D. 2015. *Foundations for Moral Relativism*. Cambridge: Open Book Publishers.
Wallace, D. 2012. *The Emergent Multiverse*. Oxford: Oxford University Press.
Westermarck, E. 1932. *Ethical Relativity*. London: Kegan Paul, Trench, Trubner.
Wittgenstein, L. 1958. *Philosophical Investigations*. Oxford: Blackwell.
Wong, D. 2006. *Natural Moralities: A Defense of Pluralistic Relativism*. Oxford: Oxford University Press.
Wootton, D. 2016. *The Invention of Science*. London: Penguin Books.
Zeki, S. 1993. *A Vision of the Brain*. London: Blackwell Scientific Publications.
Zelta, E.N. 2017. *The Stanford Encyclopedia of Philosophy*. https://plato.stanford.edu.

Index

academia for civilization, xiii, 15, 161–4, 201–5; and problems of living, 156, 174–5; and public education, 154; and symposium devoted to discussing fundamental problem, 199, 203. *See also* aim-oriented rationality; wisdom-inquiry

agriculture, modern, 6; and aim-oriented rationality, 167; beneficial, 14; and climate change, 153–4; and fundamental problem, 6; and global problems, 155, 178, 204; and human history, 152, 177; made possible by science, 14, 152, 155, 204

aim-oriented empiricism, 36, 79–91, 166, 174; and academia, 168; and aim-oriented rationality, 166–7, 178, 213; argument for, 79–89, 215, 245n13, 258n14, 267n24; and circularity problem, 220–2, 246–7n20, 269n41; and cosmological assumptions, 223–5; and decline of philosophy, 215, 219–20, 225–6; and empirical verification of theory, 222–3, 269–70n44; and Enlightenment, 165–6; exposition of, 79–89, 257n8, 258n14, 263–4n12; and fundamental

problem, 36, 89–90, 93; implications of, 88, 89–91, 198, 200, 208; and natural philosophy, 213, 215–16, 226, 268n32, 269n39; and natural science, 200, 202; and perfect simulacrum of verification of theory by evidence, 222–3, 269–70n44; and physicalism, 88, 90, 93, 177; and physics, 198, 200, 213; positive feedback character of, 91, 165–6; and scrutiny of aims and values, 174; solves Hume's problem, 219–20, 269n42; and standard empiricism, 166, 208, 219, 258n13; and success of science, 201, 203, 258n13, 263–4n12; and wisdom-inquiry, 165–6, 174, 202

aim-oriented rationality, 166–8, 173–4, 259n19; beneficial, 198; cooperative, 193; and free will, 173; generalization of aim-oriented empiricism, 167, 213; and global problems, 168, 174, 178, 201; and learning, 198, 260n3; and realizing what is of value, 173; and revolution in social science and life, 202–3; and scrutiny of aims and values, 174; and wisdom-inquiry, 173, 178

d'Alembert, Jean, 165

of perception, 24–7; and critical
fundamentalism, xii; and Darwin,
195–6, 261n1; and Democritus,
21; and education, 6, 199–200;
and flourishing of life, 5–6, 152;
formulation of, xi, 1–6; and
Galileo, 22–3; and human world,
12–13, 195, 200; includes all other
problems, 5–6; and mind-brain
problem, 68–9, 208–10, 225,
239n4, 243n34; and Newton, 23;
and perception, 234n26; and philosophy, 16–20, 31–3, 37, 195–8,
207–10, 225, 229n2, 265n8; and
problems of living, 16–17; religious formulation of, 35–6, 195,
238n61; and revolutionary implications, xii–xiii, 18; and science, 5,
199; and scientific view of the
world, 20–6; and Sellars, 210; and
sentient life, 13; and specialization,
xi, 6, 37–8, 196; and two-aspect
view, 39, 239n4; and the university, 37, 199. See also Cartesian
dualism; consciousness; critical
fundamentalism; Darwinian theory; experiential physicalism; free
will; idealism; life of value; naive
realism; philosophy; revolutionary
implications; scientific view of the
world; two-aspect view;
wisdom-inquiry
fundamental requirement for
perfect free will, 104, 105–6,
250n17; and physicalism,
105–112; and simulacrum of free
will, 106–12

Galileo, 6, 83–4, 129, 230n4,
232n11; a natural philosopher, 32,
215–16, 220; and sensory qualities, 22–3, 27, 45
Gay, P., 258,10

Gell-Mann, Murray, 84
general relativity, 48, 84, 92
global problems, xiii, 6, 14, 153–6;
and aim-oriented rationality, 168,
178, 201; caused by science,
14–15, 153–6, 177–8, 204; and
Enlightenment idea, 178; failure to
solve, 206; and irrationality of universities, xiii, 156–61; and lack of
wisdom, 14–15; and social inquiry,
213–14; universities responsible
for, 154–61; and wisdom-inquiry,
15, 174
God, problem of, 35–6
Goff, P., 243n30
Goodall, Jane, 255n24
good world, xiii, 15, 152, 206, 214;
and institutions of learning, 156;
problematic, 167
government, xii; and aim-oriented
rationality, xii, 167, 170; and funding scientific research, 161; and
wisdom-inquiry, 164
grand challenges UCL, 260n30
Gravesande, Willem, 221
Green, T.H., 31, 236n44
Greene, Brian, 245n12
Grice, Paul, 146, 255n25

Haak, Susan, on contemporary
philosophy, 266n15
habitat destruction, xiii, 14, 153, 155,
201, 204. See also global problems
Hales, S., 262n2
hard problem of consciousness, 69,
243n35; not so hard, 69–70,
243n35
Hardy, Alister, 132, 256n32
Hardy, Thomas, 12
Harman, G., 261n5, 267n28
Harries, Karsten, 197
Hasker, W., 242n26
Hayek, F.A., 258n11

unpopularity of, 245n11; scientific
fruitfulness of, 88. *See also*
aim-oriented empiricism
Mill, J.S., 30, 164, 209, 235n32
Miller, George, 250n15
mind-brain problem, 27–8, 31, 50,
53–4, 67–9; and controllism, 58;
and externalism, 50, 53–4; and fundamental problem, 68–70, 243n34,
262n23; and internalism, 50, 53;
resolution of, 50, 54, 69–70; what
creates, 50, 53, 59, 66–7
Moore, G.E., 187, 238n57
Morgan, Elaine, 256n32
Mumford, S., 244n3

Nagel, Thomas, 33, 67, 210, 239n4,
241n13, 242n26, 242n27, 262n2
naive realism, 34
Neurath, Otto, 209
Newton, Isaac, 22, 32, 35, 84, 166,
215–16, 233n16; and sensory
qualities, 23, 45
Newtonian conception of science,
216–20, 222–3; and gulf between
science and philosophy, 219–20,
269n39; and neurosis of science,
268–9n37; refuted, 218; refuted by
Hume, 218–20, 267n31
Newtonian theory, 42–4, 84, 92;
disunified versions of, 74–7, 218,
245n9; essentialistically interpreted, 42–4
Newton's *Principia*, 216; and destruction of natural philosophy, 216–18,
267n27; dishonesty of, 217, 220;
great work of natural philosophy,
216, 220; and Hume, 218–20; and
hypotheses, 216; inductive character of, 216; and inference to best
explanation, 217
Norton, J., 239n6
nuclear weapons, xiii, 14; and

aim-oriented rationality, 168; and
Enlightenment, 227; and science,
153, 155, 204
Nussbaum, Martha, 197
Nuttall, J., 262n2

Olding-Smee, F.J., 253n5
origin of life, 125
Orwell, George, 12
O'Shaughnessy, B., 242n26

panpsychism, 67–8; problems of, 68,
243n31
Papineau, D., 266n17
Parmenides, 21
partial knowability, 81–2
Penrose, R., 260n24
perception, problem of, 24–30,
49–56, 59, 197, 234n26. *See also*
argument from causal account of
perception; externalism;
internalism
perceptual qualities, xi, 4, 21–4, 28,
33, 35, 239n7; and causal account
of perception, 24–7, 49–53; and
internalism and externalism,
49–54; and objective/subjective
distinctions, 54–5; real existence,
49–55; what they are, 56
personalistic understanding, 62–5,
113–20; and animals, 255n24
philosophical zombie, 110–12;
cannot in fact exist, 112
philosophy, xi; and aim-oriented
empiricism, 215, 226; analytic, 31,
211; and anti-philosophy, 266n18;
bad implications for social life of
orthodox, 262n5; branches of, 196;
and Cartesian dualism, 207–10;
conjectural character of, 19–20;
Continental, 31; and contrast with
science, 32; and critical fundamentalism, xii–xiii, 18, 19–20, 69,

174–5, 195–210, 212–14; and
Darwin, 195–6; failures of, 27–33,
196, 203–4; and fruitfulness of critical fundamentalism, 197–8; and
fundamental problem, xii, 16–20,
32, 195–6, 207–10, 226, 230n3,
237n55; history of decline of,
211–12, 266n17; of inquiry, 203–4;
intellectual legitimacy of, 210–11;
introductory books on, 196–7; lack
of progress in, 210–11, 266n16;
lost its way, 31–3, 206; and mind-
body problem, 207–10; and natural
philosophy, 211, 213, 215, 226,
237n52, 268n32; and natural and
social sciences and humanities, 196,
212; nonsense of story of decline of,
212–15; and physics, 212; poverty
of orthodox, 197, 210–15, 219–27,
237n51; and rationality, 212; and
social sciences, 212; and specialization, 37, 196, 207, 212, 224–5,
230n3; and standard empiricism,
214–15; tasks of, 20, 195–6,
199–204; urgent need for reform
of, 226–7
philosophy, tasks for, to transform:
academia so that knowledge-
inquiry becomes wisdom-inquiry,
200–4; orthodox philosophy to
become critical fundamentalism,
195–204, 226–7; schools to give
central role to discussion of fundamental problem, 199–200;
science to put aim-oriented empiricism into practice, 198, 200; social
sciences and humanities so that
they put wisdom-inquiry into practice, 198; social world so that
thinking about fundamental problem is kept alive, 195–6, 200;
universities and social world to
put aim-oriented rationality and

wisdom-inquiry into practice,
201–4; universities to give central
role to discussion of
fundamental problem, 199
photosynthesis, 11, 244n10
physical essentialism, 42–5; explains
laws, 43–5; and Hume, 42
physicalism, 33–4, 41–5, 71; and
aim-oriented empiricism, 83–7;
argued to be a part of scientific
knowledge, 72–9, 83–7, 88; empirical fruitfulness of, 83–5; and
empirically successful, disunified
theories, 72–7; a key item of scientific knowledge, 90–1; a metaphysical thesis, 71; and necessary
connections, 42–5, 267n31; and
physical comprehensibility, 83–7; a
presupposition of physics, 72–9;
and scientific knowledge, 71; and
standard empiricism, 72–9
physical theory of everything, 40–2;
essentialistically interpreted, 42–5;
field theory, 240n9; limited predictive powers of, 239–40n8; probabilistic, 40–1
physics, incompleteness of, 40, 41,
45–9, 69, 176; reasons for, 45–9,
69, 92, 176–7, 243n33, 244n4
physics and human world, 3–6, 38–9,
41, 46–9; 176–9
physics restricted to depicting
causally efficacious, 40–5, 176
Pinker, S., 256n1
Pirsig, Robert, 187, 261n13
Plato, 19, 196
Pojman, L.P., 262n2
politics, 6, 227; and critical fundamentalism, 214; and fundamental problem, 6, 200; and knowledge-inquiry,
156; and wisdom-inquiry, 175
pollution, xiii, 14, 153, 155, 168,
201, 204. See also global problems

Popper, Karl, 33; conception of science refuted by Hume, 268n33; and Enlightenment, 258n12; and evolution, 136; and falsifiability, 157, 244n2; and Hume on induction, 268n33; and open society, 182, 237n53; and philosophy, 33, 262n5; and Plato, 230n2; and problem of knowledge, 122; and skepticism, 80; and specialization, 264n1; and standard empiricism, 165, 244n3

population growth, 14, 153–5, 204

problems of living, xii, xiii; and action, 158–9; and cooperative rationality, 159, 162, 167, 174; and fundamental problem, 6, 16–17, 19; and institutions of learning, xiii, 156, 158, 160, 167; and knowledge-inquiry, 156, 160–1; and personalistic explanation, 173; and social science, xii, 162, 173–4; and tribal and modern worlds, 152–3; and wisdom-inquiry, 173–4

Proust, Marcel, 12

purposive beings, 63–101; and aims, 249n12; and Aristotle, 249–50n14; compatibilist and incompatibilist notions of, 249–50n14; and control systems, 102–3; and Darwinian evolution, 64; and feedback mechanism, 101–3; and Galileo, 249–50n14; and physicalism, 65–6, 101–3

purposive explanation, 63–5, 113–14; and Darwinian theory, 64

Putin, Vladimir, 227

Pygmies of central Africa, 185–6; and cooperation without control, 256n2

quantum theory, 18, 48, 84, 92; disunity of, 263n8; probabilistic, 99, 248n9, 248n10; and wave/particle duality, 230n8

quark, xi, 4, 8–10, 84, 229n1

Ragland, C.P., 197, 262n2

rationality, 157; aim-oriented, 166–8, 173–4, 178, 193, 198, 201–3, 213; cooperative, 159, 167, 193; definition of, 157; and means and ends, 168, 178, 193; and philosophes of Enlightenment, 164; and physics, 213; and realization of what is of value, 178; rules of, 158–60; and skepticism, 170; universities lack, xiii, 156, 160–1, 164–5; and wisdom-inquiry, 173–4, 178. *See also* aim-oriented rationality; critical fundamentalism; wisdom-inquiry

Redhead, M., 239n6

reductionism, 37, 238n2

Reichenbach, Hans, 209

requirements for acceptance of physical theory, 72, 88; role of unity in, 72; standard empiricist account of, 72

revolutionary implications, xii–xiii, 18, 202–3; for academia, xiii, 18, 159, 161–75, 198; beneficial character of, 198; for biology, xii, 18, 126–51, 198; concerning fundamental problem, 195; for Darwinian theory, 126–51, 198; for the humanities, 198; for mathematics, 18, 263n7; for natural science, xii, 72–91, 198, 200; for neuroscience, 18, 263n9; for philosophy, xii, 72–91, 195–205; for quantum theory, 18, 198, 263n8; for social science, xii–xiii, 18, 174–5, 198; for the social world, 18, 174–5, 195, 198, 201; for theoretical physics, 72–91, 198, 200

Russell, Bertrand, 30, 221, 235n33, 239n6, 262n2; and decline of

and knowledge-inquiry, 157; need
for rejection of, 200, 202, 208; and
Newton, 217, 220; and physicalism, 72, 90, 93; refutation of,
72–9, 219; and science and philosophy, 91, 266n20, 270n45; and
specialization, 245–6n19
standard model, 84, 92
Stendhal, 12
Strawson, Galen, 67, 242n26,
243n30
string theory, 78–9, 245n12
Stroud, Barry, 197
Swain, M., 268n34

technology, 6; and aim-oriented
rationality, 168, 178; beneficial,
14, 153, 155, 177–8, 204; and critical fundamentalism, 214; and fundamental problem, 6; and global
problems, 14, 153, 155, 177–8,
204; and human world, 38; and
irrationality of institutions of
learning, 161; and modern world,
89, 142, 152, 155; and natural
philosophy, 216; and problematic
aims, 201; and social inquiry, 162;
and wisdom, 14, 161
Tolstoy, Leo, 12, 143
Tooley, M., 239n4, 240n11
Trump, Donald, 227
Tugby, M., 244n3
Turgenev, Ivan, 12
Turnbull, Colin, 185, 256n28
two-aspect view, 34–5, 38–70,
176–7, 239n4; people who uphold
versions of, 242n26; problems of,
35, 39–40. *See also* experiential
controllism; experiential
physicalism
two-aspect view, minimalist version of,
66; basic mistake of, 68; and
Chalmers, 67; and Dennett, 67; and

experiential physicalism, 66–7, 68,
243n31, 243n33; and Nagel, 67;
and panpsychism, 67–8; problems
of, 66–9, 243n32; and Strawson, 67
two great problems of learning, 204–
5; learning from the first how to
solve the second, 167, 205

unification of physics, 84–5, 245n17
unity of physical theory, 72–3, 219;
problem of, 73; solution to problem of, 73–4, 244n7; successful
discovery of, 84–5
universities, damaging irrationality
of, 154–61, 256–7n3

value in life, 179–94; and aim-
oriented rationality, 192; can leach
away, 180; and conjectural objectivism, 185–94; and consciousness,
183–4; and death, 181–2; disagreements about, 187; and dogmatic
objectivism, 185–6; and doubt,
182–3, 193; exists whether "good"
or "bad," 189–90; as fact, 186–94;
and feelings and desires, 180–1,
188; improving ideas as to what is
of, 193; and intrinsic, 187–94;
and intuition, 192; and modern
science, 181, 188; much that is of,
179–80; and open society, 182–3;
of person who has died, 193–4;
problematic character of, 179; and
reason, 191–3; and relativism,
184–6; and reliable value perceiver,
190–2; and source in purposive
life, 183–4; subjective and objective, 188–9; undefinable nature of,
187–8; unproblematic character
of, 179–80; and value realism,
186–94, 261n10
values, declared, believed, and actual,
260–1n4